THERE IS, PROFESSOR SCHEUERMANN FINDS, A GREAT deal of social protest and very little revolution in the eighteenth-century English novel. Novelists as early as Defoe descry much that needs to be changed in contemporary society, but they advocate reform of existing structures, not destruction of basic institutions. Thus when she speaks of what she characterizes as "novels of social protest," Dr. Scheuermann refers to works that show an underlying commitment to the traditional structures of English life while protesting against the corruption and debasement of those forms.

Henry Fielding uses the first volume of *Amelia* to detail the evils of the British penal system and the legal system that supported it. Henry Brooke begins his *The Fool of Quality* with a series of uncomplimentary portraits of the aristocracy and never lets up after that. Thomas Day, whose *The History of Sandford and Merton* follows Brooke's novel in almost all respects, is, if anything, harsher in his criticism than his model. Fanny Burney *(Evelina)* gently ridicules, and Robert Bage less gently satirizes. Elizabeth Inchbald *(Nature and Art)* polemicizes. Thomas Holcroft *(Anna St. Ives* and *Hugh Trevor)* laments. William Godwin *(Caleb Williams)* denounces. In each case, the underlying assumption is the same: notice must be taken of evils in society and men must make attempts to redress them.

The novel has not yet been clearly understood as a vehicle for social reform in the eighteenth century. The failings of the institutions of society are attributed to the cumulative moral weakness of corrupt individuals, whose improvement in heart and mind becomes, therefore, the means to renovation of impaired societal structures and to the restitution of the commonweal. Only William Godwin is an exception to this general rule. Only he indicts the institutions of society as corruptive of the individual. Only he postulates a society whose tyranny over the individual is so complete and so oppressive as to dash all hope for the salvation of its helpless victims.

The abuse of power—or what is more often regarded as the misuse of power (the first deliberate and malicious, the second

merely misguided and in error)—is a common theme in eighteenth-century novels of protest; and the exercise of arbitrary power is singled out for special condemnation. The attack is fueled by the prevailing spirit in the novels that the failings of society will, once they have been exposed, be ameliorated by rational men of good will.

All in all, Professor Scheuermann concludes, the social protest in the novel of the eighteenth century is a quite civilized affair. Belief in the power of education as a force for the improvement of society (through the moral regeneration of its lapsed members) colors the protest by suggesting that there is a relatively easy and likely very effective solution for much that is wrong. Irony, satire, and rationalist optimism intervene between the reader and the social pain being brought dramatically to his attention.

Mona Scheuermann is Associate Professor of English at Oakton Community College in Des Plaines, Illinois.

SOCIAL PROTEST IN
THE EIGHTEENTH-CENTURY
ENGLISH NOVEL

Social Protest in
the Eighteenth-Century
English Novel

MONA SCHEUERMANN

OHIO STATE UNIVERSITY PRESS : COLUMBUS

Library of Congress Cataloging in Publication Data

Scheuermann, Mona.
  Social protest in the eighteenth-century English novel.
  Includes bibliographies and index.
  1. English fiction—18th century—History and
criticism. 2. Social problems in literature. I. Title.
PR858.S62S34   1985   823'.6'09355   84-27157
ISBN 0-8142-0381-7

for Peter

Contents

Acknowledgments

Many friends have helped to shape my ideas about the eighteenth century, and this book would not have been quite the same without the enthusiasms of Thomas Maresca, Kenneth Graham, Paul Hunter, Jean Hagstrum, and Donald Reiman. A real regret is that the late Joseph Bennett, who taught me so much about scholarship, did not get to see this result of his teaching. John Sekora read an earlier draft and offered encouragement and good advice at a time when both were much needed. The most special debt I have is to Jerry Beasley, whose generosity as a friend and a scholar continually surprises me. Jerry read the manuscript twice, each time with such care and attention to detail that much of what is good in the book grows from his perceptiveness.

The first chapter of this book originally appeared in somewhat different form in the *Forum For Modern Language Studies* (April 1984), and I thank the editors for their kind permission to reprint it here. I am grateful to the two (to me unknown) readers for the Ohio State University Press for their many insightful comments. Susan Maltese, Sandra Wittman, Dawn Casey, and Esther Marks always have been cheerfully ready to help me track down research materials; I want to thank also the staffs of the Newberry Library and the Northwestern University Library. Maureen Koziol, who typed and retyped the manuscript at its various stages, is simply irreplaceable. My husband Peter's friendship, his interest, and his endless fund of good ideas are acknowledged in the dedication.

INTRODUCTION

There is a great deal of social protest in the eighteenth-century English novel but very little revolution. English novelists as early as Defoe see much that needs to be changed in English society, but they advocate the reform of existing structures rather than the destruction of basic institutions. Underlying almost every one of what I call the novels of social protest is a commitment to the traditional forms and institutions of English life; much of the protest, in fact, is protest against the corruption and debasement of sound institutions. Thus I speak of novelists as diverse in social and political orientation as Henry Fielding, Henry Brooke, Elizabeth Inchbald, and William Godwin as novelists of social protest, for each is disturbed at the shortcomings of what should be a felicitous social structure. The anger against corruption that each novelist expresses manifests an underlying faith in the institutions being criticized. One of the most striking examples of this impulse is Thomas Holcroft, who in successive novels writes first, in *Anna St. Ives,* of the virtually limitless potential for human development and happiness that English society affords her members, and then, in *Hugh Trevor,* of the impossibly corrupt and corrupting machinery of that same society. The other novelists I treat are not quite so ambivalent, but the same impulse to approve the basic structure of society while reproving its corruptions is basic to each work's strain of protest.

I define social protest in the novel as the author's delineation of social injustices, inequities, and failings, usually accompanied by explicit statements regarding the need for reform. The statements of protest are straightforward and often anything but subtle. Fielding takes a major portion of the first volume of *Amelia* to detail the evils of the penal system and the legal system that supports it. Henry Brooke begins *The Fool of Quality* with a series of uncomplimentary portraits of the aristocracy and never lets up on his criticism; Thomas Day, whose *Sandford and Merton* follows Brooke's novel in almost all respects, is even harsher in his criticism than his model. Bage satirizes, Inchbald criticizes, Holcroft laments, and Godwin denounces the injustices of society. The degree of anger changes, the tone of outrage is more or less shrill, but the underlying assumption is the same: men must note social evils and must attempt to redress them.

As the century wears on, the belief that action by benevolent men can indeed ameliorate bad situations grows less pervasive, and as early as midcentury the foreboding that good men may not have the power to change evil institutions already manifests itself. In *Amelia* Fielding draws so bleak a picture of men victimized by unequal social forces and corrupt social institutions that even he, as creator of a fictional world, can find no way out of misery for his protagonists within the given outlines of the novel. In order to supply the happy ending, Fielding must introduce a fortuitous but irrelevant fall into unexpected good fortune for his characters. By the end of the century, even the fortuitous happy ending is no longer possible: the young peasant girl seduced and abandoned by an unfeeling aristocrat dies of her disgrace in Elizabeth Inchbald's *Nature and Art,* and in Godwin's *Caleb Williams* every turn of the social chain produces more agony until Caleb's retribution turns, at the moment of triumph, into a corruption worse than any he had yet suffered. There is much faith in benevolence and social progress in the novels of the mid and late eighteenth century, but there is also much pessimism. All of these novelists of protest share a desire to see English society and her institutions made better; the more optimistic of them see such amelioration as being within reach—the novels of Brooke and Day simply call for benevolent efforts by individual men of educated good will—but those of bleaker view protest only, in the end, to admit despair.

The eighteenth century, like our own, was a period of immense dislocations in the ways men viewed themselves and society, but perhaps because of the difference in modes of communication, these dislocations were slower to be recognized and even slower to be publicly discussed than such upheavals are in our time. In the novel of the later eighteenth century, pervasive rather than specific discomfort with social institutions emerges. Although society seems healthy on the surface, the foundations of the social structure have somehow developed disparate cracks. Indeed, almost every one of these later novelists touches on the idea that security is fragile, and that a false step may send a respectable, responsible man to destruction. Many of these novels, in one context or another, mention that a man, often through no fault of his own, may find himself in prison for debt (for example, he may have cosigned a note for a relative who then defaulted); the very idea of prison is enough to evoke terror. John Howard in *The State of the Prisons,* writing in 1777, reminds his readers that prison reform should be very much their concern, for no man knows when he may suddenly find himself confined.

The spectre of such fearful reversals of fortune is both firmly grounded in reality and hauntingly symbolic. The perception that the orderly patterns of society may barely conceal deep flaws is evident even in a book such as Henry Brooke's *The Fool of Quality,* traditionally viewed as a cheerful sentimental novel. For example, in the rather long interpolated tale of Mr. Clement, Brooke presents a man who, starting life respectably well-off, falls so far as to commit a highway robbery to try to save his starving wife and child. But Brooke, writing relatively early (1770), firmly believes that a bit of benevolent tinkering can correct the failings of society. Mr. Clement, instructive as is his fall, is in the book to teach us how not to fail; having shown us Mr. Clement's mistakes, Brooke brings him back into society. As the century goes on, the sense that institutions and the men in them are not functioning properly becomes stronger, and characters like Mr. Clement who have missed their footing do not manage to get back in step. For Godwin, Holcroft, and

Bage there are, finally, no easy answers. Writers who try to posit easy answers fail miserably, as Inchbald does when, at the end of *Nature and Art,* she suggests that all the social problems would be solved if everyone would just go back to the simple life of the farm. Inchbald's ending does not fit her book or her time; Godwin's horror at the end of *Caleb Williams,* in contrast, seems inevitable.

The institutions of society, particularly economic institutions, changed markedly during the eighteenth century, and the novelists had not yet had time to put these changes into perspective. The novelists of the Victorian period would later analyze these changes. The novelists of the eighteenth century could only chronicle them. By the 1790s the agricultural, the industrial, the American, and the French revolutions had cast new light on British society. To these we may add a social revolution—the restructuring of traditional class lines caused by the others. The implications of the changes for British society that these movements set in motion were not immediately perceived by those living through them, as we would expect. But the cumulative effect of so many major dislocations produced that sense of uneasiness, of not being in control, that I have noted.

The agricultural revolution, whatever its benefits, displaced large numbers of workers and freeholders from the land to the city as small tracts were enclosed into the larger areas more suitable for mechanized farming. The industrial revolution changed society still more, moving even light industry out of the home into the impersonal and often brutal mill or factory. As a result of both of these basic movements, the lives of relatively large numbers of people were changed in ways over which they had not even minimal control.

On the other hand, the merchants themselves were seen as a positive force in society. England became fascinated with commerce, and manufacturing took on something of a moral as well as an economic impetus.[1] The good people are those who produce, Brooke tells us in *The Fool of Quality,* as opposed to the aristocrats, who, of course, only consume. Industry created a class of monied families who sought political power and social recognition to go with their new wealth. Fanny Burney's *Evelina* chronicles the acculturation of a young middle class girl as she learns her way into "society." The integration of these newly powerful families into what had hitherto been a hereditary aristocracy provided yet another strain on the social order. One reflection of this tension is the frequent advocacy of middle-class values in the novels, but in almost every case, such advocacy comes along with a fascination with traditional aristocracy. In Holcroft's *Anna St. Ives,* Frank is of the lower classes—but Anna is an aristocrat. In Burney's *Evelina,* Evelina seems to be middle class—but before the end of the novel we learn that she is of aristocratic lineage. And even in Bage's *Hermsprong,* a book which strongly caricatures and satirizes aristocratic values, Hermsprong himself, we learn, is the rightful heir to the estate Lord Grondale holds. Class structures, like the other structures of society, begin to lack the definite demarcations that could earlier have been taken for granted.

The political revolutions in America and in France partly reflected these other upheavals and underlined for many thinkers at the end of the century the mutability of institutions. As in the other movements, much seemed positive and exciting, but a sense of insecurity inevitably accompanied the new awareness of flux. The political reaction in England to the French Revolution culminated in the repressive measures the government tried to put into effect in the 1790s, measures that directly affected several members of the Godwin circle when Holcroft and others were put on trial in 1794 for sedition. Bage's jibes at the political paranoia of the time (Hermsprong is accused not only of reading the *Rights of Man* but of lending it to at least one friend—which must be conspiracy) records, however humorously, a real concern.[2]

The books in this study range broadly in their criticisms of society, and even the most conservative of them have some forceful criticisms to make. Institutional and personal corruption concerns not only, as we would expect, the more radical novelists of the nineties but the earlier writers as well. Fielding in *Amelia* exposes the abuses of the legal and penal systems;

Godwin, Holcroft, Inchbald and Bage all return to this theme. Political corruption is dissected repeatedly, and side by side with the corrupt politician stands the corrupt clergyman as an object of scorn. In *Hugh Trevor* Holcroft presents the two professions as sides of the same coin, and several of the novelists, Holcroft, Inchbald and Bage particularly, insist that corruption ties the two professions together; Dr. Blick's relationship with Lord Grondale in *Hermsprong* is perhaps the clearest example of this connection. Along with an awareness of institutional corruption comes a questioning of social function: how should a clergyman, an aristocrat, even a parent behave to those over whom he has power? Five of the nine novels I discuss criticize the traditional role of the parent; even that most basic social structure, the family, undergoes reexamination during this period, and the very relationship of parent to child is presented as being in need of major reforms. Finally, the novels of the nineties also criticize the traditional role of women.

But the most frequent social criticism in novels during the fifty years with which I am concerned is that the powerful (that is, the aristocrats and the clerics), individually and as a class, not only fail to take responsibility for improving society but are too often uncaring, selfish, and callous to the sufferings of those less fortunate than themselves. In novels such as *The Fool of Quality* and *Sandford and Merton,* the individual responsibility of the powerful for the less powerful is distinguished from larger social movements and made a theme in itself. This focus is not merely a function of the discussion occurring within the context of the sentimental novel, for even in a novel such as Bage's *Hermsprong* a major concern is the responsibility that individuals must assume in specific instances. These novels recurrently criticize aristocrats for consuming far more than they need while others lack bare necessities.

Brooke and Day believe that educating aristocrats to a humane outlook will cure most social problems; the later eighteenth-century novelists are not nearly so optimistic. All make the distinction between true benevolence and calculated charity; Inchbald, for example, sarcastically notes that it is prudent for the rich to give a little, lest the poor revolt and take all. Viewed in this context, the theme of benevolence, which critics have taken for granted as an aspect of the earlier sentimental novel, takes on a new dimension. None of these novelists suggests a radical redistribution of goods, but they insist on the immorality of a social system that so callously gives superfluous wealth to one small group and leaves the rest of the people in poverty. This social protest is as sharp in the sentimental novels as in those later novels that have traditionally been examined for social comment. When we recognize that novels such as *The Fool of Quality* have far more social content than has been acknowledged, we gain new insights into the development of the novel in the eighteenth century.[3]

Social criticism in the English novel has usually been associated with nineteenth-century writers, but criticism of corrupt institutions and pleas for reform emerge virtually with the appearance of the novel itself. That this tradition begins in the eighteenth century, and indeed extends back to Smollett and even Defoe, has been largely unremarked until now.[4] I have chosen to begin with Fielding's *Amelia* because social protest is already a major aspect of the work: Fielding's lengthy early description of the corruptions of the legal and penal systems sets the tone for the rest of the novel. Fielding's is a dark vision; already by 1751, he portrays social and economic forces buffeting individuals so violently that they are largely helpless. The book has been referred to as Fielding's "problem novel," but it is a problem only insofar as it is a different kind of novel from any of his earlier ones. Within its own terms, it presents a coherent picture of contemporary society.

Henry Brooke's *The Fool of Quality* criticizes many of the traditional assumptions rather than the institutions of English society, and Brooke, unlike Fielding (and unlike many of the novelists of the nineties), presents a new set of values to replace those against which he is protesting. The book celebrates the middle-class values of hard work, self-reliance, and benevolence. Brooke believes that these values can be inculcated into every class and that such proper education (or reeducation) will bring society to a state of happiness and security. Thomas Day's *The History of Sandford and Merton* was intended to spread these important lessons yet further. The books are interesting as novels of protest because of the amount of criticism of contemporary values (especially but not limited to aristocratic values) that they include within seemingly innocuous limits: the novels were essentially for children, after all.

Actually, the books were intended to educate children and their parents to an appreciation of sound social interactions, and both Brooke and Day believe fervently that education is a powerful, positive tool. Education and its potential for good or evil is a theme common to many of these novels, not only to works like Brooke's and Day's, which we may term educational novels, but to novels that seem occupied with quite other things. For example, in Matthew Gregory Lewis's *The Monk* (certainly, one hopes, not an educational novel), the monk's evil is directly attributed to his faulty education.[5] Throughout the century, novelists return to the theme of education as a shaping force; each of the novels I discuss talks about education in these terms.

Fanny Burney's *Evelina* is the only novel I include which is not basically critical of the institutions of society; on the contrary, Evelina's main concern is learning her way into society. Burney focuses on a conflict not in morals but in manners; her heroine wishes only to correct her own manners so that she can approximate the behavior of the upper classes—and enter their social circles. In Evelina's predicament, Burney portrays an important social problem of her time: in an age when new money demands social as well as economic prerogatives, how do the traditional upper classes assimilate the newly rich? The problem was an immediate one for Burney's contemporaries and, as I have noted, an additional source of pressure in the social structure. Burney's novel, in part because it is not doctrinaire and is not interested in taking a critical stance, allows us to see these social pressures at work from another view. I include the novel also because it provides a control on the novels of protest. Here from a much more tolerant perspective is the society that the other novelists view so critically.

This difference in perspective does not change the picture of society a reader gets from the novels: some of Inchbald's sharpest satire in *Nature and Art* is directed at the emptiness of social customs, while Burney, describing the same customs, has much less criticism to make. The similarity of the descriptions in the two novels suggests that the specifics are generally accurate, regardless of the interpretation a particular author gives to certain circumstances. Indeed, one of the conclusions to be drawn from a close study of these novels, critical and uncritical, is that their descriptions of eighteenth-century British life and institutions tally almost exactly. If I may take consistency of description to be a proof, the novelists I discuss seem to be attempting as much as possible to present "things as they are."

Although the strain of protest should be recognized as a major aspect of the eighteenth century, we must also remember that much of the contemporary literature, like *Evelina,* was essentially accepting of the status quo. Holcroft's *Anna St. Ives* partakes to some degree of such acceptance, for although Holcroft sees a great deal in English society and its institutions that needs to be corrected, he sees even more that is resoundingly positive. As in Brooke's *The Fool of Quality,* any imperfections can be remedied through a process of reeducation; even the most hardened villain (i.e., the most badly educated person) can be redeemed and made a contributing member of society. "We live in an age of light," the hero exclaims, and Holcroft's novel gives us no leave to doubt him. But in the years between *Anna St. Ives* (1792) and *Hugh Trevor* (1794–97), Holcroft himself had clearly begun to doubt. In *Hugh Trevor* Holcroft shows corruption in every institution of society, and the only way he can find to keep the honest Hugh from himself becoming corrupted is to have him retire on inherited money—hardly an optimistic ending! The views of society are so different from one Holcroft novel to the next that juxtaposing them gives us a good sense of the change in perspective manifested by the novelists as the century progressed. The position taken in the earlier novels is that of *Anna St. Ives:* although there are many areas of society that need to be improved, man can make his world better through his own efforts, particularly through the application of his reason; it is an age of light. But by the end of the century, as imperfectly understood social traumas take hold in people's minds, this position no longer seems tenable. The application of reason, the impulse to reform, seems at best insufficient and at worst destructive. Godwin, like Holcroft, reflects this change in successive works, for in *Political Justice* (1793) reason is seen as the prime mover in the perfecting of society; while in *Caleb Williams,* only a year later, Godwin is forced to admit that so much is wrong, so much is corrupt in the institutions of his society that even the process of revolt implies only further breakdown in the social structure. As Caleb realizes at the end of the novel, his triumph over Falkland dooms them both.

The last two novels, Inchbald's *Nature and Art* and Bage's *Hermsprong,*[6] reflect this disillusionment in different ways. Inchbald vigorously attacks corruption in society, particularly (but by no means solely) striking at the corruptions of a worldly and highly political clergy. She theorizes about the best ways to educate the young; she explores the dichotomy of nature versus art in life and education. The satire is witty and biting— until the end of the book, when her social vision collapses and she retreats into the simplistic and utterly unbelievable explanation that if the poor would not covet riches, all social problems would disappear. Having exposed so much corruption in society, she can supply no new models to replace the faulty structures, and her book simply comes up short in its own failed vision. Bage, a more consistent thinker than Inchbald and perhaps a better writer as well, does not attempt to supply a structure to replace the social institutions he has exposed. Having satirized corrupt politicians, an equally corrupt clergy, and an aristocracy whose degeneration manifests itself in the fleshly metaphor of crippling gout, he marries off his protagonist, blesses his good characters with a fond happily ever after, and ends the book. By the end of the century, it had become easy to see what was wrong in society but very difficult indeed to posit workable reforms.

1. Isaac Kramnick has argued persuasively that the "manufacturing spirit" was central to much of the most vital thought of the time, informing science, industry, social and family relations, and literature. See "Children's Literature and Bourgeois Ideology: Observations on Culture and Industrial Capitalism in the Later Eighteenth Century," in *Culture and Politics from Puritanism to the Enlightenment,* ed. Perez Zagorin (Berkeley: University of California Press, 1980), pp. 203–40.

2. Each of these movements has been examined in detail in numerous books; among the best introductory discussions are L. B. Namier's *England in the Age of the American Revolution* and Donald Greene's *The Age of Exuberance.*

3. The content of these novels is often ignored. For instance, in his respected book, *Jane Austen: A Study of Her Artistic Development,* A. Walton Litz talks about the "debased standards in current fiction" against which we are to measure Jane Austen's genius. One of the examples of that debased fiction which he cites is *The Fool of Quality,* from which Professor Litz draws examples only of passages that he finds "burlesques" of emotion. He makes no suggestion that Brooke's novel is of any further interest. Such a simplified view of midcentury fiction—that it all presented merely a "debased" standard—distorts literary history, as a closer look at these novels shows. Marilyn Butler, in *Jane Austen and the War of Ideas,* notes the need for such a reassessment; see particularly her discussion of Henry MacKenzie. It is interesting that contemporary writers could be aware of the social value inherent in such fiction: Mary Wollstonecraft, in *A Vindication of the Rights of Woman,* twice refers to the educational theories in Thomas Day's *The History of Sandford and Merton.*

4. One of the earliest and certainly one of the sharpest novelists of social criticism, Defoe targets for his skeptical inspection assumptions about social position, social responsibility, the nature of criminality, and the fairness and effectiveness of the criminal justice system. The most remarkable area of his criticism, it seems to me, is his analysis of the place of women in society. Defoe's women enjoy a wider sphere of movement than any other female characters in eighteenth-century novels, even those in works such as *Anna St. Ives* and *Hermsprong* that concern themselves so specifically with the issues of women's rights and responsibilities in society.

5. Lewis describes the effect of education on the Monk: "It was by no means his nature to be timid: but his education had impressed his mind with fear so strongly, that apprehension was now become part of his character. Had his youth been passed in the world, he would have shown himself possessed of many brilliant and manly qualities. He was naturally enterprising, firm and fearless; he had a warrior's heart, and he might have shown with splendour at the head of an army. There was no want of generosity in his nature: the

wretched never failed to find in him a compassionate auditor: his abilities were quick and decisive. With such qualities he would have been an ornament to his country: that he possessed them he had given proofs in his earliest infancy, and his parents had beheld his dawning virtues with the fondest delight and admiration." *The Monk* (New York: Grove Press, 1957), p. 237.

6. Many of these novels are available in good modern editions, and I have used these whenever possible; for the novels that have not recently been reprinted, I have cited the eighteenth-century texts. Regrettably, Martin Battestin's new edition of *Amelia* in the Wesleyan series was not published in time for me to use it, and therefore I have used the first edition of the novel.

1

AMELIA / *Henry Fielding*

Whatever is wicked, hateful, absurd, or ridiculous, must be exposed and punished before this Nation is brought to that Height of Purity and good Manners to which I wish to see it exalted.
Henry Fielding, The Champion, No. 16

For most of the eighteenth century, social criticism in the English novel is clearly to be distinguished from revolution. It is not until the hope of persuasion to reform fades that, with Godwin, a revolutionary posture becomes unavoidable. Social problems, like human relationships, are complex, and matters are further complicated because failures in the social system magnify faults in the individual. Thus a relatively small misstep by an individual can bring disaster when social institutions are unresponsive, if not simply and blatantly corrupt. Fielding's *Amelia* explores this interaction between individual and social weakness.

Henry Fielding, though a social critic, was certainly no more a revolutionary than were Daniel Defoe, John Gay, Samuel Richardson, or Tobias Smollett. Fielding's social commentary—the *Covent Garden Journal,* the essays on *Provision for the Poor* and *The Causes of the Late Increase of Robbers,* the satirical plays, the novels *Jonathan Wild, Tom Jones,* and, most of all, *Amelia*—describes and criticizes social faults which Fielding saw in common with many of his contemporaries. Like Addison and Steele and Pope, he was concerned with corruption in manners and in politics; like Smollett, he blamed many social ills, from unrest to robbery, on a meretricious desire for "luxury;"[1] like Gay, he wrote about the abuses of the legal and penal systems as manifestations of broader social problems. Much of Fielding's writing, like that of his contemporaries, is concerned with the exposure of social faults, and in *Amelia,* his last novel, Fielding brought many of these common concerns to bear in his story of the deserving but long-suffering couple, the Booths.

Fielding's comment in *The Champion* that "whatever is wicked, hateful, absurd, or ridiculous, must be exposed and punished before this Nation is brought to that Height of Purity and good Manners to which I wish to see it exalted,"[2] suggests that he takes upon himself the tasks of setting standards and exposing faults; as George Sherburn and others have pointed out, Fielding's writing is consciously moral.[3] For the most part, Fielding's morality is very practical. A pamphlet such as *On the Late Increase of Robbers* is as characteristic as *Tom Jones.* In both, Fielding exposes faults in his society and suggests solutions to these problems.[4]

The social concern of *Amelia* is made plain in its opening chapters. Fielding introduces us to the legal and penal systems of England, devoting nearly two hundred pages to a detailed description of the workings of these institutions. The novel portrays specific social ills: the inequities of justice for the poor, especially laws regarding debt; unjust social policies that fail to provide adequate pensions for soldiers; and corruptions of human institutions and relationships on every level of society, particularly the treatment of the needy by the rich.

The predominant mood of *Amelia* is suspended fear; the characters live on the edge of a precipice of penury and, even worse, in imminent danger of arrest for debt. We learn in the first pages of the novel that a man (or woman) can be thrown into prison by circumstances as capricious as walking on the wrong street or becoming involved in someone else's problems. Fielding's opening sets the narrow emotional range of the work, encompassing only the most basic human emotions. There are few gradations of character, and little growth. Even Booth, who could be expected to learn from his various follies (particularly after he repeatedly brings his family to the very brink of ruin and has to be saved by others each time), shows no real change. He does have a rather sudden religious conversion at the end of the novel, but the conversion, as critics have noted,[5] is not convincing.

In spite of the title, Fielding focuses at least as much on institutions as on characters. The novel is a portrait in fiction of the current social institutions—but it is not a fictional portrait. Virtually every abuse described is documented by historians and by Fielding himself in his pamphlets and periodical prose. This is not a "problem novel," as it has been called; it is not a "falling off of power in his last novel."[6] Rather, *Amelia* is a different kind of novel from what we have met in Fielding before. To the detriment of plot and characterization, Fielding concentrates on, as it were, current events. We should not be surprised to find him preoccupied with real social problems, for in *Jonathan Wild* Fielding had already moved the novel into the realm of social criticism, although the criticism is reserved more for the bad character than for the bad institution. But we see quite enough of bad institutions in that book for it to be clear that there is an intimate relationship between one and the other. The obviously satiric tone in *Jonathan Wild* allows the social criticism to be cutting yet not unduly disturbing. It is perhaps hard to tell to what degree Fielding is being witty rather than simply angry at any given point: Heartfree is the positive character, the one the reader hopes will come to no harm, but he is not the hero—in fact, he is so naive that the reader is inclined, with Wild, almost to feel that Heartfree gets what he deserves.

The case is quite different in *Amelia,* where the character who suffers is the heroine, and where plaints against injustice are directly stated. When Fielding writes here about how the evil take advantage of the good, he remarks in his own voice that the good are victimized by the bad simply because their minds do not run in the same nefarious paths as their more evil acquaintances:

> The Truth is, that it is almost impossible Guilt should miss the discovering of all the Snares in its Way; as it is constantly prying closely into every Corner, in order to lay Snares for others. Where-

as Innocence, having no such Purpose, walks fearlessly and carelessly through Life; and is consequently liable to tread on the Gins,
which Cunning hath laid to entrap it. . . . it is not Want of Sense,
but Want of Suspicion by which Innocence is often betrayed. . . .
many an innocent Person hath owed his Ruin to this Circumstance
alone, that the Degree of Villainy was such as must have exceeded
the Faith of every Man who was not himself a Villain.[7]

That Fielding largely avoids satire in *Amelia* makes his criticism
relatively straightforward, without a stylistic intermediary between the author's voice and the reader. Reading the book for
its blunt statements on social questions does much to lessen our
struggles with it as a problem novel. The first chapters of *Amelia*
make Fielding's plan quite clear. Although these early chapters
seem almost like a separable section of the book, they are part
of Fielding's larger structure: he does not change his method in
the novel after he closes the introductory prison scenes, but, on
the contrary, he keeps to the same mode for four volumes.

As we know from scholars such as Dorothy Marshall and
E. P. Thompson, eighteenth-century England was not kind to
the poor.[8] The laws and the legal system severely aggravated,
rather than ameliorated, social problems. Fielding's chapter
one of *Amelia* is a statement that living conditions are created by
men themselves, and that it is not "Providence" but men who
are responsible for them. The magistrate Fielding surely had
seen enough evidence firsthand of the social and legal abuses
he was to chronicle in *Amelia* to be able to write: "To speak a
bold Truth, I am, after much mature Deliberation, inclined to
suspect, that the Public Voice hath, in all Ages, done much
Injustice to Fortune, and hath convinced her of many Facts in
which she had not the least Concern. I question much, whether
we may not by natural Means, account for the success of
Knaves, the Calamities of Fools, with all the Miseries in which
Men of Sense sometimes involve themselves by quitting the
Directions of Prudence . . ." (vol. I, pp. 1–2).

As if to prove the point, having paused for this comment
right at the beginning, Fielding opens the second chapter by
getting into the action. The action is not domestic, nor even

social—it is legal: "On the first of *April,* in the year _____, the Watchmen of a certain Parish (I know not particularly which) within the Liberty of Westminster, brought several Persons whom they had apprehended the preceding Night, before *Jonathan Thrasher,* Esq; one of the Justices of the Peace for that liberty" (vol. I, pp. 3–4). Chapter two surveys some of the abuses of the legal system. The next chapters are scenes of prison life; we do not get out of the prison until the third chapter of Book the Fourth, an entire volume later.

Booth, Amelia's husband, is a poor soldier on half pay (his inadequate pension itself is one of the injustices Fielding notes), and his poverty is exacerbated by his several failings. An inclination to gamble and a rather innocent attitude allow him to be taken advantage of at every turn by those of greater means and fewer scruples. Amelia is a good and understanding woman, but, as a woman, she can do little more than scrimp, pawn her extra nightdress, and say forgiving words. Both Amelia and her husband are good people. And yet they will be in trouble with the law for most of the book. Though respectable, they are poor—and thus at the mercies of their creditors and the courts. Fielding wants his readers to be aware both of the quality of impending disaster that such a lifestyle presupposes and of the gross callousness, not to mention unfairness, of the judicial and punitive system that is in the background. It is not accidental that Fielding opens his book with such a long section of court and prison scenes: the reader's perception of the situation of the protagonists is colored by the same awareness of looming disaster under which they suffer.

Amelia insists that the human condition is a fragile one, but Fielding sees this fragility not in terms of an unavoidable human fate but of a correctable social system. Justice Thrasher's court is a glaring example of that corrupt system:

Mr. *Thrasher* . . . had some few Imperfections in his magistratical Capacity. I own, I have been sometimes inclined to think, that this Office of a Justice of Peace requires some Knowledge of the Law: for this simple Reason; because in every Case which comes before him, he is to judge and act according to Law. Again, as these Laws are contained in a great Variety of Books; the Statutes which relate to the Office of a Justice of Peace making of themselves at least two large Volumes in Folio; and that Part of his Jurisdiction which is founded on the common Law being disbursed in above a hundred Volumes, I cannot conceive how this Knowledge should be acquired without reading; and yet certain it is, Mr. *Thrasher* never read one Syllable of the Matter. (vol. I, pp. 7–8)

Not simply ignorant, Justice Thrasher is also unfeeling, blind to reason, and open only to arguments of class. Fielding states his case against Thrasher so strongly that he seems to be drawing a caricature. If it were not for the work of scholars such as Marshall and Thompson, we might think Fielding is exaggerating. He is not; Thrasher must be based on many a "Justice" whom Fielding had known. Fielding continues that Justice Thrasher's never having read any law

perhaps was a Defect; but this was not all: for where mere Ignorance is to decide a Point, it will always be an even Chance whether it decides right or wrong; but sorry am I to say, Right was often in a much worse Situation than this, and Wrong hath often had Five hundred to one on his Side before that Magistrate; who, if he was ignorant of the Law of England, was yet well versed in the Laws of Nature. He perfectly well understood that fundamental Principle so strongly laid down in the Institutes of the learned Rochefoucault; by which the Duty of Self-love is so strongly enforced. . . . To speak the Truth plainly, the Justice was never indifferent in a Cause, but when he could get nothing on either Side. (vol. I, p. 8)

The ignorance and venality which Fielding records in Justice Thrasher were quite common, as B. M. Jones has documented in some detail.[9] Jones shows that these shameful faults in the legal system were a recurring theme for Fielding, as in *Tumble-Down Dick, or Phaeton in the Suds* (1736), and he reminds us that Fielding was "unsparing in his denunciation of the ignorance, dishonesty, corruption and partiality of the 'trading justices:' 'Sir, that's a Justice of the Peace; and the other is a schoolmistress teaching the Justice to spell; for you must know, Sir, the Justice is a very ingenious man and a very great scholar, but happen'd to have the misfortune in his youth never to learn to read'" (*Tumble Down Dick*).[10] Jones continues, "In Justice Squeezum (the forerunner of Justice Thrasher in *Amelia*), Fielding has given us a picture of a justice of the time, who decides all cases brought before him only after his clerk has informed him whether the accused has offered a sufficient bribe [and] who is obsequious to men of fashion."[11] So bad was the repute in which the office was held that Fielding actually suffered opprobrium when he took it on, and he found it necessary to vindicate his character.[12] I should note that it was only the corrupt justice who found the office lucrative; Fielding himself had to request an additional magistracy in order to increase his income.[13]

In earlier books like *Joseph Andrews* and *Jonathan Wild,* Fielding had made reference to the weaknesses and corruptions of the legal system; most obviously, there are recurring references in *Jonathan Wild* to the blindness of the law and to its virtual prejudice against the honest (but poor) citizen. The law is only one of many targets *Jonathan Wild* satirizes, the reader's attention being divided over a number of objects. In *Amelia* the reader's attention focuses directly on the legal and penal systems. The novel, having disposed of the idea that providence causes all men's evils and having presented Justice Thrasher to prove the point, introduces us to the course of justice which Justice Thrasher oversees: the first case is that of a man who, streaming with blood and clearly the worse for wear, is accused of battery against a much stouter man who bears no mark of violence. The accused pleads to be allowed to bring forward witnesses in his defense, "but the justice presently interrupted him, saying, "Sirrah, your Tongue betrays your Guilt. You are an Irishman, and that is always sufficient Evidence with me" (vol. I, p. 10). The second case concerns a maid servant who was arrested for street walking when she was found outside her house during the night. Her explanation that she was seeking a midwife for her mistress is ignored and she, too, is sent off to jail. Next, a pair of genteel people are brought before the justice, but upon receiving a sign from his clerk, they are dismissed.

British justice of the time apparently was much like this. Treatment hung on appearance—appearance of the ability to pay a bribe or a fee; some of the "trading justices" would even order mass false arrests in order to take fees and bail money (which they kept) from those arraigned.[14] Thus the case of poor Booth when he comes before the justice in *Amelia* should be no surprise to us, and surely was not to any reader of Fielding's time who was even minimally aware of legal goings-on. Booth is accused of "beating the watchman in the execution of his office." The justice is able to decide the case without any fuss: "The Justice, perceiving the Criminal to be but shabbily drest, was going to commit him without asking any further Questions" (vol. I, p. 13). Booth insists on being heard, however, and tells his story: on his way home, he saw two men beating a third; he stopped to help the person being beaten and was, with the original three combatants, arrested by the watch. The two assailants bribed the officers and were released; he was offered liberty "at the Price of Half a Crown," but he unfortunately had no money on his person. Justice Thrasher is far too venal to listen to such a story. "In short, the Magistrate had too great an Honour for Truth to suspect that she ever appeared in sordid Apparel; nor did he ever sully his sublime Notions of that Virtue, by uniting them with the mean Ideas of Poverty and Distress" (Vol. I, p. 9). So both Booth and the man he had tried to help are sent off to prison. The assailants never even come before the justice.

Just as Fielding chronicles real abuses when he describes the proceedings in Justice Thrasher's court, so he writes of current practice when he comes to the prison scenes. Prisons are not correctional institutions designed to aid society by reshaping its untoward members; they are profit-making concerns, there to make as much money as possible for their (unsalaried) heads. All of the abuses Fielding had described more than twenty-five years earlier were still current in 1777 when John Howard wrote *The State of the Prisons*. Howard, who visited the prisons himself, recorded and publicized his findings. His testimony moved Parliament to make a few, but largely insufficient, reforms. (I discuss some of his most shocking findings as verification of the details in the prison scenes in Godwin's *Caleb Williams;* the following details are specifically relevant to *Amelia.*[15])

Prisoners were subject to a range of fees—fees upon entry, fees upon leaving (even if he were acquitted of any wrongdoing, a man could not leave until he had paid all the accumulated fees), fees for the putting on and taking off of chains, fees for room, fees for the privilege of having guests, and most horribly, fees for food and drink. One of Howard's major complaints is that the keepers are permitted to sell food and drink to the prisoners and are therefore essentially keeping a public house; it is in their interest to encourage consumption, especially of liquor, and therefore to contribute to the degeneracy of their charges. The man without money might just about starve, since almost no food was provided for him by law. Debtors, obviously, would be hard put to pay for themselves; absurdly, in many cases the law specifically omitted debtors from provisions made for the support of felons. Beyond the many fees demanded by keepers, the prisoner was also subject to garnish, the fee demanded of incoming prisoners by those already in jail. If the newcomer had no cash, he was obliged to give up some part of his clothing. Finally, on the subject of fees, Howard objects also to the "extortion of bailiffs. These detain in their houses (properly enough denominated spunging-houses), at an enormous expense, prisoners who have money."[16]

Howard complains also about laxness of discipline, promiscuity, and gambling. "The prisoners," he says, "spend their time in sloth, profaneness and debauchery, to a degree which, in some of those houses that I have seen, is extremely shocking."[17] All sorts of prisoners, he complains, are confined together: "debtors and felons, men and women, the young beginner and the old offender . . . ."[18] Riot and drunkenness thrive, encouraged by the jailor's sale of spirits. In addition,

"gaming in various forms is very frequent: cards, dice, skit-
tles . . . abound as accomplished gamblers ply their trade."[19]
The whole is a scene of "such confusion and distress, and such
shrieks and outcries, as can be better conceived than described," with "numbers of both sexes . . . shut up together for
many days and nights in one room."[20]

Fielding's drawing of prison life in *Amelia* corresponds in
every point to conditions documented by Howard. Fielding
closes chapter two by dispatching the "delinquents" to prison.
The first sentence of chapter three, "Containing the Inside of a
Prison," deals with garnish; Booth immediately is accosted and
garnish demanded of him. "Garnish," Fielding explains, is the
custom that requires every incoming prisoner "to give something to former Prisoners to make them drink" (vol. I, p. 16).
When Booth explains that he has no money, he is stripped of
his jacket.[21] Thus begins chapter three, which largely catalogs
the abuses in the penal system. The prison crowds human
beings together without regard to sex, physical condition, or
even crime. The first offender, or the simply unfortunate, re-
sides with the most hardened criminal, resulting in an increase
in the criminality of those who had perhaps only come to prison
by accident in the first place. Fielding inveighed against this
practice not only in *Amelia* but in his legal writings. In *Amelia* he
slowly and carefully sets these and other horrors of the system
before us.

Not least of these is the fact that the punishments seem to
afflict the least criminal man much more heavily than the hardened felon. In chapter four, "Disclosing further Secrets of the
Prison-House," Fielding sends Booth on a tour of the prison,
during which we meet all classes of men. (Note that Booth, like
most of the other prisoners, has a great deal of freedom within
the prison.) First, he meets three men in fetters, "who were
enjoying themselves very merrily over a Bottle of Wine, and a
Pipe of Tobacco" (vol. I, p. 24). These are three street robbers,
"certain of being hanged the ensuing Sessions" (vol. I, p. 24).
Their impending fate clearly makes no difference to their present enjoyment. "A little farther [he] beheld a Man prostrate on

the Ground, whose heavy Groans, and frantic Actions, plainly indicated the highest Disorder of Mind" (vol. I, p. 25). Was this a repentant felon, castigating himself for his crimes? "This person was, it seems, committed for a small Felony; and his Wife, who then lay-in, upon hearing the News had thrown herself from a Window two Pair of Stairs high, by which means he had, in all Probability, lost both her and his Child" (vol. I, p. 25). Among the women it is the same—the hardened criminals find incarceration a joke; the innocent and unfortunate find it a horror. Booth passes a street walker who "as she past by Mr. *Booth* . . . damn'd his Eyes, and discharged a Volley of Words, every one of which was too indecent to be repeated" (vol. I, p. 25); on the other hand, he passes "a little Creature sitting by herself in a Corner and crying bitterly." Also a street-walker? No, she "was committed, because her Father-in-Law, who was in the Grenadier Guards, had sworn that he was afraid of his Life, or of some bodily Harm, which she would do him, and she could get no Sureties for keeping the Peace: for which Reason Justice *Thrasher* had committed her to Prison" (vol. I, pp. 25–26).

The imprisonment itself is as unjust as the commitment process. Money buys not only privilege but also freedom from punishment. At the same time, prisoners often take matters into their own hands in the case of crimes odious to themselves and may nearly put an end to transgressors against their community's rules before any authority bothers to intervene. Thus, Booth sees a man prepared for whipping as a punishment for petty larceny; the man pays an additional sixpence and is saved. He sees a man being set upon by several of the prisoners; only at the latest moment is he rescued from them by the authorities. If commitment and punishment are unjust, equally so are the bail laws. Booth notices a "young Woman in Rags sitting on the Ground, and supporting the Head of an old Man in her Lap, who appeared to be giving up the Ghost." He learns that they are father and daughter, "the latter . . . committed for stealing a Loaf, in order to support the former, and the former for receiving it knowing it to be stolen" (vol. I, pp. 26–27). At the same moment, Booth notices a well-dressed man walk by and is told that this man's crime was "a most horrid Perjury"—he is expected to be bailed that same day. The "horrid" crime of the "gentleman" is bailable; that of the father and daughter is not. Even worse, because perjury is bailable, "methods are often found to escape any punishment at all" (vol. I, p. 27).

Finally, there is the case of the veteran, who "hath served his Country, lost his Limb, and received several Wounds at the Seige of Gibraltar. When he was discharged from the Hospital abroad, he came over to get into that of *Chelsea*, but could not immediately, as none of his Officers were then in England; in the mean time, he was one Day apprehended and committed on suspicion of stealing three Herrings from a Fishmonger. He [had been] tried several Months ago for this Offence, and acquitted; indeed his Innocence manifestly appeared at the Trial; but he was brought back again for his Fees, and here he hath lain ever since" (vol. I, pp. 28–29). Fielding ends Booth's survey of the prison with reference to one of the unfairest practices of all—the taking of fees that could keep a man in prison even when no charges were outstanding against him. As I noted earlier, because prisons levied fees on every necessity and act, without money a man could not leave even on acquittal. The prisoner with money could have all the comforts; the poor prisoner might even starve. The poor were often imprisoned on the strength of their appearance or their circumstances; once there, they had neither redress nor escape.

At the end of Booth's tour, he notices a woman prisoner being introduced to the prison. Some time later, he ascertains that she is Miss Mathews, a lady with whom he had formerly been on somewhat friendly terms. She soon arranges that they spend the night together and seduces the good Booth into an affair. Aside from the moral implications for Booth's character (he longs for his virtuous wife all the while he is having the affair with Miss Mathews), these seduction scenes show that, among the amenities money could purchase in prison, not the least of them was the right to a private chamber where fellow prisoners or guests from outside could be entertained. Promiscuity among the prisoners, thefts of each other's goods, mixing hardened criminals with first offenders—or even totally innocent persons—and, not least, the gross cupidity of the jailors make the prison system that Fielding details in *Amelia* a clear target for reform. Indeed, as Jones shows in his chapter on "Fielding and Prison Reform," Fielding was strongly concerned to implement, or at least to make public the necessity for, reform. As Howard's *The State of the Prisons* attests, little was to change in the next quarter of a century.

But the question in dealing with the novel *Amelia* is to discover not what attempts at reform Fielding made in the course of his career as magistrate, but to determine why he would begin his novel with such a detailed account of the inequities, injustices, and evils of the judicial and penal system. The helplessness of the individual in the face of corrupt institutions is in large part the subject of the book, and although Fielding in later chapters deals with the individual as he relates to various social institutions, it is clearly the legal and penal system that is most threatening. Once this framework has been established, it stands as a necessary backdrop to the action, for we as readers must—and do—feel the same sense of danger that haunts Booth and his Amelia.

Fielding explores the relationship between faulty societal institutions and the people whose lives are shaped by them. The characters always act within an institutional context: just as we watch Booth and Miss Mathews within the confines of the prison in the early chapters, we watch Booth and Amelia as they struggle with patrons, pawnbrokers, and bailiffs throughout the later ones. The sense of threat is always present and always external to the relationship. Fielding defines very supportive human relationships for his protagonists, yet society's institutions keep them constantly in a state of anguish.

Most frighteningly, the evils that engulf them are not of their own making. Booth may be weak, and he loses the little money he and Amelia get together. But they never can acquire enough money to be safe; no matter what they do, debt is always a spectre that any misstep turns into a reality. Similarly, Booth first finds himself in jail through no fault of his own. All of Booth's troubles, including that first conviction, come about because he is poor in the first place. He is convicted, we remember, because he does not look respectable. His very poverty is a social injustice: although he has served his country well, he has been retired on a most insufficient half pay. Fielding emphasizes that one injustice leads to another. Because Booth is poor, he is at the mercy of creditors and his wife is at the mercy of great men; when he is robbed by a dishonest servant girl, the little he had is too small an amount to be covered by law. Booth and Amelia are a deserving couple. Why should they suffer poverty, and, further, why should they constantly be exploited by others who are clearly less virtuous and even less wise? Fielding is explicit. Merit should be, but is not, rewarded by society; vice can triumph over virtue because virtue is not prepared to recognize the devious traps which vice manufactures. Fielding is blunt in saying that, on virtually every front, merit is not properly rewarded by society. Booth's inadequate half pay and the treatment of the soldier who was imprisoned because he could not get into a hospital are two examples. Later, after the reader has met a number of such cases, Fielding explicitly comments that the rewards in society ought to go to the deserving rather than the insistent. The first context is literary; later, Fielding returns to the topic in a more general setting.

The earlier discussion takes place, as so much of the novel does, in the baliff's house as Booth awaits the posting of bail. He has been treated to a lengthy conversation with an "author," a man of no particular learning or talent, who asks Booth to subscribe to his newest work, and Booth avoids doing so. When Booth's two friends, the Colonel and Sergeant Atkinson, come to post bond, the "author" asks the colonel to subscribe, and without any consideration, the colonel hands over double the subscription rate. Booth is distressed by this clear reward for lack of merit and by the social implications of the act; he apologizes to the colonel:

"it may look uncharitable in me, to blame you for your Generosity; but I am convinced the Fellow hath not the least Merit or Capacity; and you have subscribed to the most horrid Trash that ever was published."

"I care not a Farthing what he publishes. . . . Heaven forbid, I should be obliged to read half the Nonsense I have subscribed to."

"But, don't you think . . . that by such indiscriminate Encouragement of Authors, you do a real Mischief to the Society? By propagating the Subscriptions of such Fellows, people are tired out, and with-hold their Contributions to *Men of real Merit.* . . ."

"Pugh . . . I never consider these Matters. Good or bad, it is all one to me. . . ." (vol. III, pp. 155–56) [italics mine]

This indifference to quality, whether in the treatment of a soldier or a writer, a rich man or a poor one, is disturbing to Fielding on two grounds: the deserving are not rewarded, and even more importantly, society as a whole may lose the services of the good and the competent, to be left impoverished "with all the Scurrility, Indecency, and Profaneness with which the Age abounds . . ." (vol. III, p. 156).

When Fielding returns to this theme later, he is even more forceful. Here it is Dr. Harrison (always the approved voice of Fielding) and a "nobleman of his acquaintance" who discuss at length the system of reward prevailing in society. The nobleman argues that merit can have little relation to reward in a real, as opposed to an ideal, society. The doctor, of course, argues on the other side. Dr. Harrison has come to the nobleman to ask a favor—that a young soldier of considerable merit (Booth) be placed back on full pay so that he can support his wife and children. After the requisite social amenities,

the Doctor open'd his Business, and told the Great Man, that he was come to him to solicit a Favour for a young Gentleman who had been an Officer in the Army, and was now on Half-Pay. "All the Favour I ask, my Lord . . . is, that this Gentleman may be again admitted *ad eundum.* I am convinced your Lordship will do me the Justice to think I would not ask for a worthless Person; but indeed the young Man I mean hath very extraordinary Merit. He was at the Seige at *Gibraltar,* in which he behaved with distinguished Bravery; and was dangerously wounded at two several Times in the Service of his Country. I will add, that he is at present in great Necessity, and hath a Wife and several Children, for whom he hath no other Means of providing; and if it will recommend him further to your Lordship's Favour, his Wife, I believe, is one of the best and worthiest of her Sex."(vol. IV, p. 121)

The doctor's argument rests solely on merit. Booth is deserving, even his wife is deserving; justice demands that they be aided. The nobleman's answer is instructive. He tells the doctor that he needs his help in getting a friend elected. When the doctor protests that he cannot work in the cause of that particular man, the nobleman says he cannot help Booth. Dr. Harrison responds, "Is his own Merit, then, my Lord, no Recommendation?" (vol. IV, p. 125).

Clearly the nobleman and the doctor are talking at cross purposes, the one viewing reward only in terms of bargains reached, the other in terms of absolute worth. The remainder of the rather long scene is a debate between the two points of view. Note that Fielding chooses for his debators the middle-class doctor and the aristocratic nobleman who clearly represents the socially destructive power of an insensitive aristocracy. George Sherburn reminds us that we should look at these scenes within the literary context of the time:

Amelia was published in December, 1751. Its attack on the aristocracy for callousness and lack of recognition of merit was, of course, nothing new. About two months before the death of Alexander Pope, much of whose writing decries the bad taste and corruption of the aristocracy, Dr. Johnson had published his Life of Richard Savage, which told a story motivated much as Booth's was to be. In 1748 in Roderick Random Smollett had displayed the acidity of his heart in the story of the difficulties of Melopoyn in securing a patron for his tragedy—transparently the story of Smollett's own difficulties over his Regicide. Four years after Amelia, Dr. Johnson penned his famous letter to the Earl of Chesterfield about patronage, and in 1759 Goldsmith's Enquiry reiterated this tale of the lack of recognition of merit. In brief, this sort of thing, always evident in literary circles, was in the eighteenth century by way of becoming an agent to dissipate respect and regard for noble lords.[22]

Fielding's attack may not have been new, but it was certainly angry. None of the aristocratic characters in *Amelia* comes off with high marks, and the nobleman with whom the doctor discusses this issue of rewards in society is no exception. Fielding, through Dr. Harrison, insists that merit must be rewarded, both for the sake of the individual and for the health of the community. The nobleman argues that the doctor's position is hopelessly idealistic, that in the real world merit and reward simply do not presuppose one another.

The doctor notes that Booth is an excellent officer.

> "Very probably!" cries my Lord _____. "And there are Abundance with the same Merit, and the same Qualifications, who want a Morsel of Bread for themselves and their Families."
> "It is an infamous Scandal on the Nation. . . ."
> "How can it be otherwise?" says the Peer. "Do you think it is possible to provide for all Men of Merit?"
> "Yes, surely do I," said the Doctor. "And very easily too."
> "How, pray?"—cries the Lord _____.
> "Only by not providing for those of none." (vol. IV, pp. 126–27)

For the doctor, the relation between the individual and society as a whole is very close indeed:

> "to deny a Man the Preferment which he merits, and to give it to another Man who doth not merit it, is a manifest Act of Injustice. . . . Nor is it only an Act of Injustice to the Man himself, but to the Public, for whose Good principally all public Offices are, or ought to be instituted. Now this Good can never be completed, nor obtained, but by employing all Persons according to their Capacities. Wherever true Merit is liable to be superseded by Favour and Partiality, and Men are intrusted with Offices, without any Regard to Capacity or Integrity, the Affairs of State will always be in a deplorable Situation." (vol. IV, pp. 130–31)

Thus, injustice to the individual is always injustice to the society at large. But lack of reward for merit has even worse consequences: "it hath a manifest Tendency to destroy all Virtue and all Ability among the People, by taking away all that Encouragement and Incentive, which should promote Emulation, and

raise Men to aim at excelling in any Art, Science, or Profession"
(vol. IV, p. 131). The lack of moral integrity and the destruction of ambition, again, have broad consequences, for such a
nation becomes "contemptible among its neighbours" (vol. IV,
p. 131).

This theme of the interdependency between morality and
government, between individual and society, had already begun to be explored by Fielding in *Jonathan Wild.* In that earlier
novel, Fielding repeatedly seems to suggest that evil usually
lives better than good, and that, therefore, to borrow a phrase,
the times are out of joint. Fielding's criticism of governmental
corruption is obviously more intense in *Jonathan Wild*—in some
scholars' readings it is the subject of the book. That is not the
case in *Amelia;* Fielding's range of social targets is broader in
Amelia than in *Jonathan Wild.* But government is central to that
range because so many personal misfortunes can be traced to
corrupt, or at best, wrong-headed government policies. Thus,
amelioration of the social situation requires the improvement
of government, which Dr. Harrison sees as not only simple but
natural. Dr. Harrison tries to convince the nobleman that virtue
in a minister of government is not only socially useful but politically expedient:

> "But if . . . he will please to consider the true Interest of his
> Country, and that only in great and national Points; if he will
> engage his Country in neither Alliances nor Quarrels, but where it
> is really interested; if he will raise no Money but what is wanted;
> nor employ any civil or military Officers but what are useful; and
> place in these Employments Men of the highest Integrity, and of
> the greatest Abilities; if he will employ some few of his Hours to
> advance our Trade, and some few more to regulate our domestic
> Government: If he would do this, my Lord, I will answer for it he
> shall have no Opposition to baffle. Such a Minister may, in the
> Language of the Law, put himself on his Country when he pleases
> and he shall come off with Honour and Applause." (vol. IV, pp.
> 133–34)

The nobleman cannot believe that "there ever was such a Minister, or ever will be." The doctor responds, "Why not. . . . It

requires no very extraordinary Parts, nor any extraordinary Degree of Virtue. He need practise no great Instances of Self-denial. He shall have Power, and Honour, and Riches, and perhaps all in a much greater Degree than he can ever acquire, by pursuing a contrary System" (vol. IV, p. 134). If this is true, that expediency so neatly fits with honor, why then are there so many corrupt men, especially corrupt politicans? Or, as his lordship asks, "Do you really believe any Man upon Earth was ever a Rogue out of Choice?" To which the good doctor has to reply, "I am ashamed to answer in the Affirmative; and yet I am afraid Experience would almost justify me if I should" (vol. IV, p. 134).

This interchange is central to Fielding's moral explorations in the book, for from this discussion it seems quite clear that morality consists simply in the doing of meritorious acts by the individual and the rewarding of those acts by the society. On every level, from the personal to the societal, good and expediency should go together—that is, not only honor but reward should dictate that a man choose to act according to the highest standards. Evil and injustice on any level, therefore, cannot be ignored simply because "that is the way things are." Whatever is, clearly is not right; rather, much of what is wrong results from manmade error or corruption, and that corruption needs to be addressed by men of good will. *Jonathan Wild* and *Amelia* seem to indicate that Fielding would like to apply himself to reform on a much grander scale than he had ever been able to do as magistrate at Bow Street.[23]

The question of why the good always seem to lose to the bad is a nagging one. Amelia and Booth do not thrive, as Heartfree does not in *Jonathan Wild;* Fielding has observed that such people are always at the mercy of the unscrupulous. Fielding answers the question directly. Why are the bad able to hoodwink the good?

> It is not, because Innocence is more blind than Guilt, that the former often overlooks and tumbles into the Pit, which the latter foresees and avoids. The Truth is, that it is almost impossible Guilt should miss the discovering of all the Snares in its Way; as it is

constantly prying closely into every Corner, in order to lay Snares for others. Whereas Innocence, having no such Purpose, walks fearlessly and carelessly through Life; and is consequently liable to tread on the Gins, which Cunning hath laid to entrap it. To speak plainly, and without Allegory or Figure, it is not Want of Sense, but Want of Suspicion, by which Innocence is often betrayed. Again, we often admire at the Folly of the Dupe, when we should transfer our whole Surprize to the astonishing Guilt of the Betrayer. In a word, many an innocent Person hath owed his Ruin to this Circumstance alone, that the Degree of Villainy was such as must have exceeded the Faith of every Man who was not himself a Villain. (vol. III, pp. 190–91)

Fielding does not discount individual evil; he recognizes it and rather wryly wishes good men could protect themselves somewhat more effectively from it. But he also recognizes that, on the individual level, the good have at least some chance against evil designs. Although Colonel James, under cover of his friendship for Booth, attempts to seduce Amelia, she can and does defend herself: she refuses to go to the masquerade, and she will not stay as a guest in his house. Booth, were he a bit stronger of character, could have withstood Captain Trent's invitations to the card table and not fallen into his debt. On the individual level, the possibility exists that one can ward off the blows. Fielding reserves most of his anger for societal corruptions and for legal injustices because, on that institutionalized level, the individual stands no chance at all. Clearly, for Fielding, institutionalized evil is far more dangerous than mere human weakness.

As we have seen, the law in *Amelia* operates with little regard to justice. Often worse than arbitrary, it is at times ridiculous. For example, at the end of the novel, it is discovered that Amelia's property had been fraudulently taken from her upon the death of her mother. The relevant deeds are locked in the home of Murphy, the unscrupulous lawyer who had engineered the plot. *But there is no legal way to search for the papers.* Papers, even if they are worth huge sums of money, cannot be stolen property. Fortunately, the papers are in a worthless box that *is* property, and therefore everything can be recovered.

Recovery of stolen goods, too, is subject to arbitrary and unfair treatment by the law. When Booth's servant runs off with the paltry goods he and Amelia have left after their financial embarrassments, neither she nor the pawnbroker to whom she sells the goods can be taken to task because the goods are not quite worth the legal amount (arbitrarily set at forty shillings) for "stolen goods under a servant's care." The girl is discharged, much to Booth's dismay, and

> "If the Girl is discharged," cries the Justice, "so must be the Pawnbroker: For if the Goods are not stolen, he cannot be guilty of receiving them, knowing them to be stolen. And besides as to his Offence, to say the Truth, I am almost weary of prosecuting it; for such are the Difficulties laid in the Way of this Prosecution, that it is almost impossible to convict any one on it. And to speak my Opinion plainly, such are the Laws, and such the Method of Proceeding, that one would almost think our Laws were rather made for the Protection of Rogues, than for the Punishment of them." (vol. IV, pp. 183–84)[24]

The great punishable crime seems to be lack of money. Being in debt is not socially frowned on; neither the debt nor going to prison for it carries much (if any) moral sanction. It is not shameful when Booth has to hide in his house to avoid his creditors. Booth and Amelia are not embarrassed in the face of their friends, and the friends are not embarrassed either. As Sherburn has pointed out, debtors for Fielding are a group for which he had "an especial sympathy."[25] Although debt carries little moral onus, it is punishable by imprisonment at the instigation of the creditor. In prison, unless the debtor has friends outside, nothing can be earned toward the paying of the debt. And so the punishment of the debtor becomes not a matter of justice but of vengeance. Arrest, bail bond, and imprisonment become parts of a nightmarish game in which the only people who stand to win are the officers of the law. In the prison scenes of the early part of the novel, Fielding emphasizes the corruption of the judicial and penal systems—both judge and jailor, clearly, are unfit to bear their offices—but, ironically, with "things as they are," the corrupted fit perfectly into the present state of corruption. The other link in the chain, arrest and internment, is equally bad. It is as if the entire legal system has nothing to do with justice but merely with profit. At every level, from the street, to the bar, to the prison, the evil-doer may escape punishment by paying, while the innocent will suffer simply through lack of funds.

Fielding portrays those who represent the system of justice as crafty and grasping creatures who make up in cupidity what they lack in humanity. Booth, for example, is called from his house on the pretext that his wife suddenly has been taken gravely ill. In reality, he is the victim of a bailiff's ruse to lure him from the safety of his home. Apprehended, he is taken by cab to the bailiff's house—and charged double the legal rate for cab hire. At his request, he is placed in a room by himself—and informed that he must buy refreshments whether he wants them or not because the bailiff "can't afford Gentlemen a Room to themselves for nothing" (vol. III, p. 112).

Fielding's account of Booth at the hands of the bailiff epitomizes his plaint against bad institutions and those whose corruption serves to exacerbate already bad conditions. In the eyes of Booth's jailor, respect is due only to those who can pay for it,[26] and Booth's misfortunes are made even heavier by the bailiff's treatment. Because he cannot hope to gain much money from Booth in the way of incidental expenses, the bailiff's only interest is to find additional actions against him, and he tries to keep Booth as long as possible. Jones has reminded us that for each "action" charged to the debtor, the bailiff was entitled to an additional fee, so it is in his interest to detain the debtor, neither to send him on to prison nor to release him.[27] When Booth's friends come to serve bail for him, the bailiff manages to put off his release for one extra night and, in the meantime, finds an additional writ against Booth. He treats Booth more and more disrespectfully as he realizes how little he can expect to extort from him. When it becomes impossible to hold him any longer, "the Bailiff stepped up to *Booth*, and told him he hoped he would remember Civility Money" (III,

209). Booth, remarking on the many incivilities he had endured at the man's hands, refuses to honor the custom.[28]

Thus the debtor, by definition poor, has no right to dignity or fair treatment. He is almost entirely at the mercy of the representatives of society, and those are, Fielding clearly shows us, not of the highest sort. The lack of logic shown by society in arresting a man for debt, so that he has no means of earning the money to pay that debt, is too obvious to require comment. Fielding contents himself only with the observation that, as Booth notes, "by the old Constitution of *England* . . . Men could not be arrested for Debt" (vol. III, p. 117).[29]

Amelia has been viewed by critics as Fielding's "problem novel" because it is so different from his other works, but the significant difference is not of form or even topic, but of tone. *Amelia* is an angry book; Fielding has written a relatively straightforward account of the social and legal injustices with which he was so intimately involved in his work as magistrate. He accounts for the distortions of relationships caused by human weaknesses, as when the colonel pursues his friend Booth's wife. But such social explorations are present in other novels of the century as well. Fielding's extended depiction of institutionalized injustice, coming as early as it does, is unique. The book has a vaguely nightmarish tone throughout, which, as I have noted, initially is struck in its earliest chapters. There is constant danger—as if to walk outside one's house is to invite disaster.

Fielding indeed recognizes that there are wonderful human relationships (friend, wife, husband) that improve the human condition. The relationships between Dr. Harrison, Sergeant Atkinson, and the Booths, or between Booth and Amelia, are all warm, caring, and virtually ideal. Amelia is always ready to support Booth. When she learns that he has had an affair with Miss Mathews, when she learns that he has gambled away the last money they have, Amelia's only concern is that her dear husband should not bear any additional guilt. She defends him from any pain she can; she willingly does without even food as long as he is with her. Booth returns her affection; to him she is the perfect woman, and (his lapse with Miss Mathews notwithstanding) his life and desires revolve around her well-being. Amelia and Booth are not so fortunate only in their relations with each other, for they have friends who are almost as loving and supportive to them as they are within their marriage. Sergeant Atkinson and his wife are important characters in the book, as is Dr. Harrison. All of them would, indeed on more than one occasion do, give the Booths their last reserves of money. When Sergeant Atkinson thinks he sees a suspicious character near the Booths' house, he offers to stand guard—and does. When Booth is arrested, Sergeant Atkinson runs up and down the town finding people to stand bond, keeps Amelia informed, and so on. Whatever small sums of money he has are at the disposal of the Booths at any time. Dr. Harrison is an equally good friend; it is he who stands bail for Booth, up to his own financial limits. Not only his money but his guidance are at Booth's disposal, and he tries in all ways to advance the welfare of the young couple, even, as I have noted, by trying through political means to secure a post for Booth. Although Fielding does include a number of unpleasant portraits, generally of the aristocracy, he gives most of the novel's attention to these relationships between friends and spouses. The overwhelming impression, looking at the Booths, the Atkinsons, and Dr. Harrison, is that human relationships are for the most part positive.

Then how is it that the impression of the book as a whole is one of unease, even of fear? Even the best of relationships, Fielding seems to say, cannot protect us from our faulty institutions; at best, they can afford us temporary buffers. Booth and Amelia cannot escape their situation by their own exertions, not even with all the goodwill and help of their friends. In order to give the novel a happy ending, Fielding has to drag in a *deus ex machina*: Amelia wonderfully enough comes into the fortune that had been stolen from her years earlier, and so all is saved. Fielding the moralist gives his book a moral ending. When Amelia regains her fortune, virtue is rewarded. All of her suffering, all of the Booths' distresses, are somehow repaid. Fielding ends his novel by assuring the reader that "as to *Booth* and *Amelia,* Fortune seems to have made them large Amends for the Tricks she played them in their Youth. They have, ever since the above Period of this History, enjoyed an uninterrupted Course of Health and Happiness" (vol. IV, p. 295). Each of the other characters, we learn in this last chapter, is rewarded according to his merits as well.[30] It is a very moral— and a very neat—ending for the novel.

But Fielding is not being entirely serious as he accounts for the fates of his heroes and his villains, for Fielding the realist, Fielding the magistrate, knew well that such neat apportioning of rewards and punishments is more pleasing than true. And he expects his readers to know it, too. At least, his hint is broad enough. For if on the last page of his novel Fielding tells us that "Fortune seems to have made [Booth and Amelia] large Amends for the Tricks she played them in their Youth," he expects us to remember that on the very first page of the novel he had warned:

> To speak a bold Truth, I am, after much mature Deliberation, inclined to suspect, that the Public Voice hath in all ages done much Injustice to Fortune, and hath convicted her of many Facts in which she had not the least Concern. I question much, whether we may not by natural Means account for the Success of Knaves, the Calamities of Fools, with all the Miseries in which Men of Sense sometimes involve themselves . . . ; in short, for all the ordinary Phenomena which are imputed to Fortune; whom, perhaps, Men accuse with no less Absurdity in Life, than a bad Player complains of ill Luck at the Game of Chess.
>
> But if Men are sometimes guilty of laying improper Blame on this imaginary Being, they are altogether as apt to make her Amends, by ascribing to her Honours which she as little deserves. (vol. I, pp. 1–2)

Fielding, however, has no other way to account for the change in Booth and Amelia's life, except for a change of "Fortune," for they have done nothing in particular to regain Amelia's inheritance. It is only by accident that they are saved, and so the accident must seem contrived. We have seen throughout the novel that none of their own efforts, nor those of their friends, could otherwise save them. Ironically, the very falsity of the ending proves the truthfulness of the book, for Fielding has so accurately reproduced for us the corruptions of his age that we, like his characters, can see no way out.

1. John Sekora in *Luxury: The Concept in Western Thought, Eden to Smollett* (Baltimore: The Johns Hopkins University Press, 1977) provides an excellent analysis of the meaning of luxury to the eighteenth-century English. See especially the chapters which deal specifically with Smollett.

2. *The Champion*, No. 16, December 22, 1739.

3. George Sherburn, "Fielding's Social Outlook," *Philological Quarterly,* XXXV, No. 1 (1956), pp. 1–23 passim.

4. Martin Battestin says in his essay "Fielding, *Amelia*, and the 'Constitution' of England," in *Literature and Society: The Lawrence Henry Gipson Symposium,* ed. Jan Fergus (Bethlehem, Pa.: The Lawrence Henry Gipson Institute, 1978) that "*Amelia* . . . deserves to be honored as the first novel of social protest and reform in English" (p. 1). His excellent analysis remarks on the relationship between Fielding's zeal as magistrate and his social protest in *Amelia*.

5. Robert Alter, *Fielding and the Nature of the Novel* (Cambridge: Harvard University Press, 1968), p. 165, is typical. "Booth's conversion . . . is hardly credible because it comes so suddenly, without any psychological preparation: the metamorphosis of Booth the deist into Booth the good Christian is a final reflection of a tendency in *Amelia* to moral schematism. . . ."

6. Robert Alter titles his chapter on *Amelia* "Fielding's Problem Novel," and he begins his discussion with the following definition: "Fielding's last work of fiction can be thought of as a problem novel in much the same way that the troubled comedies of Shakespeare's middle period are often regarded as problem plays. One gets a disconcerting sense that the tone of the writing is not always fully under the writer's control . . ." (p. 141). J. Paul Hunter in *Occasional Form: Henry Fielding and the Chains of Circumstance* (Baltimore: The Johns Hopkins University Press, 1975) argues more convincingly that we should not take "the easy view . . . that Fielding's talent was, sadly, depleted at the age of forty-four" in trying to understand *Amelia*, but that we should realize that "the radically different tone of *Amelia* . . . involve[s] a diminished vision of rhetorical possibility rather than talent gone soft or just gone" (p. 193).

7. Henry Fielding, *Amelia*, 4 vols. (London: A. Millar, 1752), vol. III, pp. 190–91. All references in the text are to this edition.

8. Dorothy Marshall, *The English Poor in the Eighteenth Century* (London: George Routledge and Sons, 1926); see also Marshall's *The English Domestic Servant in History* (London: George Philip and Son, 1949) and E. P.

Thompson, *Whigs and Hunters: The Origin of the Black Act* (London: Penguin Books, 1975).

9. *Henry Fielding: Novelist and Magistrate* (London: George Allen and Unwin, 1933). Jones does not do a great deal in the way of critical reading; rather, his accomplishment is to make much of the relevant historical information available in one essay and to suggest some of the many correspondences between fact and fiction in Fielding's world.

10. Jones, pp. 36–37. His discussion of "legal allusions in the plays" begins on p. 30.

11. Jones, p. 38.

12. Jones, p. 119; see also pp. 113–27 passim.

13. Nishan Parlakian, Pref., *An Enquiry into the Causes of the Late Increase of Robbers, &c,* by Henry Fielding (New York: AMS Press, 1975), p. 4.

14. Ibid.

15. The following discussion draws particularly on Howard's second section, "Bad Customs in Prisons." All references are to *The State of the Prisons*, ed. Kenneth Ruck (London: J. M. Dent; New York: E. P. Dutton, 1929).

16. Howard, pp. 2–3.

17. Howard, p. 1.

18. Howard, p. 5.

19. Howard, p. 11.

20. Howard, p. 13.

21. John Gay's *The Beggar's Opera* presents a picture of prison life which corresponds on many points to Fielding's. In addition to the general corruption of Peachum and Lockit and the freedom of movement and action they allow their charges, compare specifically Gay's reference to the custom of garnish with Fielding's. The scene is Macheath's entrance to Newgate (Act II, scene vii).

> *Lock.* Noble Captain, you are welcome. You have not been a Lodger of mine this Year and half. You know the custom, Sir. Garnish, Captain, Garnish. Hand me down those Fetters there.
> *Mach.* Those, Mr. Lockit, seem to be the heaviest of the whole sett. With your leave, I should like the further pair better.
> *Lock.* Look ye, Captain, we know what is fittest for our Prisoners. When a Gentleman uses me with Civility, I always do the best I can to please him.— Hand them down . . . I say.—We have them of all Prices, from one Guinea to ten, and 'tis fitting every Gentleman should please himself.
> *Mach.* I understand you, Sir. [Gives Money.] The Fees here are so many, and so exorbitant, that few Fortunes can bear the expense of getting off handsomely, or of dying like a Gentleman.

22. "Fielding's *Amelia:* An Interpretation," *ELH*, III (1936); rpt. in *Fielding: A Collection of Critical Essays,* ed. Ronald Paulson (Englewood Cliffs, N.J.: Pren-

tice Hall, 1962), p. 14. Sherburn's essay remains one of the best examinations of the novel.

23. Sherburn in "Fielding's Social Outlook," (p. 5) notes that "Fielding's central idea . . . concerning the relation of the classes to each other would be the concept of all classes working together for the good of the whole."

24. Fielding devotes an entire chapter of *An Enquiry into the Causes of the Late Increase of Robbers* to the problem of punishing "Receivers of Stolen Goods" (p. 68 ff.). His conclusions are precisely those he states here in *Amelia*.

25. "Fielding's Social Outlook," p. 5.

26. The bailiff's distortion of perspective is complete:
[the bailiff] acquainted [Booth] that one of the Prisoners was a poor Fellow. "He calls himself a Gentleman . . . but I am sure I never saw any thing genteel by him. In a Week that he hath been in my House, he hath drank only part of one Bottle of Wine. I intend to carry him to *Newgate* within a Day or two, if he can't find Bail. . . . He hath run out all he hath by Losses in Business, and one way or other; and he hath a Wife and seven Children.— Here was the whole Family here the other Day, all howling together. I never saw such a beggarly Crew; I was almost ashamed to see them in my House. . . . To be sure, I do not reckon him as proper Company for such as you, Sir; but there is another Prisoner in the House that I dare say you will like very much. He is, indeed, very much of a Gentleman, and spends his Money like one. I have had him only three Days, and I am afraid he won't stay much longer. They say, indeed, he is a Gamester; but what is that to me or any one, as long as a Man appears as a Gentleman? I always love to speak by People as I find. And, in my Opinion, he is fit Company for the greatest Lord in the Land; for he hath very good cloaths, and Money enough. He is not here for Debt, but upon a Judge's Warrant for an Assault and Battery . . . (vol. III, pp. 118–19).

27. Jones, p. 216.

28. Jones, pp. 208, 216.

29. Fielding begins *An Enquiry into the Causes of the Late Increase of Robbers* with references to the "constitution," and the whole of the work is sprinkled with allusions to this institution. Battestin notes that for Fielding "the term implies not only the laws of the nation but the essential spirit and character" (p. 3).

30. In every case the good characters, Fielding tells us, live happy, healthy lives—the unpleasant or evil characters all suffer just fates. In a particularly characteristic twist, for example, the false witness Robinson, who had helped Murphy steal Amelia's fortune years before, repents and is instrumental in helping the Booths to reclaim it. "The Witness for some Time seemed to reform his Life, and received a small Pension from Booth; after which he returned to vicious Courses, took a Purse on the Highway, was detected and taken, and followed the last Steps of his old Master [i.e. Murphy, who had been 'hanged at Tyburn']" (vol. IV, pp. 293–94).

2

THE FOOL OF QUALITY / *Henry Brooke*
THE HISTORY OF SANDFORD
AND MERTON / *Thomas Day*

The novelists of the 1740s, Richardson, Smollett, Fielding, and a host of lesser contemporaries, regularly incorporated the social issues of their time into their novels, as Jerry Beasley recently has so persuasively shown us in *Novels of the 1740s.*[1] In chapter one, I examined the remarkable precision of Fielding's descriptions of current concerns in *Amelia. Amelia,* published in 1751, brings us to the 1750s; the 1760s and 1770s are represented by *The Fool of Quality* and *Evelina,* and *Sandford and Merton* brings us to the 1780s. The second half of my book looks at the novelists of the 1790s. Beasley's thesis, that the novel grew up as a form shaped by its ties to contemporary events, illuminates the entire span. Each of the novels I discuss responds to specific social stimuli.

The novels' early interest is economic issues; in the 1790s, the center shifts to politics. Only Inchbald of these novelists really combines the two perspectives, and, interestingly, hers is structurally the least satisfying of the novels of the 1790s. In this last decade, it is clear enough why politics would be in the forefront—the offshoots of the French Revolution and the English Treason Trials, for example, were much on people's minds. The 1760s through the 1780s were decades of immense economic change in England, and the novels of this time reflect society's attempts to learn to deal with these new conditions. Part of the response to the economic conditions of the second half of the eighteenth century is the creation of a body of children's literature, that is, literature written specifically for children, that itself makes reference to social issues.

The Fool of Quality and *Sandford and Merton* are children's books and take children as their heroes.[2] Both authors see their work as educational and want their novels to be used in the teaching of children and the shaping of their moral perceptions. The element of social protest is as strong in *The Fool of Quality* and *Sandford and Merton* as it is in *Amelia,* although the emphasis is different: it is not institutions so much that are to blame as it is men—specifically, aristocrats. It is not society, or the legal system, or the prison system that angers Brooke and Day, it is the rich parasitic idler who takes what the poor work to produce, squanders it, and leaves both himself and the poor man whose produce he has consumed no better off. Brooke and Day never stop to consider any larger forces that can disrupt ideal relationships among men. They assume that the individual is the guiding force and that, through proper education, he can be helped to develop into a productive and benevolent member of society. Education is central to this process, and once such people are created, society will prosper. Brooke and Day do not set out to change the basic inequities in social relationships; they are not going to do away with poverty, for example, but they are going to make the "supporting" of "that condition of life" more bearable "for those who must support it always" (*Sandford,* vol. II, p. 207). It is a realistic, in some senses very humane vision: since the individual can be shaped, he must be made as benevolent and as societally useful as humanly possible. The means to that improvement is education, and education, therefore, becomes one of society's most sacred duties. The books are tools in this sacred process.

Both stories show in detail the education of a child, or, more specifically, the education of a pair of children. The children in *The Fool of Quality* are the sons of the aristocrat Richard Moreland. We see little of the older son, also named Richard. His is not the preferred plan of education: he is kept at home through his childhood and quite thoroughly spoiled there; as a young man, he goes abroad to finish his education and dies there of the pox (!). The younger son, Harry, is separated early from the pernicious influences of an aristocratic education. As an infant, he is put out to nurse and does not even visit the paternal mansion until he is five years old. Soon after, he is taken away from his nurse by Mr. Fenton, his father's (long-lost) brother, who raises him to adulthood. Mr. Fenton, a second son, is a successful merchant—in Brooke's terms, he produces rather than consumes. He teaches Harry to be a useful member of society. Social usefulness, the quality most applauded in the book, implies both benevolence towards others and self-sufficiency for oneself. Aristocratic values, which imply almost total dependence on others combined with a disdainful, frivolous outlook are condemned. The pattern is virtually identical in Thomas Day's *Sandford and Merton*. Again, aristocratic and wholesome educations are contrasted, and the aristocratic child is removed from his family in order to be properly educated—that is, raised to be a benevolent and productive member of society. Tommy Merton, the spoiled rich child, is sent to the house of Farmer Sandford to be educated with the farmer's son Harry. As in *The Fool of Quality,* the education is carefully plotted for the reader, and during its presentation, Day repeatedly finds the opportunity to attack the values of the upper classes and to praise the less artificial values exemplified by Farmer Sandford and his son Harry. In both books, disapproval of the upper classes is always sharp and sometimes even shrill.

Brooke's criticism begins on the first page. The description of Richard Moreland, the father of Henry, sets the tone for most of the comments on the aristocracy. Richard returns to England from his "grand tour" shortly before the Restoration,

and being too gay and too dissolute for the plodding and hypocrisy of Cromwell . . . he withdrew to the mansion house of his fore-fathers.

In the country, he amused himself with his bottle, hounds, hawks, race-horses. . . . But, on the restoration of his majesty, of pleasurable memory, he hastened to court, where he rolled away and shone as in his native sphere. He was always of the party of the king . . . where virtue was laughed out of countenance, and where all manner of dissoluteness became amiable and recommendable by the bursts of merriment and zest of wit. But toward the latter end of this droll reign, Earl Richard, being advanced in age, and being still older in constitution than years, began to think of providing an heir to his estate; and, as he had taken vast pains to impair it, he married a citizen's daughter who wanted a title, and with her got a portion of one hundred thousand pounds, which was equally wanting on his part. (*Fool,* vol. I, pp. 34–35)

It is not a flattering picture, certainly, and part of its bite is that the earl is not the exception but the rule of the man of inherited wealth. As we become better acquainted with Richard Moreland, we realize that he is not an evil man nor even an unduly profligate one. Rather, he acts in conformity with the general order of his class.

When Brooke describes "a brilliant concourse of the neighboring gentry" which takes place at the Moreland mansion some years after Richard's marriage, he is obviously much influenced by the grosser comic naming devices of Restoration comedy (e.g., *The Way of the World*). Aristocratic society has a most inflated sense of its own importance and a singularly deficient degree of worth and intelligence:

There was Sir Christopher Cloudy, who knew much but said nothing; with his very conversable lady, who scarce knew by halves, but spoke by wholesale. In the same range was Sir Standish Stately, who in all companies held the first place, in his own esteem. Next to him sat Lady Childish; it was at least thirty years since those follies might have become her, which appeared so very ridiculous at the age of fifty-five. By her side were the two Stiltons; a blind man would swear that the one was a clown and the other a gentleman, by the tones of their voices. Next to these were two pair of very ill mated turtles; Mr. Gentle, who sacrificed his fine sense and affluent fortune to the vanity and bad temper of a silly and turbulent wife; and Squire Sulky, a brutal fool, who tyrannized over the most sensible and most amiable of her sex.

On the opposite side was Lord Prim, who evidently laboured hard to be easy in conversation; and next to him was Lord Flippant, who spoke nonsense with great facility. By his side sat the fair but dejected Miss Willow; she had lately discovered what a misfortune it was to be born to wit, beauty, and affluence, the three capital qualifications that lead the sex to calamity. Next to her was Colonel Jolly. . . . Had he known how to time his fits, the laugh might have grown catching. Below him was seated Mrs. Mirror, a widow lady, industriously accomplished in the faults of people of fashion. And below her sat the beloved and respected Mr. Meekly, who always sought to hide behind the merits of the company. Next to him was Major Settle—no one spoke with more importance on things of no signification.

These were the principal characters. The rest could not be said to be of any character at all. (*Fool*, vol. I, pp. 37–39)

The assembly lacks values, though it is prodigiously supplied with affectations. The few characters in this brief survey who might claim our respect are tyrannized by convention into giving up their good sense and blending in with their peers. And this society molds the children who inherit aristocratic position and power. Brooke finds the prospect of continuing traditions of shallowness and frivolity unacceptable, and his book is, in large part, directed at the education of the parents so that they can properly educate the children. Richard Moreland is not a bad man: he is rather insufficiently influenced by appropriate values. Even his wife, who seems to us a very frivolous, even silly person, reflects her society's values rather than a personal, deliberate evil.

Such people raise children who are callous, unthinking, and ungenerous. The children reflect their parents' values as they interact with each other and, even more, as they interact with someone like Harry, who is not guided by aristocratic values but who reacts guilelessly and humanely to any overture. When Harry is introduced to the company of his brother Richard and Richard's friends, the little aristocrats play several cruel tricks on him—most of the tricks, we should note, proposed by the lady of the house. The children taunt and even assault Harry; he bears with a great deal and only retaliates when he is maliciously injured. The other children and his mother see him as a simpleton; to the reader, however, it is clear that Harry behaves far better than his peers.

Typical of the tests given Harry, and of the difference in

values shown by the aristocrats and the simpleton, is the following game set up by Harry's mother:

> My lady . . . told the earl that she resolved . . . to prove the wits of the youngster . . . and, whispering to Dicky, he immediately went out and took with him his companions. Soon after, Dick returns without his shoes, and with a pitiful face, cries, Brother Harry, I want a pair of shoes sadly, will you give me yours? Yes, I will, said Harry, and instantly strips and presents them to him. Then entered another boy and demanded his stockings in the like petitioning manner; another begged his hat, another his coat, another his waistcoat, all of which he bestowed without hesitation; but, when the last boy came in and petitioned for his shirt, No, I won't, said Harry, a little moody, I want a shirt myself. My lady then exclaimed, Upon my conscience, there is but the thickness of a bit of linen between this child and a downright fool. But my lord rose up, took Harry in his arms, and having tenderly embraced him, God bless thee, my boy, he cried, and make thee an honour to Old England! (*Fool*, vol. I, pp. 64–65)

Harry's generosity is tempered only by his good sense. His father recognizes that Harry's behavior is exemplary, but the constraints of society are so strong that even such recognition does not allow the father actually to change the behavior within his house.[3] Harry's mother, mistaking his strength of character for deficiency of wit, considers that he is "a stock of a child . . . a statue" (*Fool*, vol. I, p. 67). The last of her tests is the entrance of a ghost; all the other children are terrified of the ghoulish figure which comes through the door. Only Harry stands unafraid. Brooke's description of the incident is a pointed comment on the character of the "better classes": "The panic grew instantly contagious, and all this host of little gentry who were, thereafter, to form our senates, and to lead our armies, ran, shrinking and shivering, to hide themselves in holes and to tremble in corners" (*Fool*, vol. I, p. 71).

Children such as these, for Brooke, require a better education not just for their own sakes but for that of society. In Brooke's perspective, such children grow into selfish, cowardly, unmotivated adults whose only societal function is to consume the fruits of other men's labor and whose personal satisfactions are momentary and, upon any kind of introspective examination, not very satisfying at all. Richard Moreland, for example, is educated to be an oldest son. Too late he realizes that the values he had always accepted are productive neither of social nor of personal satisfaction. He laments the fact that he "had the misfortune to be born to a title and a vast estate" because, continually beset by "sychophants and deceivers," he was "trained from . . . infancy to . . . prejudices, errors, and false estimates of every thing" (*Fool,* vol. I, p. 93)—just as his son would be if Harry were to be educated at home.

Aristocratic education results in a lack of discrimination, a snobbery so intense that it leads Richard as a young man to reject his own brother, merely because the brother has been apprenticed to a trader. This is not just the conditioned reflex of a callow youth, for years later when he meets his brother again, he makes the same mistake. When he is introduced to the man whom he later discovers to be his lost brother, Richard is struck by the stranger's dignity and grace. The man has come to Richard as the representative of a group of citizens who seek redress for certain infringements on their charter. Richard does not even wait to hear the arguments; it is enough for him that the advocate's appearance is impressive. But when he hears that the man is a merchant, he is as quick to dismiss him as he had been to accept him when he thought the man was an aristocrat. Richard is angry that he was "deceived by the dignity of his appearance" and makes it clear that he finds it objectionable that those of the "lower ranks" should "confound . . . themselves with gentlemen" (*Fool,* vol. I, pp. 95–96).

Aristocratic education places inordinate value on appearance and rank. Brooke wants to teach his young readers that such values are wrong, that a man's contribution to society rather than his appearance or his hereditary rank must be judged. Part of what comes into play here is the contemporary debate about what place trade should assume (had assumed, in fact) in the conduct of the nation's affairs. Responding to Richard's patronizing remarks, his brother the merchant gives him—and the reader—a lecture on the producers in society. While Richard continues to insist that it is all well and good to use the services of those of lesser rank—the "baker, barber, brewer, butcher, hatter, hosier, and taylor" (*Fool,* vol. I, p. 97)—as long as he need not have anything personally to do with them, the brother explains that those who produce goods and services are of inestimable value to society and should be respected accordingly. In fact, he makes it clear, in the visit of the trader to the peer, it is the peer who is honored. Richard is told that he should not "despise some, merely for being of use to others," for

> the wealth, prosperity, and importance of every thing upon earth, arises from the TILLER, the MANUFACTURER, and the MERCHANT; and that, as nothing is truly estimable, save in proportion to its utility, these are, consequently, very far from being contemptible characters. The tiller supplies the manufacturer, the manufacturer supplies the merchant, and the merchant supplies the world with all its wealth. It is thus that industry is promoted, arts invented and improved, commerce extended, superfluities mutually vended, wants mutually supplied; that each man becomes a useful member of society; that societies become further of advantage to each other, and that states are enabled to pay and dignify their upper servants with titles, rich revenues, principalities, and crowns. (*Fool,* vol. I, pp. 96–98)

A lively debate follows, with Richard trying very hard to put the merchant "in his place"; the merchant, however, rather obviously has the better of the argument. The exchange helps Brooke to expose the pretensions and social irresponsibilities of the hereditary rich while it underlines the positive role of the newly powerful merchant classes. It begins with Richard taunting the merchant that he would

> have no quarrel . . . to the high and mighty my lords the merchants, if each could be humbly content with the profits of his profession, without forming themselves into companies, exclusive of their brethren, our itinerant merchants and pedlars. I confess myself an enemy to the monopolies of your chartered companies and city corporations; and I can perceive no evil consequence to the public or the state, if all such associations were this instant dissolved.

The merchant retorts:

> I am sensible that the gentlemen of large landed properties are apt to look upon themselves as the pillars of the state, and to consider their interests and the interests of the nation, as very little beholden to or dependent on trade; tho' the fact is, that those very gentlemen would lose nine parts in ten of their returns, and the nation nine tenths of her yearly revenues, if industry and the arts (promoted as I said by commerce) did not raise the products of lands to tenfold their natural value.[4] The manufacturer, on the other hand, depends on the landed interest for nothing save the materials of his craft; and the merchant is wholly independent of all lands, or, rather, he is the general patron thereof. I must further observe to your lordship, that this beneficent profession is by no means confined to individuals, as you would have it. Large societies of men, nay, mighty nations, may and have been merchants. When societies incorporate for such a worthy purpose, they are formed as a foetus within the womb of the mother, a constitution within the general state or constitution; their particular laws and regulations ought, always, to be conformable to those of the national system, and, in that case, such corporations greatly conduce to the peace and good order of cities and large towns, and to the general power and prosperity of the nation.
>
> A nation that is a merchant has no need of an extent of lands, as it can derive to itself subsistence from all parts of the globe.
>
> Should England ever open her eyes to her own interest, she will follow the same prosperous and ennobling profession; she will conform to the consequences of her situation. She will see that, without a naval pre-eminence, she cannot be safe; and that, without trade, her naval power cannot be supported. Her glory will also flow from this source of her interests. . . . She will then find that a single triumph of her flag will be more available for her prosperity, than the conquest of the four continents; that her pre-eminence by sea will carry and diffuse her influence over all lands; and, that universal influence is universal dominion.
>
> Avarice . . . may pile; robbery may plunder; new mines may be opened . . . conquerors may win kingdoms; but all such means of acquiring riches are transient and determinable; while industry and commerce are the natural, the living, the never-failing fountain, from whence the wealth of this world can alone be taught to flow. (*Fool,* vol. I, pp. 99–102)

Richard, still unable to get beyond his own prejudices of rank,

wonders that the merchant "can have the effrontery to insinu-
ate a preference of [himself] and [his] fellow-cits, to our British
nobles and princes, who derive their powers and dignities from
the stedfast extent of their landed possessions" (*Fool,* vol. I, p.
102). With obvious contempt, he directs the merchant to seek
elsewhere for redress of his grievances. The merchant, having
finally had enough, drops the hint that he is the long-lost Moreland brother—and stalks out. Too late, Richard realizes that his
initial valuation of the man, based on bearing and conduct, had
been correct and that only his prejudice had kept him from
acknowledging the merchant's obvious worth.

Kingsley's statement of the subject of the book, that it is about
the education of an ideal nobleman by an ideal merchant
prince, gives us some indication of how to read these passages.[5]
Brooke is clearly on the side of the merchant prince, but he is
not against the aristocrats. He is, rather, against propagation of
a class that frivolously consumes but never produces—exactly
the complaint of the radicals such as Inchbald thirty years
later.[6] Brooke's perspective is that all members of society, aristocrat and laborer, have contributions to make and that, in the
case of the upper classes, people must be educated to their
duties. Although their exchange reads against the aristocrat, it
should be borne in mind that Brooke makes the point that the
king, the chief aristocrat, recognizes the merchant's worth and
honors him accordingly.

The book unmistakably admires the TILLER, the MANU-
FACTURER, and the MERCHANT, especially the merchant.
Fascination with the power and potential of trade already had
been voiced fifty years earlier by Addison and Steele, who in
their character Sir Andrew Freeport describe a merchant

> of great eminence in the city of London. A person of indefatigable
> industry, strong reason, and great experience. His notions of trade
> are noble and generous. . . . [He] will tell you that it is a stupid and
> barbarous way to extend dominion by arms; for true power is to be
> got by arts and industry. . . . A general trader of good sense is
> pleasanter company than a general scholar; . . . having a natural
> unaffected eloquence, the perspicuity of his discourse gives the
> same pleasure that wit would be in another man.[7]

Britain had always been a trading nation, and during the eighteenth century, trade absorbed an ever-increasing share of the British consciousness, as economic movement was accompanied by growing awareness of the social implications of that expansion.[8] Donald Greene notes that by midcentury "with Britain's technological superiority over the rest of the world, it seemed reasonable to many (such as Adam Smith and his disciple, the younger Pitt) for her to put all her economic eggs in the one basket of unrestrained commercial and industrial expansion, buying raw materials from the outside, manufacturing them cheaply, and selling the finished product back to the rest of the world at a profit sufficient to enable her to buy food for her population."[9] Brooke's fascination with the role of the merchant, and with the concept of the merchant state, reflects contemporary events and attitudes. In a novel concerned as his is with the appropriate education of a child, the discussion between the aristocrat Moreland and the merchant Moreland is presented as a lesson in a (vastly) simplified economics. The social bias of the whole book is that "nothing is truly estimable save in proportion to its utility," and Brooke explains that "each man becomes a useful member of society" by being part of the commercial system, which he sees as a chain stretching from tiller to manufacturer to merchant. In the same way, nations are useful to each other, and relations among nations are improved. Brooke has, essentially, redefined the great chain of being; it no longer stretches from god to man and beyond, but instead is a continuous cycle of commercial interaction.

Isaac Kramnick shows that the economic changes in England were largely responsible for the development of children's literature as a separate genre in England, and further he ties the growth of children's literature to the new bourgeois ideology that he sees as defining much of English consciousness in the later eighteenth century. Until the industrial revolution created a middle class with both the leisure and the economic means to provide a special culture for and of the child, children had been merely small adults; the development of a literature designed specifically for children had to wait until they were perceived as beings different from adults. Naturally, Kramnick suggests, the books written for children stressed the values of their parents, and the parents buying books were essentially middle class. Such children's books as *The History of Little Goody Two-Shoes* (1765), Sarah Trimmer's *Fabulous Histories Designed for the Amusement and Instruction of Young People* (1786), Maria Edgeworth's *The Purple Jar, The Little Merchants,* and, especially, *Harry and Lucy* all stress for Kramnick the values and concerns of the new bourgeois age.[10] From *The History of Sandford and Merton,* to which I shall turn shortly, he quotes the "catalogue and summary" of these values: "I don't know that there is upon the face of the earth a more useless, more contemptible, and more miserable animal than a wealthy, luxurious man without business or profession, arts, sciences, or exercises." Kramnick's point, which is valid for *The Fool of Quality* as well as for the novels he discusses, is that these books are precise expressions of contemporary preoccupations. With their instructive little tableaux, they teach the same values of self-reliance, responsibility, prudence, resourcefulness, and thrift that were at the very center of the bourgeois society they reflect.

The values expounded in these children's novels are the values of the producers; the businessmen and scientists whose methods were changing the economy were also responsible for shaping the English view of morality. When Josiah Wedgwood speaks to his workers in 1783, he sounds precisely like a character in *The Fool of Quality:* "From where and from what cause did this happy change take place? The truth is clear to all. Industry and the machine have been the parent of this happy change. A well directed and long continued series of industrious exertions, has so changed, for the better, the face of our country, its buildings, lands, roads and the manners and deportment of its inhabitants, too."[11] As Kramnick points out, "Industry had changed manners and deportment. . . . The new economic order required a new ethic. . . ."[12] Science, of course, is very much part of industry, and as a contemporary scientist, Thomas Cooper, insisted, "It is to science, chemical and mechanical, that England is indebted for having made her island the storehouse of the world, for having compelled the nations of the earth to pour into her lap their superfluous wealth; for having acquired the undisputed command of the sea her merchants are as princes."[13]

In *The Fool of Quality* these values are expressed with the same enthusiasm. And, as I have shown, joined with the enthusiasm for the producers is a marked disrespect for those who do not produce. For Brooke, as for Wedgwood and Cooper, productivity and morality are tied together, and this idea is perhaps the major lesson of his book. It is the merchant "who furnishes every comfort, convenience, and elegance of life; who carries off every redundance, who fills up every want; who ties country to country, and clime to clime, and brings the remotest regions to neighborhood and converse; who makes man to be literally the lord of the creation, and gives him an interest in whatever is done upon earth; who furnishes to each the product of all lands, and the labours of all nations; and thus knits into one family, and weaves into one web, the affinity and brotherhood of all mankind" (*Fool*, vol. I, p. 98). Even more telling, however, is his appraisal of "gentlemen of large landed properties" who, he says, like to see themselves as standing above, and separate from, the rest of the economy but who are in fact more dependent on trade than any other class. The merchant does not need land to trade, but the landowner depends on the trader to raise the value of his land.

What is the function, then, of the large landowner, of the rich man whose riches are not connected to his own production? For Brooke, that man's social function is to ameliorate unfortunate social conditions through the judicious application of his wealth. The education of the child who will grow up to have that power is paramount, for the child must be taught to revere true human, rather than artificial, values; he must be taught to be responsible and compassionate. Harry, having been removed from his parents for just this purpose of education, approaches the ideal. Brooke is concerned with practical rather than utopian solutions, and the education he gives to Harry can be provided for any child.

Harry's education comes in a series of specific lessons, each

designed to teach human virtue. Mr. Fenton, Harry's precep-
tor, does not assume that Harry will be responsible,
compassionate, or serious-minded; he teaches him to be these
things. Mr. Fenton's note to Harry's parents promises to return
to them "the most accomplished and most perfect of all human
beings" (*Fool*, vol. I, p. 166). The period of Harry's education—
that is, his abduction by Mr. Fenton and his subsequent training—follows closely on the "social necessity" passages about
merchants, making the connection between social utility and
education clear.

Harry's education, a judicious mix of instruction and action,
is intended to create a socially sensitive, self-sufficient man who
appreciates individual merit rather than social station. Thus,
one of the first lessons to which the child is exposed upon his
arrival at Mr. Fenton's house is one in human equality. After
Harry and the family have eaten, Mr. Fenton proposes that
Harry and the family serve the servants, "for God made us all
to be servants to each other: one man is not born a bit better
than another; and he is the best and greatest of all who serves
and attends the most, and requires least to be served and attended upon. And . . . he that is a king today . . . may become a
beggar tomorrow and it is good that people should be prepared against all that may happen" (*Fool*, vol. I, pp. 171–72).
Harry enters wholeheartedly into the spirit of the reversal and
learns that human interaction like this between upper and
lower classes is indeed natural and only made unnatural by
imposed restrictions between men. Similarly, Harry finds his
greatest pleasure in searching out objects of need and in applying his own resources to their aid. To encourage the development of Harry's benevolent instincts, Mr. Fenton on several
occasions deliberately provides Harry with opportunities to exercise his generosity. He sets Harry up with a collection of
simple but presentable clothes, and it is Harry's work and pleasure to give them away; he sends Harry to aid the deserving
unfortunates in a debtor's prison, where, again, Harry finds
tremendous satisfaction in distributing his largesse. A conscious
commitment to the systematic aiding of one's fellows is for

Brooke an inherent part of being human and, especially, of being upper class.

Brooke does not imply, as Fielding does before him and as the novelists of the 1790s will later on, that the institutions of society need changing. Unconcerned with social institutions as such, he sees them simply as given aspects of the human condition. Help for the poor or afflicted must come from individuals who are better off, and it must come on a personal level. Brooke seems convinced that personal benevolence is effective in ameliorating the condition of the unfortunate, whether the action is on the small scale of little Harry's distribution of clothing or on the only slightly larger scale of the adult Mr. Fenton's regular program of alms and dinner for the deserving poor.

Every Sunday Mr. Fenton invites to dinner the heads of deserving local families. In addition to a fine dinner, they are treated to the warmth and good fellowship of the family and servants, as well as "a crown in silver" (*Fool*, vol. I, p. 176) to take home. The results of this benevolence are truly heartwarming:

> after a saturating meal and an enlivening cup, they departed, with elevated spirits, with humanized manners, and with hearts warmed in affection toward every member of this extraordinary house.
>
> By the means of this weekly bounty, these reviving families were soon enabled to clear their little debts to the chandlers, which had compelled them to take up every thing at the dearest hand. They were also further enabled to purchase wheels and other implements, with the materials of flax and wool, for employing the late idle hands of their houshold. They now appeared decently clad, and with happy countenances; their wealth increased with their industry; and the product of the employment of so many late useless members became a real accession of wealth to the public. So true it is that the prosperity of this world, and of every nation and society therein, depends solely on the industry or manufactures of the individuals. And so much more nobly did this private patron act, than all ancient legislators, or modern patrons, and landlords; whose selfishness, if they had but common cunning, or common-sense, might instruct them to increase their proper rents, and enrich their native country, by supplying the hands of all the poor,

within their influence, with the implements and materials of the prosperity of each. (*Fool,* vol. I, pp. 176–77)

To speak of social protest is not necessarily to speak of revolutionary ideas and social violence. For Brooke, protest is an immensely comfortable exercise in repeating what seems very obvious: those who are well-off in society are in no way responsible for the ill luck of others; however, they do have the duty to provide some succor to the less fortunate. The social dividends earned by such actions seem to Brooke almost limitless. A very small investment of advice and material help can set the poor on the road not only to happiness but to financial prosperity. They became MANUFACTURERS, and not only is the problem of poverty solved, but the very economy—and therefore the strength—of the nation is enhanced as these initial burdens become contributing members of society. All of this, for Brooke, can be accomplished "by the means of this weekly bounty."

Brooke implies that the England of his day provides adequate economic potential for anyone who wishes to avail himself of the opportunities (the poor, somehow set apart from such potential, are ignored within this context). The traditional role of the aristocracy, that of consumer, must change, and each man, regardless of rank, must develop socially useful skills. When that happens, the result is a man like the productive and happy Mr. Fenton; when it does not, we get the sad Mr. Clement.

Harry, ever on the watch for "poor travellers" (*Fool,* vol. I, p. 179), finds Mr. Clement

> sitting on the ground. His clothes seemed, from head to foot, as the tattered remainder of better days. Through a squalid wig, and beard, his pale face appeared just tinctured with a faint and sickly red. And his hollow eyes were fixed upon the face of a woman, whose head he held on his knees; and who looked to be dead, or dying, though without any apparent agony; while a male infant, about four years of age, was half stretched on the ground, and half across the woman's lap, with its little nose pinched by famine, and its eyes staring about, wildly, though without attention to any thing.

Distress seemed to have expended its utmost bitterness on these objects, and the last sigh and tear to have been already exhausted. (*Fool,* vol. I, pp. 179–80)

Mr. Clement's misfortune is due entirely to his faulty education. The son of a wealthy man, he was educated to be a gentleman; that is, his education was in classical languages and philosophy. He studied nothing practical and, in fact, looked down on his ungentlemanly father—" a trader, a mechanick, I sighed for his reptile state . . ." (*Fool,* vol. I, p. 218).

When the trader and mechanic disowns the gentleman, the gentleman is lost. Mr. Clement has no skills that will enable him to earn a living; there is call for a bookkeeper, an engineer, or a navigator, but not a gentleman. He sinks lower and lower into poverty, until finally he finds his metier; he will sell his ideas: he will write pamphlets! Clement has some success at this game, but unwittingly he offends a minister of the government and is jailed. His young wife and her widowed mother exhaust all their resources to bail him out, and from that point they fall ever deeper into poverty until they are left with nothing. In desperation, he "disguises" himself as a poor man and hires himself out as a porter. This attempt to eke out a subsistence comes to an abrupt halt when he is assaulted by four men, porters, who beat him because, they tell him, he is a "gentleman" and "yet, thief as you are, you must steal into our business, and glean away the few pence by which we get our daily bread . . ." (*Fool,* vol. II, pp. 40–41). Finally, Mr. Clement is reduced to staging robberies in the street to steal money to buy food for his wife and child. Such, as Brooke sees it, is the evil of a misdirected education!

The concept of "the gentleman" is one that bothers Brooke a great deal.

In the habits, manners, and characters, of old Sparta and Old Rome, we find an antipathy to all the elements of modern gentility. Among those rude and unpolished people, you read of philosophers, of orators, patriots, heroes, and demigods; but you never hear of any character so elegant as that of—a pretty Gentleman.

When those nations, however, became refined into what their
ancestors would have called corruption; when luxury introduced,
and fashion gave a sanction to certain sciences, which Cynics would
have branded with the ill-mannered appellations of debauchery,
drunkenness, whoredom, gambling, cheating, lying, &c, the practitioners assumed the new title of Gentlemen, till such Gentlemen
became as plenteous as stars in the milky-way, and lost distinction
merely by the confluence of their lustre. (*Fool,* vol. II, pp. 76–77)[14]

Brooke continually emphasizes that individuals must question
society's determination of distinction; further, he demands that
children be educated to revere value rather than show. If Mr.
Clement had had his head filled with ideals of usefulness rather
than those of gentlemanly grandeur, he would have been of
service to his community and of value to himself and his family.
Children have no inherent regard for finery and frippery,
Brooke insists, but misdirected adults instill those false values.
Little Harry, having been educated by Mr. Fenton, disdains the
trappings of the gentleman and is happier for it.

The perversion of real needs into artificial social and institutional formuli causes much of the distress men suffer. Mr.
Clement's misfortunes are largely caused by his misplaced values, which have institutional correlatives as well. Brooke, like so
many others (Fielding, Holcroft, Inchbald, Godwin), focuses
particularly on the grossly distended legal system, a monstrous
apparatus that consumes those who come into contact with it,
sending people into bankruptcy long before it settles their
claims against one another. Brooke, if he could, seems ready to
tear it apart, as Harry did his fancy lace-covered coat, to get at
the bare, useful garment underneath. The legal process makes
justice virtually impossible for a poor man to come by (*Fool,* vol.
II, p. 116), and it ruins any who come to it with money. The
only people who benefit from the legal process are the lawyers:
"English property, when once debated, is merely a carcase of
contention, upon which interposing lawyers fall as customary
prize, and prey during the combat of the claimants. While any
flesh remains on a bone, it continues a bone of contention; but
so soon as the learned practitioners have picked it quite clean,

the battle is over, and all again is peace and settled neighborhood" (*Fool,* vol. II, p. 115).

We must be careful to define Brooke's anger at certain institutions of his society. It is not, in any case, the basic structures
of English society that he is attacking, for in fact the book is
virtually a celebration of the English and their society. For
Brooke, the basic structures are perfectly sound; in the section
on the judiciary, for example, Brooke emphasizes that the jury
system itself is a fair, efficient, praiseworthy institution, only
the apparatus that has grown up around it and too often re-
places it is to be blamed. Similarly, although he is angered by
specific faults in government, the constitutional system itself is
treated to an elaborate and very positive examination (*Fool,* vol.
III, p. 245 ff.). Brooke directs his ire at corruptions of sound
institutions, not at the institutions themselves. He wants his
book to help create gentlemen—real gentlemen—and thus he
must teach his young readers and their parents what is valuable. Just as Mr. Clement's perception of his role as gentleman
needed redefinition, so do some social institutions need reor-
dering. But just as Mr. Clement is regarded as a worthwhile
human being, so the institutions that need reform are in themselves good. Brooke wants to repair, not to destroy.

Brooke's approach, and his lessons, were highly esteemed in
his own time. Thomas Day found Brooke's work so significant
that he rewrote it in slightly simplified form so that it would be
the more readily available to children. In the rewriting, he
sharpened the social comment markedly, so that while the spirit
of rebuke remained the same, the tone became more acerbic.
Day's *The History of Sandford and Merton,* like *The Fool of Quality,*
is primarily concerned with educating middle and upper-class
children so that they grow up to be sensitive, contributing
adults. A principal point in their education must be the break-
ing down of the child's concept of his role as gentleman, and to
this end the book contains repeated and lengthy discussion of
what that role really implies. Even more emphatically than
Brooke, Day insists that the social definition of a gentleman as
one who dresses with care and does no useful work is per-

nicious not only to society in general but to the well-being of the child himself.

Tommy, the aristocratic child, is six years old at the beginning of the book. He has none of the mental and physical accomplishments to be expected of a child his age because he has been raised as a gentleman and has therefore never been required to do anything for himself. Servants carry him about; he is so "delicately" brought up that "the least wind or rain gave him a cold, and the least sun was sure to throw him into a fever" (*Sandford,* vol. I, p. 14). He isn't required to learn to read, write, or do arithmetic because it makes his head ache. "By this kind of education . . . Master Merton . . . could neither write, nor read, nor cypher; he could use none of his limbs with ease, nor bear any degree of fatigue; but he was very proud, fretful, and impatient" (*Sandford,* vol. I, p. 14).

Little Tommy's father realizes that his child must receive another kind of education if he is to grow into a worthwhile adult, and he puts Tommy into the hands of Mr. Barlow, the clergyman of the parish, who also has the care of Harry Sandford, a local farmer's son. Harry, having been "simply" brought up, has none of the handicaps of Tommy; he is physically fit, mentally alert, and morally well developed. Tommy, the aristocrat, continually must learn from Harry, the farmer's son. The social lesson of the book is summed up in their relationship. Tommy indeed learns a great deal, and slowly he develops into a benevolent, responsible child. Day emphasizes that education can counter the malicious influences of a society that worships false values. About halfway through the book, Tommy is reintroduced to his aristocratic society. The impressionable child reverts to the worst mannerisms of his class and ignores Harry and Mr. Barlow in favor of the young gentlemen of rank he meets in society. He is led into malicious, rowdy behavior and grows crass and ungenerous toward his former friends. But slowly his better education—acting on a nature that, Day repeatedly assures us, is essentially (naturally) kind and good— reasserts itself, and he moves away from the misplaced values of his peers to a renewed, and this time unshakeable, inclination toward the simple and the humanly valuable.

Antiaristocratic remarks are constant throughout *The History of Sandford and Merton*. The first page analysis of Tommy's education is contrasted almost immediately with the description of the wholesomeness of the young farm boy's upbringing. Day uses juxtaposition to show his reader true values as opposed to aristocratic ones. When Harry Sandford, having saved the life of the helpless aristocrat Tommy, is invited to dinner at the Mertons', Mrs. Merton expects him to be awed by the luxury he sees and impressed by the quality of the artifacts and the company. When she tries to make him a present of a silver goblet, however, Harry declines, insisting that he has a better one at home. It is better, he says, because it is made of bone and is not valuable, so it serves the purpose without making him nervous about loss or breakage. Mrs. Merton thinks he's an idiot, for as she says, "he makes such strange observations."

Always when Day places Harry in aristocratic company, the aristocrats show up badly. In this instance, Harry's values of simplicity and utility are clearly more praiseworthy than Mrs. Merton's ostentation. As the conversation continues, ostentation comes to symbolize the value system of the rich who live their lives with much consumption but little productivity. Tommy has been raised to believe that he should not work because he is a gentleman, and repeated lessons are required before he learns that all human beings should be prepared to produce as well as to consume. This primary theme of the book is announced early when the two children are asked what they want to be when they grow up. Tommy wants to be king, because the king "has nothing to do, and every body waits upon him, and is afraid of him" (*Sandford*, vol. I, p. 25). Harry's response to the question is rather different: "I hope I shall soon be big enough to go to plough, and get my own living; and then I shall want nobody to wait upon me." Mrs. Merton, "looking rather contemptuously upon Harry," remarks on "what a difference there is between the children of farmers and gentlemen" (*Sand-*

ford, vol. I, pp. 25–26)! Her husband, to give him due credit, isn't too sure the advantage goes to his son.

When Tommy goes from his home to the tutelage of Mr. Barlow, one of the first lessons he learns is that if he has the same needs as other people, he must work like them.

> The day after Tommy came to Mr. Barlow's, as soon as breakfast was over, he took him and Harry into the garden: when he was there, he took a spade into his own hand, and giving Harry an hoe, they both began to work with great eagerness. Every body that eats, says Mr. Barlow, ought to assist in procuring food; and therefore little Harry and I begin our daily work; this is my bed, and that other is his; we work upon it every day, and he that raises the most out of it, will deserve to fare the best. Now, Tommy, if you chuse to join us, I will mark you out a piece of ground, which you shall have to yourself, and all the produce shall be your own. No, indeed, said Tommy, very sulkily, I am a gentleman, and don't chuse to slave like a ploughboy. Just as you please, Mr. Gentleman, said Mr. Barlow; but Harry and I, who are not above being useful, will mind our work. In about two hours Mr. Barlow said it was time to leave off, and, taking Harry by the hand, he led him into a very pleasant summer-house, where they sat down, and Mr. Barlow, taking out a plate of very fine ripe cherries, divided them between Harry and himself. (*Sandford,* vol. I, pp. 53–54)

Tommy is shocked that anyone could expect him to work; the next day, naturally, Tommy is most eager to do his part—not because he is starving, for kind Harry had given him food from his own share, but because he feels that he too should, literally, earn his bread. Such lessons are reinforced by precept ("So you see now that if nobody chose to work, or do any thing for himself, we should have no bread to eat. But you could not even have the corn to make it of without a great deal of pains and labour" [*Sandford,* vol. I, p. 121]) and by example.

The lessons in the book for children are for the most part wholesome and rational, but Day, like Brooke, occasionally inserts a passage that in its implications seems directed more at the parents of his young readers than at the children themselves. Such, I think, is the case when Day continues a discussion about the making of bread and turns it into a polemic against the rich who take goods and services but return nothing to their producers—money having no intrinsic value of its own:

> What then, answered Mr. Barlow, must not gentlemen eat as well as others, and therefore is it not for their interest to know how to procure food as well as other people? Yes, sir, answered Tommy, but they can have other people to raise it for them, so that they are not obliged to work themselves.
> How does that happen, said Mr. Barlow? T. Why sir, they pay other people to work for them, or buy bread when it is made, as much as they want. Mr. B. Then they pay for it with money. T. Yes, sir. (*Sandford*, vol. I, pp. 123–24)

But what is that money with which the rich buy the work of the poor? When Mr. Barlow asks the question of Tommy, the child responds, logically enough, that "Money, sir, money is—I believe little pieces of silver and gold, with an head upon them (*Sandford*, vol. III, p. 86). The dialogue that follows is, in its social implications, one of the most cutting in the book and, although couched in a child's language, fully as revolutionary as anything Godwin or any of the other radicals of the latter part of the century were to write:

> Mr. Barlow: And what is the use of these little pieces of silver and gold?
> Tommy: Indeed, I do not know that they are of any use. But everybody has agreed to take them, and therefore you may buy with them whatever you want.
> Mr. Barlow: Then, according to your last account, the goodness of the rich consists in taking from the poor houses, cloaths, and food, and giving them in return little bits of silver and gold, which are really good for nothing.
> Tommy: Yes, sir; but then the poor can take these pieces of money, and purchase every thing which they want.
> Mr. Barlow: You mean, that, if a poor man has money in his pocket, he can always exchange it for cloaths, or food, or any other necessary.
> Tommy: Indeed I do, sir.
> Mr. Barlow: But who must he buy them of?—For, according to your account, the rich never produce any of these things: therefore the poor, if they want to purchase them, can only do it of each other.

Tommy: But, sir, I cannot think that is always the case; for, I have been along with my mamma to shops, where there were fine powdered gentlemen and ladies that sold things to other people. . . .

Mr. Barlow: But . . . do you imagine that these fine powdered gentlemen and ladies made the things which they sold?

Tommy: That, sir, I cannot tell, but I should rather imagine not; for all the fine people I have ever seen are too much afraid of spoiling their cloaths to work.

Mr. Barlow: All that they do, then, is to employ poorer persons to work for them, while they only sell what is produced by their labour. So that still you see we reach no farther than this; the rich do nothing and produce nothing, and the poor every thing that is really useful. (*Sandford,* vol. III, pp. 86–89)

Tommy, like his peers, has always taken privilege and uselessness as his prerogative. He has to be taught that he must use his means for the betterment of society, thereby improving his own character as well. Neither Brooke nor Day suggests that the wealth itself should be redistributed, nor even that it is to be hoped that poverty might be eliminated. Rather, they take as a condition of life that there are rich men and poor men—Day even goes so far as to assert that poverty is a natural condition of life (*Sandford,* vol. I, p. 36)—and the responsibility of the rich toward the poor is simply to make poverty as bearable as possible. The line between sanctimonious self-congratulation and genuine benevolence is perhaps difficult to define, but certainly Day skirts it rather narrowly when he describes, with a tone of total approbation (this, he implies, is surely how things should be), Mr. Barlow's annual dinner for the local poor; Mr. Fenton, in *The Fool of Quality,* at least made it a weekly affair!

He had a large hall, which was almost filled with men, women, and children; a chearful fire blazed in the chimney, and a prodigious table was placed in the middle for the company to dine upon. Mr. Barlow himself received his guests, and conversed with them about the state of their families and their affairs. Those, that were industrious and brought their children up to labour, instructing them in the knowledge of their duty and preserving them from bad impressions, were sure to meet with his encouragement and commendations. (*Sandford,* vol. II, pp. 205–6)

It is hard for a modern reader to swallow Mr. Barlow's presumption in generously "commending and encouraging" on the basis of people being "deserving poor," although the rhetoric of our own time and place often seems not too far removed from Mr. Barlow's. The passage continues:

> Those, that had been ill, he assisted with such little necessaries, as tended to alleviate their pains, and diffuse a gleam of chearfulness over their sufferings. How hard, he would say, is the lot of the poor, when they are afflicted with sickness! How intolerable do we find the least bodily disorder, even though we possess every convenience that can mitigate its violence! Not all the dainties which can be collected from all the elements, the warmth of downy beds and silken couches, the attendance of obsequious dependents, are capable of making us bear with common patience the commonest disease. How pitiable then must be the state of a fellow creature, who is at once tortured by bodily suffering and destitute of every circumstance which can alleviate it; who sees around him a family that are not only incapable of assisting their parent, but destined to want the common necessaries of life, the moment he intermits his daily labours! How indispensable then is the obligation, which should continually impel the rich to exert themselves in assisting their fellow creatures, and rendering that condition of life which we all avoid, less dreadful to those who must support it always? (*Sandford*, vol. II, pp. 206–7)

In addition to an annual dinner and occasional help during sickness (which the poor should surely appreciate),

> there is yet a duty, which he thought of more importance than the mere distribution of property to the needy, the encouragement of industry and virtue among the poor, and giving them juster notions of morals and religion.
>   If we have a dog, he would say, we refuse neither pains nor expence to train him up to hunting; if we have an horse, we send him to an experienced rider to be bitted; but our own species seems to be the only animal which is entirely exempted from our care. (*Sandford*, vol. II, pp. 207–8)

As I have suggested, the modern reader finds it difficult to accept Day's formula for social justice in quite the same spirit he offers it. Part of the problem is that without realizing it, Brooke and Day implicitly assume that one of the functions of the poor is to provide objects of benevolence for the rich.

Both Brooke and Day criticize society, and often the criticism is strong indeed. To say, in so many words, that the rich take goods and services from the poor and give in return only useless bits of metal is not a gentle criticism. But neither Brooke nor Day wants to change anything basic in society. They assume that things will—and indeed should—remain as they are.[15] The protest, then, no matter how strongly made, demands largely cosmetic changes. Neither Brooke nor Day asks that the rich give up their privilege and their wealth to the poor; rather, they ask merely that the rich be considerate of the poor and, as long as the poor are "deserving," that the rich give of their largesse to ameliorate individual suffering whenever possible. Both books emphasize the improvement of the rich person's character through the development of social responsibility and personal benevolence, an incredibly comfortable kind of social protest. Within the constructs of their perspective, Brooke and Day can look realistically at the world and see all the suffering and inequity in it. They do not have to ignore all that, for it forms a necessary part of their whole vision. If there is no need, there can be no benevolence; the suffering of the poor serves to give the rich a purpose. This view is not the anger at corruption that we found in Fielding and that we will see again in the novelists of the 1790s. But it is a form of social protest, a comment that some things—in this case a major reeducation of the upper classes—must be changed. If this, in perspective, does not seem like much of a protest, we should turn to a contemporary of Day's, Fanny Burney, who sees very little wrong with society at all and whose major concern is "the entrance of a young lady into the world." Of the novels I discuss, hers has the least social criticism to make. I include it to help put into perspective the strains of criticism that we have seen in some of the novels that precede *Evelina* and the increasingly strident demands for change which we shall find in many of the novelists who follow Burney in the turbulent nineties.

1. *Novels of the 1740s* (Athens: University of Georgia Press, 1982), pp. 13–15, 17–20, 146, 189, et passim.

2. Henry Brooke, *The Fool of Quality; or, the History of Henry Earl of Moreland,* 4 vols. (London: Edward Johnson, 1776); Thomas Day, *The History of Sandford and Merton, A Work Intended for the Use of Children,* 3 vols. (London: John Stockdale, 1787–89). All references in the text are to these editions.

3. As I noted in an earlier discussion of these two novels, "the families from which the children are taken are almost identically drawn in each book. The father is intelligent and fair-minded; the mother is far less admirable intellectually, and, in fact, seems to be impressed only by the frivolous and the gaudy. In both homes the fault is always with the mother. It is the female parent whose misplaced values threaten to ruin the child, and it is in each case the male parent who sees beneath the surface of aristocratic 'graces' to the truer values. In each book, the mother even makes sport of the child who shows such traits of character as benevolence, simplicity of taste, and innocence, while the fathers appreciate these finer qualities but raise much less forceful voices in praise than their wives do in blame." "More Than A Few Passages: Henry Brooke's *The Fool of Quality* as the Source for Thomas Day's *The History of Sandford and Merton,*" *Durham University Journal,* 75 (June 1983), p. 58.

4. The struggle to bring respectability and political power to the merchant was an ongoing one. Compare Brooke's statement with this pronouncement (in capital letters) of Bolingbroke's which John Sekora calls to our attention: "THE LANDED MEN ARE THE TRUE OWNERS OF OUR POLITICAL VESSEL; THE MONEYED MEN, AS SUCH, ARE NO MORE THAN PASSENGERS IN IT." *Luxury: The Concept in Western Thought, Eden to Smollett* (Baltimore: The Johns Hopkins University Press, 1977), p. 70.

5. Charles Kingsley, Biographical pref., *The Fool of Quality,* by Henry Brooke (London: George Routledge and Sons, 1906), p. iii.

6. See, for example, my discussion of *Nature and Art* in chapter seven.

7. *Spectator,* No. 2, quoted by Donald Greene in *The Age of Exuberance* (New York: Random House, 1970), p. 43. Greene's chapter on "The Business Community: The Industrial Revolution," pp. 42 ff., is an excellent summary of the issues involved.

8. I will discuss these social implications in some detail in the next chapter.

9. Greene, p. 46.

10. "Children's Literature and Bourgeois Ideology: Observations on Culture and Industrial Capitalism in the Later Eighteenth Century," in *Culture and Politics from Puritanism to the Enlightenment,* ed. Perez Zagorin (Berkeley: University of California Press, 1980), p. 232.

11. *An Address to the Young Inhabitants of the Pottery* (Newcastle: J. Smith, 1783), p. 22; quoted by Kramnick, p. 206.

12. Kramnick, p. 206.

13. *Introductory Lectures on Chemistry* (Columbia, S.C.: Daniel Faust, printer, 1820), p. 96; quoted by Kramnick, p. 207.

14. John Sekora, pp. 107–8, has shown that the indictment of aristocrats for wastefulness and excessive consumption—for luxury—as it begins to appear in novels of the late 1760s and the 1770s is actually a reversal of target. Earlier, he suggests, it had been the poor who were accused of moral degradation caused by an excessive fascination with luxury. Fielding in his *Enquiry into the Causes of the Late Increase of Robbers* accounts for the increase by claiming that the poor have set themselves to crime in order to satisfy their aspirations "to a Degree beyond that which belongs to them."

15. In Day's *The History of Little Jack,* 1778, this sense is even more pronounced. The young hero, orphaned in earliest childhood, rises through the exertion of his own energy and intelligence to become "one of the most respectable manufacturers in the country" (*Little Jack* [New York: Garland Publishing, 1977], p. 111), and all his success is due to the strength and goodness of his character. Surely a society which affords a young man such a possibility has much to recommend it. Naturally, in his success our hero does not become haughty or proud and "to all his poor neighbours he was kind and liberal, relieving them in their distress . . . (pp. 112–13).

3

EVELINA / *Fanny Burney*

Burney's *Evelina,* like *The Fool of Quality* and *Sandford and Merton,* is a middle-class book, and while her commentary shades over closer to social satire than social protest, her subject is much the same as theirs: the assimilation of the newly monied middle class into the traditional social hierarchy. All three books respond to the same economic change, and they share the happy sense that the change has been markedly for the best. Brooke and Day complacently explain to the aristocracy their role in the new system, but the elucidation is not for the benefit of the supposed aristocratic audience but the satisfaction of the intended readers of the books, the middle-class parents. Burney's novel, essentially a "how-to" book on easing the social transition, is directed at those same middle-class readers. As the newly rich merchant class entered into social as well as financial commerce with the aristocracy, it had to learn to imitate the behavior of the upper classes and to be aware of their social customs and social organization—all of which, as the young, middle-class Fanny Burney knew, was an education in itself.

Burney chronicles this kind of social education in *Evelina.* The seventeen-year-old Evelina comes from her rural retirement to the gay world with only her moral education and her own good sense to guide her. With the exception of small blunders, she does remarkably well. To the young woman writing the book, herself hardly older than her heroine, social success—which she never differentiates from personal fulfillment—is perfectly accessible to the wise, albeit naive, heroine. *Evelina* is written by a very young woman for whom the world of the fashionable and near fashionable is a most exciting place. With each novel she writes, some of the bloom wears off. The four years between *Evelina* and *Cecilia* bring her to an almost bitter ending for her novel. Subsequent books, colored by her struggles to support herself, her forced "marriage" to a life at court as Queen Charlotte's second keeper of the robes, as well as various personal disappointments, reflect an even more markedly changed outlook. The values are the same: wisdom, benevolence, and chastity, of course. But all of these no longer seem to have the power they have in *Evelina* to insure a happy ending.

Perhaps the charm of *Evelina* is the assurance of its happy ending. *Evelina's* world is well ordered, every character ensconced in a secure niche by the end of the novel. It is a morally comfortable world; Burney makes it easy for the reader to sympathize with the good characters and to look with gentle scorn on the less pleasant types. She makes easy moral judgments about who is or is not a worthwhile human being, and conveniently it happens that the rewards indeed fall to the worthwhile. More than that, as in fairy tales, the worthwhile are princes and princesses. Although we do not learn that Evelina is an aristocrat until the end of the book, Burney is sure to let us know then, and of course Orville is always "Lord." *Evelina* mixes the fairy-tale glow of "they lived happily ever after" with a sharply realistic picture of middle and upper-class society in eighteenth-century England. When we read her diaries, we become even more aware of how realistic Burney's novels are in their images of eighteenth-century life. To read the diaries is to find that social engagements are indeed among the principle concerns of the young, and the not-so-young, lady's life; having a benevolent nature and doing benevolent deeds are part of a lady's daily consciousness; the lady is aware of her own education in terms not so much of intellectual but of personal and social growth. Of course we have to be careful: the diaries were written by a very conscious writer and revised years later by an even more self-conscious woman. Yet the reflections of the life around her that we find in Burney's journals, and that in *Evel-*

ina she colors with such gay pastels, tally with other evidence of social and personal outlook in the century.

The changes that England had undergone by the 1770s in distribution of population, wealth, and power had brought a great deal of pressure to bear on established patterns of society. The industrial revolution and the consequent migration to the cities had put economic power into the hands of the mercantile class in two ways. First and most obviously, the merchants ran industry and reaped its money and power. Second and perhaps less obviously, with the workers concentrated in the cities, and not as in all earlier times on the land, England by the latter part of the century had become unable to feed herself. Thus, the power to feed the nation was under the control of the same merchant class whose power was growing so quickly by virtue of the industrial expansion. All of this economic strength demanded political expression as well. The merchant class, increasingly dominating the life and growth of the country, desired—demanded—to have a voice in the running of that country. L. B. Namier notes that already in the early years of the century, "wealth amassed in trade was laid out in landed estates and used to secure seats in the House of Commons, for both helped to lift their holders into a higher social sphere."[1] Later, the merchant class entered the House of Lords as well. In the 1780s and 1790s, William Pitt the younger was to harness their drive for his own purposes: to gain lasting control of the House of Lords he created over 140 new peers who were, naturally, to be loyal to him.[2] Thus the merchant princes became members of the government, even of the aristocracy, and gained with their titles the social recognition as well as the political power they desired. By the time *Evelina* was published in 1778, the middle class had acquired huge economic power and was gaining more and more political power to go with it. What remained was to acquire the social graces that were necessary to be comfortable with their new status.

The newly monied classes were not looked down upon by the hereditary aristocracy;[3] on the contrary, they were viewed as a vital force in the country's growth. Lord Orville is not being unusually democratic when he treats Evelina simply as a human being rather than as a member of a given social class. Namier describes the relationship in the eighteenth century among trade, class, and social rank:

> Trade was not despised in eighteenth-century England—it was acknowledged to be the great concern of the nation; and money was honoured, the mystic, common denominator of all values, the universal repository of as yet undetermined possibilities. But what was the position of the trader? There is no one answer to this question. A man's status in English society has always depended primarily on his own consciousness; for the English are not a methodical or logical nation—they perceive and accept facts without anxiously inquiring into their reasons or meaning. Whatever is apt to raise a man's self-consciousness—be it birth, rank, wealth, intellect, daring, or achievements—will add to his stature; but it has to be translated into the truest expression of his sub-conscious self-evaluation: uncontending ease, the unbought grace of life. Classes are the more sharply marked in England because there is no single test for them, except the final, incontestable result; and there is more snobbery than in any other country, because the gate can be entered by anyone, and yet remains, for those bent on entering it, a mysterious, awe-inspiring gate. . . .

He goes on to add that

> In the phylogenetic history of the Englishman the Oxford undergraduate of my own time corresponded to the eighteenth-century man, and with him nearly foremost among social qualifications was that a man should be amusing. Anyone can enter English society provided he can live, think, and feel like those who have built up its culture in their freer, easier hours.[4]

Everything Namier describes as a historian is reflected by Burney in *Evelina*. There are no hard and fast class lines in *Evelina*, but there are definitely consciousness lines. Evelina's problems throughout the book are caused by social misunderstandings; she learns, in Namier's words, how to "live, think, and feel" like the aristocrats. Once Evelina learns how to act properly, she is ready to take her place in society.

The education of a young lady into the ways of "the world"[5] might seem of little note except, perhaps, to the young lady herself and, possibly, to other young ladies for whom her adventures could serve as harmless entertainment. Tea table stuff, in short. But, as I have suggested, entry into society is serious societal business. The intermixing of the social classes is a prime movement of the time, immeasurably important to the participants, of course, but with a vital social function as well. Burney's chronicle, charming as it is as a novel, is equally instructive for us as a record of this melding process. Evelina makes the transition from middle class to aristocrat before our eyes; Burney makes it clear that breeding rather than rank determines the aristocrat, and Evelina works hard at becoming a lady. In a society as concerned with social movement as Burney's, this is as it must be: there has to be an earned way to become an aristocrat so that those late in the field may be accommodated. Thus, a title may be hereditary, but "aristocracy," assuming either requisite financial or hereditary background, comes with the acquisition of adequate social knowledge.

In *Evelina,* Burney focuses on the attempts of a young, socially inexperienced but carefully brought up young woman to learn to cope with new situations. One of the things that Evelina has to learn is to make her distinctions between people on the basis of real human value rather than on social position. Once she can make these distinctions, she can begin to function within the social forms of her milieu in a healthy, mature way; she has, at that point, come far along the way towards being a real lady. A significant signpost in the course of Evelina's education comes when she learns to distinguish between personal merit and inherited rank. Early in the novel, she is shocked to find that the vulgar Lovel is a nobleman. Evelina says that she "naturally concluded him to be some low-bred and uneducated man" and she is amazed to hear him addressed as "your Lordship." "*Lordship!*—how extraordinary! that a *nobleman,* accustomed, in all probability, to the first rank of company in the kingdom, from his earliest infancy, can possibly be deficient in *good manners,* however faulty in morals and principles" (p. 106). A little later, with more experience of the world, she begins to make

finer distinctions, but she still associates rank with good breeding. Notice her surprise that a lord can be uncouth: "In all
ranks and stations of life, how strangely do characters and manners differ! Lord Orville, with a politeness which knows no
intermission, and makes no distinction, is as unassuming and
modest as if he . . . was totally ignorant of every qualification
which he possesses; this other Lord . . . seems to me an entire
stranger to real good-breeding . . ." (p. 113).

Evelina the character must learn these lessons; Burney the
author already knows them. Evelina is surprised into equating
personal merit with hereditary place only because she is young
and inexperienced. She should know better, with the education
she has had from Mr. Villars, and indeed she soon does learn to
make better distinctions. Burney, in pointing out Evelina's mistake, records for us that eighteenth-century mentality that we
have already seen described by Namier. Evelina learns that
personal merit and carriage are more important than birth: to
recall Namier's point, "Whatever is apt to raise a man's self-
consciousness—be it birth, rank, wealth, intellect, daring, or
achievements—will add to his stature; but it has to be translated
into the truest expression of his sub-conscious self-evaluation;
uncontending ease, the unbought grace of life." When Evelina
can recognize that grace in others, and even more when she
manifests it, she has become a lady. As Evelina becomes more
accustomed to society and to making discriminations according
to her own judgments, she stops basing those judgments on
social position and instead concentrates on the value of the
individual regardless of his station. Similarly, the more discrim-
inating of her acquaintances value her for her own qualities of
benevolence, charm, and intelligence, and are willing to over-
look her deficiency in social education—and its attendant lack
of poise. Throughout the book, Burney emphasizes that high
social position and human value are not automatically concomitant. When the wise Orville introduces the newly proclaimed
Belmont heiress to a rather snobbish Mrs. Beaumont, he teases
her by saying "give me leave to present to you the daughter of
Sir John Belmont; a young lady who, I am sure, must long since

have engaged your esteem and admiration, tho' you were a stranger to her birth" (p. 381). Notice that he specifically refers to the distinction between worth and birth. Burney satirically describes that same Mrs. Beaumont and all those ladies like her: "She is an absolute *Court Calendar bigot;* for, chancing herself to be born of a noble and ancient family, she thinks proper to be of opinion, that *birth* and *virtue* are one and the same thing . . ." (p. 284).

Burney, in making her heroine appear middle class[6] and by having her interact both with those higher and lower on the social scale, allows herself enough scope so that she can move freely among several classes of English society. In making her subject the social education of a young, middle-class woman, she addresses one of the most salient social concerns of her time. Burney's novel, about social factors and social pressures, is concerned with external forms and forces, and leaves attempts to deal with the psychological effects of social initiations to other, later, novelists. *Evelina* is one of the earliest novels that grow out of society's need to place the new merchant class, and it begins to answer the question of how people become culturally secure after they have become socially equal—that is, after they have made the money. The fullest examination of the problem comes almost 130 years later in 1906 with Galsworthy's *The Forsyte Saga,* which follows an English family through all phases of its economic and social development. In *The Forsyte Saga,* times and people act on each other; institutions and perceptions of the socially appropriate evolve as the new middle class makes itself felt in society. In *Evelina,* however, there is little sense that the social norms should undergo any kind of evolution. Although Burney realizes that a man's worth cannot be judged by his rank, she does not see anything wrong with the social institution of class. Evelina is educated to be a lady, and there is no sense that this is wrong. Burney ridicules not the concepts of "lady" or "gentleman" but the idea that money can buy gentility. Although many of the other novelists of the period, Brooke, Day, and Inchbald, for example, object to the concept of class stratification, Burney objects to the attempts of the gauche nouveau riche to break into the upper classes by assuming a culture they do not have.

In *Evelina* Fanny Burney knows exactly which human and social values she approves. There are good traits in a human being: truthfulness, honor, reason, friendship, love,—and some that are bad: snobbishness, deceitfulness, stupidity. Through a combination of instinct and education, one learns to appreciate the good qualities, to cultivate them in oneself and in others, and to avoid those persons who are ruled by the bad. Her novel is much less concerned with social betterment than are those of many of her contemporaries: no attempts at all are made to improve or reform the less-than-virtuous characters such as Lovel and Sir Clement Willoughby, as would certainly be the case if they were in a Brooke, Day, or Holcroft novel. On the contrary, the lesson to be learned is for the positive characters and not for the reprobates, and seems to be, at least in part, how to avoid the discomfort that such unpleasant people can cause.

Evelina is largely a novel of education, and the object of Evelina's education, as I suggested, is to make her a lady of discrimination and of moral and social worth. Burney emphasizes this aspect of the book in her preface:

> To draw characters from nature, though not from life, and to mark the manners of the times, is the attempted plan of the following letters. For this purpose, a young female, educated in the most secluded retirement, makes, at the age of seventeen, her first appearance upon the great and busy stage of life; with a virtuous mind, a cultivated understanding, and a feeling heart, her ignorance of the forms, and inexperience in the manners, of the world, occasion all the little incidents which these volumes record, and which form the natural progression of the life of a young woman of obscure birth, but conspicuous beauty, for the first six months after her ENTRANCE INTO THE WORLD. (pp. 7–8)

Evelina is the most uneducated young lady possible in terms of the world; she is not only very young (seventeen) but has lived a totally secluded life. Burney, like so many contemporary novelists, carefully plots for her reader all of the significant points in her protagonist's education. We, therefore, are given ample opportunity to watch her meet and learn from new experiences. The popular eighteenth-century values of truth, benevolence, and reason have been instilled by her guardian Mr. Villars; we are to see how these values help her to meet new and perhaps difficult situations.

Evelina is the third generation that Mr. Villars has educated. Her grandfather, Mr. Evelyn, was his first charge; the young man, dying soon after his unfortunate marriage to Mme. Duval, left to his tutor "a legacy of a thousand pounds, and the sole guardianship of his daughter's person till her eighteenth year, conjuring [him], in the most affecting terms, to take the charge of her education till she was able to act with propriety for herself . . ." (p. 14). The terms of the request are significant: the guardian was not asked to take care of her, or to look after her, but to "take charge of her education." This young woman, who grows up to be Lady Belmont, Evelina's mother, entrusts Evelina to the Reverend Villars in exactly the same terms: "Lady Belmont, who was firmly persuaded of her approaching dissolution, frequently and earnestly besought me," says Mr. Villars, "that if her infant was a female, I would not abandon her to the direction of a man so wholly unfit to take the charge of her education" (p. 126). The word "education" is used in its most general sense; Burney, in the tradition of Locke and Rousseau, stresses that the educative aspects of upbringing are primary. And thus when Mr. Villars describes the responsibility given, the terms are that the father "would not, to a woman low-bred and illiberal as Mrs. Evelyn, trust the mind and morals of his daughter" (p. 14). "Mind and morals" are significant; physical, emotional, pecuniary, and social well-being will follow from, or are at least subservient to, this foremost concern.

Evelina has been raised in seclusion by Mr. Villars. The test of the education he has given her will be how she acts in the world. Education in its more abstract sense can take one only so far; then the other kind of learning, finding out how to act in given circumstances, must be allowed to function. As. Mr. Villars tells Evelina, "You must learn not only to *judge*, but to *act* for yourself" (p. 164). For even when things seem right to others, one must make decisions on the basis of one's own good sense. Thus when Evelina is to spend a month with Mme. Duval, he tells her she "will have occasion . . . for all the circumspection and prudence [she] can call to [her] aid" (p. 164) because, even though Mme. Duval would not willingly propose that Evelina do something wrong, Evelina must judge each issue at the time it comes up and act at her own, not Mme. Duval's, discretion. The novel is concerned in very large part with Evelina's continuing (and sometimes rather unsuccessful) attempts to deal with situations as they arise. In this, the novel is of rather smaller scope than many contemporary works for, like the Jane Austen novels which will come later, it confines itself to a limited set of situations and problems. Burney is concerned not with reforming the world but rather with how to function within certain social—but at the same time moral—guidelines.

As soon as she is out in the world, Evelina is sorely aware of her inexperience in handling social occasions. She undergoes trials of embarrassment that seem perhaps a little colored by her own prejudices of class and rank and yet are rather justifiable. The social occasions during which she meets her more refined friends, especially Lord Orville, while in the company of her quite unrefined family of Mme. Duval and the cousins would be uncomfortable for any reasonably sensitive person. Mme. Duval and the cousins are the embodiments of the very worst traits of the nouveau riche; they are brash, loud, insensitive, and presuming. Evelina repeatedly finds herself embarrassed by the actions of her family. For example, she does not quite know what to do when, at a dance while in their company, she comes upon Sir Clement Willoughby. She writes to Mr. Villars: "I was extremely vexed, and would have given the world to have avoided being seen by him: my chief objection was, from the apprehension that he wou'd hear Miss Branghton call me *cousin*.—I fear you will think this London journey has made me grow very proud, but indeed this family is so low-bred and vulgar, that I should be equally ashamed of such a connexion in the country, or any where" (p. 94). At the time, she tries not to talk to him but later feels that she acted in error: "I am afraid you will think it wrong; and so I do myself now,—but, at the time, I only considered how I might avoid immediate humiliation" (p. 94). At first her reactions do seem rather proud, yet who would not be ashamed to be found in such low company? When the same party goes to Vauxhall gardens, and she is first separated from them in the lonely groves and then annoyed by the undue attentions of a rather common acquaintance of her cousins, Mr. Smith, she is cha-grined that Sir Clement should find her in these situations: "Perhaps I was too proud,—but I could not endure that Sir Clement,—whose eyes followed him [Smith] with looks of the most surprised curiosity, should witness his unwelcome famil-iarity" (p. 201). Evelina's discomfort shows not that she is a snob but that her good sense makes her aware in these situations of what decorum and delicacy call for. Her vulgar family, in con-trast, epitomizing social ignorance, has no sense of the appropriate.

There are a great many instances of Evelina's embarrassment as she learns her way in the world, all of them building towards the moment not when she will be through blundering but when, at least, she has met the situations enough times so that she is able to cope. When the Reverend Villars sends her off to Mrs. Mirvan, he knows that "she is quite a little rustic, and knows nothing of the world . . . I shall not be surprised if you should discover in her a thousand deficiencies of which I have never dreamt" (p. 19), and Evelina herself thinks in these terms. For example, at her first dance she worries what Lord Orville will think of her, "How will he be provoked . . . when he finds what a simple rustic he has honoured with his choice! one whose ignorance of the world makes her perpetually fear doing something wrong" (p. 30). Her fears, of course, quickly are justified. An unwelcome swain at her first ball is moved to ask, "My dear creature . . . why where could you be educated?" (p. 44), and poor Evelina can only write home that she leaves Lon-don without regret, realizing that "I am too inexperienced and ignorant to conduct myself with propriety in this town, where every thing in new to me, and many things are unaccountable and perplexing" (p. 48). The moral to be found in these early experiences is not that she was awkward in the new situations, but that her early education had taught her how to handle such disappointments. Her reaction is entirely sensible, perhaps even too sensible for a seventeen-year-old girl. She realizes simply that her experience has not fitted her for these adventures.

She learns at each point, as all who desire entry into society must learn, what proper modes of conduct are. For there are inevitably moments when her instinctive reactions are not the best, as when she loses her way and finds herself in the very alarming company of a pair of prostitutes. As the three of them are walking along, she sees Lord Orville, and her only fear is that he shall see her—she is not aware that she needs his protection from any possible danger. No, her only thought is of her pride. When he repasses and does see her, "I thought I should have fainted, so great was my emotion from shame, vexation, and a thousand other feelings, for which I have no expressions" (p. 235). When Orville questions her on her strange situation, her first reaction is one of hurt pride, which under his kindness turns to "delight and gratitude." And yet, in the next similar situation, again her pride is foremost; by her own admission, she finds herself in trouble through her "heedlessness:" in trying not to be seen by Orville, she cautions her cousin Miss Branghton not to call attention to her, which leads to a great deal of attention indeed. Had she not been so self-conscious, there would have been no incident. Instead, Orville's coach is borrowed against her will but seemingly at her request, is slightly wrecked, and so forth. In addition to the light this incident sheds on Evelina's not-quite-polished sophistication, it allows Burney a quick comment on the view from the other side. For all along the Duval-Branghton set has been quite awed by Evelina's familiarity with the Lord Orvilles and Sir Clements. So that when young Branghton goes to apologize to Orville, he expects him to be "so proud he'll hardly let me speak" and is extremely surprised to find "he's no more proud than I am, and he was as civil as if I'd been a lord myself" (p. 248). True breeding, then, of which Lord Orville is certainly the best specimen in the book, does not stand on distinctions of rank but treats each person as a human being of worth.

Not quite seeing the lesson, Evelina is hysterical: she is sure that the actions of her cousin have forever lost her the esteem of Lord Orville. "I was half frantic; I really raved; the good opinion of Lord Orville seemed now irretrievably lost . . ." (p. 248). It was her mistake in the first place that had led to this awkward situation; she did not know how to "know" both the refined Orville and the vulgar Branghtons at the same time. Later when she meets Mr. Macartney in the garden, she is so inadept that she cannot keep the scene from seeming like a lovers' rendezvous to Orville: "unused to the situations in which I find myself, and embarrassed by the slightest difficulties, I seldom, till too late, discover how I ought to act" (p. 301). Given enough time and trust, however, she learns to confess her inexperience to Orville, to stop trying to act as if she is in control, and instead to ask that his "indulgence—will make some allowance, on account of my inexperience . . ." (p. 307). She is "new to the world, and unused to acting for myself,—my intentions are never wilfully blameable, yet I err perpetually" (p. 306). Interestingly enough, she makes no further errors during the course of the book, for Evelina's education has brought her to the point at which she feels secure enough to confess her lack of poise. In the very acknowledgment, she finally opts for simply being herself, and thus the charm that attracted Orville, Willoughby, and all the rest is now free to function without the hindrance of her attempts to cope by herself with situations that are beyond her.

Of course it is to Orville that she brings these confessions, for as Edward Bloom points out in his introductory essay, it is Orville who will be her guide after their marriage.[7] Bloom considers that the lesson she learns is "prudence," but that is only a small part of the awareness she picks up in the course of the book. Perhaps as importantly, she learns, as Mr. Villars in the first pages of the novel had said she must, to make decisions and to act on her own judgment. One aspect of this new confidence is her new self-awareness; another, perhaps, is her new prudence. She has learned, too, to trust her own judgments even when they seem to go against the opinions of people she respects, such as the Reverend Villars. This is the most significant lesson of all, because it allows her to function as a free, mature individual in society. For example, when Evelina receives a letter from Orville that suggests that she has been quite wrong about him and that he is not a good man, Mr. Villars tells her to have no more to do with him. She sees that Orville's actions do not match this verdict; in fact he is still the paragon she had thought him. Evelina, after a brief struggle, follows her own promptings and reacts not to the rules set down by Mr. Villars but to the exigencies of the reality she is experiencing. From her lament about the letter that she must find herself "in a world so deceitful, where we must suspect what we see, distrust what we hear, and even doubt what we feel" (p. 259), she learns to trust her feelings to the point of deciding to marry. The letter is a fake, and her feelings are proved to be well founded.

Other feelings also based on her education as a human being are found to be justified. These come under that popular eighteenth-century banner of benevolence: in *Evelina* acts of kindness are done simply, with little fanfare (in contrast to the seemingly endless examination and discussion of each benevolent act in Brooke's, Day's, and Holcroft's novels) and so seem, after all, simply a part of human nature. There is no discussion in Burney's novel about whether benevolence is natural or learned behavior. The fact that benevolence does exist, whether Evelina learned it from Mr. Villars or from her own instincts, or from a combination of the two, is what is important. Thus, Evelina's reaction to her father's neglect of her is pity: "I forget how much more *he* is the object of sorrow, than I am! Alas, what amends can he make himself, for the anguish he is hoarding up for time to come! My heart bleeds for him, whenever this reflection occurs to me" (p. 159).[8] And when she comes upon a wild-looking Mr. Macartney holding pistols, her immediate reaction, with no thought whatever for her own safety, is to prevent him from harming himself. What else is expressed but the spirit of eighteenth-century benevolence when she writes of the incident that "I am sure . . . you will be much concerned for this poor man, and, were you here, I doubt not but you would find some method of awakening him from the error which blinds him, and of pouring the balm of peace and comfort into his afflicted soul" (p. 184). She puts her feeling into action in ways less dramatic than the pistol episode, as when she insists on including Mr. Macartney in the company as the Branghtons prepare to go out: "and I looked towards Mr. Macartney, to whom I wished extremely to shew that I was not of the same brutal nature with those by whom he was treated so grossly" (p. 192).

Her benevolence is always the product of generosity and sensitivity—pains are always taken so that its object (unlike the beneficiaries in many other eighteenth-century novels) is subjected to as little need for acknowledgment as possible. When she suspected that Mr. Macartney needed money, she "let fall [her] purse upon the ground, not daring to present it to him, and ran up stairs with the utmost swiftness" (p. 215). She does not even talk of "benevolence," but only of her "opportunity . . . for . . . contributing what little relief was in my power" (p. 216). For Burney, real ladies are benevolent but need not and do not advertise their own generosity. It remains for the Reverend Villars to give a name to Evelina's actions towards Mr. Macartney and others. He considers that "you have but done your duty; you have but shewn that humanity without which I should blush to own my child. . . . O my child, were my fortune equal to my confidence in thy benevolence, with what transport should I, through thy means, devote it to the relief of indigent virtue" (p. 216). Again, Burney reflects current trends of thought—here, the familiar eighteenth-century belief that part of the education of a human being is his education in benevolence (*The Fool of Quality, Nature and Art, Anna St. Ives*) and that it is in the exercise of that benevolence that he is most truly worthy. The Reverend Villars encourages

Evelina to "be ever thus ... dauntless in the cause of distress! ... Though gentleness and modesty are the peculiar attributes of your sex, yet fortitude and firmness, when occasion demands them, are virtues as noble and becoming in women as in men: the right line of conduct is the same for both sexes, though the manner in which it is pursued may ... be accommodated to the strength or weakness of the different travellers" (p. 217).

As in *Anna St. Ives,* the responsibilities of women for doing good in the world are as great as those of men. Burney, however, suggests that the means of doing good may differ, a concession that neither Godwin nor Holcroft would be likely to make. But then she makes other distinctions that they would probably find rather abhorrent: when discussing Mrs. Selwyn, Evelina says that "she is extremely clever; her understanding, indeed, may be called *masculine*," but she sees in her a "want of gentleness; a virtue which ... seems so essentially a part of the female character" (pp. 268–69)—as if it is not a part of the male! She finds herself very uncomfortable with this strange woman who "in studying to acquire the knowledge of the other sex ... has lost all the softness of her own" (p. 269). One can imagine the scorn with which the intimates of Mary Wollstonecraft would have greeted such sentiments. But Burney, although reacting against the too-masculine woman, also makes fun of those who would refuse woman a mind. Mrs. Selwyn herself ridicules such distinctions when she teases a silly fop who wonders how a woman not attending the assembly can pass her time "in a manner ... extraordinary ... for the young Lady *reads*" (p. 275). The despicable creature Lovel is made the mouthpiece for the obviously unapproved doctrine that "I have an insuperable aversion to strength, either of body or mind, in a female," an opinion which the silly Lord Merton seconds, "Deuce take me if ever I wish to hear a word of sense from a woman as long as I live" (p. 361). Burney's view, in this as in everything else in the book, seems to be the moderate one: women have a right and a duty to exercise their minds but not to forget that they are women. It is in this sense, then, that Mr.

Villars suggests to Evelina that she has a duty to perform acts of benevolence, though those acts may sometimes be of a sort particularly suited to a woman.[9]

The object of Evelina's education is not to be supposed to be out of the ordinary; she is to grow up into a sensitive, intelligent girl, hopefully someday to be "bestow[ed] . . . upon some worthy man, with whom she might spend her days in tranquillity, chearfulness and good-humour, untainted by vice, folly, or ambition" (p. 127). This seems such a natural course within the novel's context that it is not until we are faced with another possibility, such as the scheme which Mme. Duval might construct, that Mr. Villar's plan even seems like a philosophy of education. Mme. Duval is the epitome of everything that should not be imitated. She is vulgar, ignorant, and opinionated—marriage to her is such a terrible mistake for the sensitive young Evelyn that he dies soon after it is contracted. Thus, anything she says on the matter of education we may assume to be wrong. Evelina recounts Mme. Duval's proposed course:

> She talked very much of taking me to Paris, and said I greatly wanted the polish of a French education. She lamented that I had been brought up in the country, which, she observed, had given me a very *bumpkinish air*. However, she bid me not despair, for she had known many girls, much worse than me, who had become . . . fine ladies after a few years abroad . . . a Miss Polly Moore, daughter of a chandler's-shop woman, who . . . happened to be sent to Paris, where, from an awkward, ill-bred girl, she so much improved, that she has since been taken for a woman of quality. (p. 67)

In other words, Mme. Duval's idea of a proper education is based not on making a person worthwhile but on giving her the appearance of a society belle. Mme. Duval assures Evelina that she will "make quite another creature of [her]" (p. 121): Evelina is to become a fashionable lady who will "despise almost every body and every thing [she] had hitherto seen"—she is to marry "into some family of the first rank in the kingdom" and "spend a few months in Paris" where her "education and manners might receive their last polish" (p. 121). Appearance, for Mme.

Duval, is all. Unlike Mr. Villars, who is constantly reminding Evelina to keep her hopes and expectations within the bounds of what she may reasonably expect, Mme. Duval is ready to pump her full of grandiose plans. She proposes just the sort of scheme one might expect from a woman Mr. Villars describes as "too ignorant for instruction, too obstinate for entreaty, and too weak for reason" (p. 127). Mme. Duval's proposal is included not only as a foil to the rational and healthy plan adopted for Evelina by Mr. Villars but also as a detail in Burney's rendering of contemporary English society; undoubtedly, there were as many foolish Mme. Duvals ready to misguide their charges as wise Mr. Villars ready to help them. Mme. Duval's ideas would be ridiculed by any of the novelists mentioned in this study.

While for the most part accepting the societal structures of class and hereditary rank that some of her more liberal contemporaries question, Burney still agrees with them in her basic assessment of what constitutes a worthwhile human being. She agrees that the healthy adult's development depends on the child's education in benevolence, sensitivity, and reason. Her novel has a slant different from most others in the period in that it examines the specific problems of the rising monied classes as they attempt to mix with those of hereditary rank, but the human values she emphasizes are the same as Day's, Holcroft's, and Godwin's. Evelina is not nouveau riche, but her problems are very much the same as theirs, for she must learn manners and mores. In addition, she must learn to tell the difference between true breeding and false sophistication on each occasion that they are manifested by any of the several social groups in which she finds herself. She has a great deal of natural good sense and a generally good instinctive appreciation of what is proper or graceful in society; she is a kind of natural lady and has but to learn the specific forms of manners to fulfill her social potential.

There is no anger in the book. Burney's satire, for the most part aimed at those who would ape their betters, is a satire born not of social ire but of social incongruity. The social satire in *Evelina* is to be distinguished from the far stronger protests found in the other novels I discuss and serves to suggest some of the range of social commentary in the second half of the century. Burney criticizes Lovel, Mme. Duval, and the Branghtons not as representatives of their class but as corruptions of an ideal. Aristocrats should comport themselves well; when they do not, it is to their personal shame. Those who behave genteelly are to be admired and emulated. Burney in *Evelina* did not set out to fight ideological battles or to delineate social problems but to write a book that would chronicle the education into society of a young lady of good breeding but little experience. The adjectives "frothy" and "charming," so often used of *Evelina*, are not misplaced. There is none of the argumentative intellectualizing that marks many of the contemporary novels and that gives Burney's late *The Wanderer* an almost comical awkwardness in its debates about the ideals of the French Revolution.

Evelina is a reflection rather than a critique of society. There is no awareness in *Evelina* of the poor; we are not often aware that social problems can encompass much more than avoiding the making of a faux pas at a ball.[10] As I have noted, Evelina is too preoccupied with learning the steps of the social dance to criticize the forms themselves. Burney presents her eighteenth-century, upper-middle-class world just as she, and Evelina, perceives it. It is an oversimplified world, in some ways naive. And yet for all those 140 new peers and the countless others on their way up in mobile eighteenth-century society, the awkwardness of Evelina and the social anxieties she faces had very real correlatives to their own lives. Burney's novel affirms the growing eighteenth-century conviction that nobility of mind and spirit matters. That is, in a real sense, a democratic ideal. At one time—and that rather recently too—it had been revolutionary. Burney's polite novel, as devoted to preservation as the novels of Holcroft and Godwin ostensibly are to change, has this very important philosophical link to them.

1. *England in the Age of the American Revolution*, 2nd ed. (New York: St. Martin's Press, 1961), p. 10.

2. Stanley Ayling, *George the Third* (New York: Alfred A. Knopf, 1972), p. 312, footnote 2. Remarking on events in the 1784 election, only six years after the publication of *Evelina,* Ayling quotes Horace Walpole: "They are crying peerages about the streets in barrows." During the years of Pitt's ministry the membership of the House of Lords virtually doubled.

3. Remember that the aristocratic Richard Moreland in Brooke's *The Fool of Quality* is clearly wrong and finally recognizes his own error in supposing himself superior to a merchant merely on the score of rank; see my discussion in chapter two.

4. Namier, pp. 13–14. This tallies precisely with what we have already seen in *The Fool of Quality* and *Sandford and Merton.*

5. Burney's preface to *Evelina* tells us that she is planning to record the first six months of an inexperienced young lady after her "ENTRANCE INTO THE WORLD." Fanny Burney, *Evelina, or the History of a Young Lady's Entrance into the World,* ed. and introd. Edward A. Bloom (London: Oxford University Press, 1968), p. 8. All references in the text are to this edition.

6. Evelina, it turns out, is in fact a lord's daughter and quite Lord Orville's social equal. Social consciousness is a fact of social life, and even the exemplary Orville admits that he had planned to make some inquiries into Evelina's background. Burney finds herself living in a society that would like to believe that a man or woman is valued as an individual but knows quite well that it operates by other prejudices. The Macartney marriage, for example, must take place quickly because, even though he is very much in love with the now displaced heiress, he would find it quite distasteful should it become common knowledge that the young lady is not the true daughter of Sir John Belmont but a mere servant's child.

7. Introd., *Evelina,* pp. xix ff.

8. Her reaction here is also colored by eighteenth-century paternalism; the father can do no wrong. There are many examples of such devoted children, especially in the gothic novels. In Ann Radcliffe's *The Italian,* for example, the evil cleric is not held at all accountable by his forgiving daughter.

9. In her own personal life, Burney closely approximated this ideal. Was she not self-supporting from a very early age (her father, Charles Burney, was a very successful music teacher and dinner companion but never, it seems, quite comfortably solvent), yet always girlishly obedient to the suggestions of her father and Daddy Crisp?

10. Mr. Macartney is poor, but his poverty is genteel and easily taken care of by a good marriage. This is quite different from the case of the laborers in *Nature and Art,* for example, who cannot and never shall be able to make ends meet.

4

ANNA ST. IVES / *Thomas Holcroft*

Holcroft is very optimistic in *Anna St. Ives*. He expresses no doubt that human progress has any visible limits; men are almost infinitely improvable and as they improve, so must their social institutions. Baseness, cruelty, dishonesty, evil of every sort is but a result of the ignorance of good; we have only to educate men to the good, and they will live by it. Thus the duty of those already enlightened is to educate their less fortunate brothers. Holcroft posits, in effect, a kind of reverse Garden of Eden, where it is lack of knowledge that brings evil.

The plot of *Anna St. Ives* is simple. Anna St. Ives is the respectful daughter of the fairly well-off baronet, Sir Arthur. She loves Frank Henley, son of her father's steward Abimelech, but feels that she cannot give in to her emotional attachment because "the world," that is, her relations and her peers, would not believe that she loves him only for his outstanding qualities of mind and character; she fears that people would consider that hers is not a rational attachment, since he is so far below her in station, and that she had been carried away by her passions. If these people were to believe that she had been moved by passion rather than reason, she would lose all her power to influence them to rational behavior. Frank disagrees with her and insists that because their love is a product of mutual rational attachment, nothing should stand in the way of their union and of the good that such a union would do society. They discuss this issue from any number of angles; this tension is the main plot. The secondary plot concerns the attempts by the villainous Coke Clifton to seduce the virtuous Anna. He doesn't succeed; instead, the power of reason triumphs, and in the last pages of the novel, Clifton is brought to the path of reason and virtue. In *Anna St. Ives* even the blackest villain, even Coke Clifton, can be reformed through reason.

All human virtues are products of our reason. A man who is not virtuous need only be educated to understand the irrationality of his misanthropy, and he will reform and become a contributing member of society. Holcroft discusses a broad range of social issues, from the function of education to the role of women, from the definition of fatherhood to the definition of criminality. Always, he emphasizes the potential for good that society, through its enlightened members, holds out to individuals. It is therefore necessary to the plot that both of Holcroft's protagonists be exemplars of virtue. Anna never has a mean thought, and Frank—Frank hardly ever has even an inaccurate thought; he almost never makes mistakes. Anna, for example, has some confusion about the proper considerations in choosing a marriage partner, but Frank never vacillates. Thus (except for Anna's hesitation about marrying Frank), we are assured of being on the right side of an issue if we accept Anna's or Frank's judgments.

Holcroft begins in the first pages of the novel to make us aware of the extraordinary virtues of Anna and Frank; at the same time, he introduces a number of significant social issues, so that within perhaps six or seven pages, a reader has already entered the lists on the side of Anna and Frank, of truth and virtue. We have, within these few pages, already begun to doubt the wisdom of traditional conceptions of rank, education, and, even, of fatherhood. The first letter is Anna's to her friend Louisa. From it, we learn that she and her father are in the midst of setting off on a trip to Paris, where she hopes to meet Louisa's brother, Coke Clifton. The brother, she is sure, "cannot but resemble his sister. He cannot but be all generosity, love, expansion, mind, soul."[1] These are the qualities Anna admires. They are to be contrasted, for example, with the qualities of someone like her father's steward Abimelech Henley, who, she tells Louisa, is "artful, selfish, and honest enough to seek his own profit, were it at the expence of his employer's ruin" (p. 2). She complains that Abimelech is slowly destroying her father through unlimited expenditures for unneeded improvements.[2] The "meanness of the father," however, is more than compensated for by "the amiable qualities of the son," Frank, of whom she notes, "he has many good, nay . . . many great, qualities" (p. 3). There is also a line in the letter about the "duty" of marriage and, last but not least, a comment, about her bird, that "the development of mind, even in a bird, has something in it highly delightful" (p. 3).

Thus many of Holcroft's themes are announced at the outset. We are told what the admirable qualities are in a human being (generosity, love, mind) and what the negatives are. We learn that Frank is "great" but somehow not being considered for marriage. And we learn that "the development of mind" is of extraordinary import—even in a bird! The next letter, from Louisa to Anna, tells us that Anna is really admirable and reiterates that Frank is wonderful—indeed (dare she even suggest it?) he might be a perfect mate for Anna. With two letters, Holcroft has set out the most important lines of his plot, given the reader the essentials of Anna's and Frank's characters, and introduced several of his primary themes. These themes all cluster around Holcroft's central concern, the application of reason—or "truth"—to human, to personal, affairs. Education is the means of spreading truth; it is what shapes the human being, and a human being who acts in antisocial ways simply needs to be reeducated so that he understands the import of his actions. As more and more people become enlightened, the problems of society will diminish, even disappear. This reeducation is a primary duty of the already good and virtuous people; Anna's fear that by marrying Frank she will lose her power to influence others is a fear that she will no longer be able to fulfill this primary duty. When Frank tells her that he believes their marriage would be socially useful, he means that together they could go about educating others productively.

The first step in the improvement of society is to improve oneself, or to be improved, to the greatest possible degree. Thus we learn in the early letters that Frank feels he must travel, and Anna insists on his travel because it is his duty "to seize on every opportunity which can tend to enlarge [his] faculties." She continues, "You have no common part to act; and, that you may act it well, you should study the beings with whom you are to associate." Further, he must accompany her to France, for, she tells him, "the journey will be of infinite service to you. A mind like yours cannot visit a kingdom where the manners of the people are so distinct as those of the French must be from the English, without receiving great benefit" (p. 45). If Frank's father won't give him the money, Anna insists that she be allowed to provide it, for that is her duty. Improving the mental faculties enlarges the moral core. Knowing more, Frank would be a better human being and thus a better mentor for others. His father Abimelech, a narrow, selfish, ignorant man, understands nothing of this, and Frank and his father argue over Frank's need to learn by travel. This lack of understanding between them is nothing new, for we are told that Frank owes all his education not to his own father but to the father of his friend Oliver Trenchard. Frank considers Mr. Trenchard his real father, for as Anna says, "a true father feeds the mind" (p. 9).

Some of the most interesting social commentary in the book is on the liberated child-parent relationship; that is, the child must only respect a parent who deserves respect and need only comply with parental wishes that bear the stamp of reason. Thus the parent who neglects or subverts his child's education has no right to the respect that otherwise might be considered his due. If we consider the attitudes of other eighteenth-century children toward their parents—Clarissa's in Richardson's novel, or Evelina's in Burney's,[3] or even those daughters of devilish daddies in the gothic novels—we see that Holcroft has moved his characters some distance. Frank's rational disapproval as he talks of his father's perspective is interesting for itself as well as for what he says about education. He tells his friend Oliver:

he [Abimelech] has kept me in ignorance, as much as was in his power. Reading, writing, and arithmetic is his grand system of education; after which man has nothing more to learn, except to get and to hoard money. Had it not been for the few books I bought and the many I borrowed, together with the essential instruction which thy excellent father's learning and philanthropy enabled and induced him to give me, I should probably have been as illiterate as he could have wished. A son after his own heart! One of his most frequent and most passionate reproaches is "the time I *waste* in reading." (p. 8)

Holcroft in *Anna* insists that the familial relationship is not more important than the simply human relationship. *Anna St. Ives* suggests that each man owes his fealty to society first and to his personal relations second. Each has the responsibility to improve society as a whole in whatever way possible. The influence of Godwin rather clearly lies behind Holcroft's thinking in many parts of *Anna St. Ives,* quite obviously so here if we remember Godwin's famous anecdote about Archbishop Fénelon.[4]

This social responsibility extends both to the self and to others. Because each person has the duty to improve himself, he must allow others to help him improve. Thus if Anna has the money to allow Frank to travel, she must offer it to him and he must accept it because the final object is the betterment of humanity through the improvement of each of its members (especially members of whom great deeds may be expected). Frank cannot allow his pride to prevent him from accepting offers for his own improvement because that would deprive humanity of some share of the potential social improvement he could contribute. Even Frank does not have a quite perfect vision, and Anna finds it a bit difficult to overcome his foolish hesitation about taking money from her. She does, however, insist—and Frank later saves a whole family from grievous harm with the twenty pounds she had forced on him.

The episode begins when Anna's father tries to reward Frank with twenty pounds for fighting off a highwayman. Frank refuses, annoyed that "a man cannot behave as he ought, and as it would be contemptible not to behave, but he must be paid!" (p. 33). He finally accepts the money only because Anna begs him to. While walking one day soon after, he sees a commotion in the street and notices "a decent, well looking, and indeed handsome young woman, with a fine child in her arms" (p. 33) who is running after her husband, himself pursued by bailiffs who are trying to arrest him. As Frank relates to Oliver, "Her grief was so moving, so sympathetic, that it excited my compassion, and made me determine to follow her" (p. 34). Frank learns that the bailiffs were trying to arrest the husband for a debt of sixteen pounds, plus costs, for which he was liable because he had cosigned a note for his wife's brother and the latter had defaulted. These good people (Frank notes that "it seemed they are a young couple, who by their industry have collected a trifling sum, with which they have taken a small shop. . . . She serves her customers, and he follows his trade, as a journeyman carpenter. It did not a little please me to hear the young creature accuse her brother of being false to his friend; while the husband defended him, and affirmed it could be nothing but necessity" [p. 34]) are saved by Frank, who just happens to have with him the twenty pounds he had accepted with such hesitation from Anna's father. This relatively small sum is the difference between safety and disaster for this deserving young couple. There are several points to be noted here. One is that, although benevolence like Frank's is part of any man's duty, nevertheless it is important that recipients be themselves deserving. The worthiness of the couple is emphasized not only by their desire to work hard and live simply but also by their responsible, generous attitude toward each other and towards those in need. The husband apologizes for the brother-in-law, generously excusing the man of any fault; the wife is critical of her brother, thus proving herself unbiased by family ties. Altogether, in Frank's terms, they are a model couple and helping them clearly contributes to the larger needs of society as well.

The discussion of the woman's terror of the bailiffs affords Holcroft a brief opportunity to allude to the corruption of the legal and penal system of England, the same sore spot that had been the subject of Fielding's probing nearly fifty years earlier. The woman's terror for her husband, Holcroft makes clear, is well founded. The bailiffs are totally corrupt; when the wife begs to be allowed to sell her family's goods so that her husband will not be taken to jail, Frank is sure that "the bailiffs would have paid no other attention to her panic than to see how it might be turned to profit. The miscreants talked of five guineas, for the pretended risk they should run, in giving him a fortnight to sell his effects to the best advantage. They too could recommend a broker, a very honest fellow . . ." (p. 351). Frank is moved to ask his friend, "By what strange gradations . . . can the heart of man become thus corrupt?" (p. 35). But we know that the heart of man does become so corrupt, for these bailiffs act just like the ones we have seen in *Amelia*. Their corruption is part of the same penal system Fielding had described, and which Godwin so bitterly denounces in *Caleb Williams*. Frank describes the young wife's agonized pleading at the very thought of her husband going to jail:

> The horrors of a jail were so impressed, so rooted in her fancy, that she was willing to sell any thing, every thing; she would give them all she had, so that her Harry might not be dragged to a damp, foul dungeon; to darkness, bread and water, and starving. Thou canst not imagine the volubility with which her passions flowed, and her terrors found utterance, from the hope that it was not possible for Christian hearts to know all this, and not be moved to pity. (pp. 34–35)

We know, from Godwin and from John Howard, that her fears are not at all exaggerated, and this fact lends an element of horror to the scene that Holcroft may not have intended. In fact, it is only chance that this young man was not condemned to slime and starvation; it is only chance that Frank happened to be where he was and that he happened to have the money with him. Although Holcroft does not emphasize it here, such a system seems shaky at best. The fragility of human security is a constant theme in these eighteenth-century novels, as we have seen in Fielding and as will be apparent when we look at Godwin and Inchbald as well. Holcroft suggests this lack of control at several points in *Anna St. Ives*, but a much heavier sense of helplessness becomes apparent in *Hugh Trevor*. It is as if Holcroft, peripherally aware of the basic problems in his society, attempts in *Anna St. Ives* to suppress them with the sweeping theoretical solution of educating men to benevolence. But individual benevolence is, in the last resort, an uncertain proposition on which to stake personal safety. Although Holcroft does not face this problem openly in *Anna St. Ives,* in his next book, *Hugh Trevor,* he not only recognizes but is overwhelmed by it.

In *Anna St. Ives,* however, individual benevolence is still presented as adequate social insurance. That is why Frank is wrong to resent having Anna or her father give him money. A good man like Frank must always have money with him because he never knows when he may need to do a benevolent deed. Frank is wrong when, as Anna says, "he is desirous to confer, but not to accept obligations; he is ready enough to give, but not to receive" (p. 39). And she knows the argument that can overcome his hesitation. When she learns where the twenty pounds has been spent, she determines to reimburse him, noting that "there is one thought which will make him submit . . . quietly. I have but to remind him that the good of others requires that men, who so well know the use of it, should never be without money" (p. 41). Philosophically, this opens rather a can of worms—the same can that Godwin opens in *Political Justice.* Frank asks "what is the thing called property? What are *meum* and *tuum?* Under what circumstances may a man take money from another?" (p. 36). Godwin says and acts on the notion that each man must do what he does best for society; for example, the philosopher should philosophize. That is why, of course, the philosopher has the right to be supported by others while he does his thinking; even further, the others have a duty to support him. In practice, we remember the rather notorious image of Godwin sponging off, most notably, poor Shelley.[5]

Acting with benevolence is merely reasonable and deserves no special praise, or so Frank protests repeatedly when he is thanked by the various recipients of his goodness. Holcroft insists throughout *Anna St. Ives* that benevolence consists not only of the giving of charity, as with the poor family Frank saved, but of the saving of mistaken minds. In fact, he emphasizes the latter. Much of the book analyzes the flaws and the reformation of the misguided Coke Clifton, and one of the earliest detailed episodes of Frank's benevolence concerns his own reformation of a highwayman who had attacked Anna's party and wounded him. The story of the highwayman seems intended by Holcroft as a paradigm of how the enlightened man of good will (in Holcroft's terms a redundancy—for to be enlightened is to be of good will) can change the course of another's life for the better and so can improve society. Frank, who "abhor[s] the taking away the life of man, instead of seeking his reformation" (p. 17), does not identify the highwayman to the authorities and convinces Anna's father to do the same. Holcroft's morality is a little muddled here, for Frank claims that it was impossible for him to identify the man but that he "luckily prevail [ed] on Sir Arthur to do the same" (p. 17). Presumably, he would not have identified him even if he could, but it is less awkward, or more fortunate, if he needn't lie. After refusing to identify the assailant, Frank then visits him. Frank describes the interview:

> I paid the poor wretch a visit, privately, and gave him such a lecture as, I should hope, he would not easily forget. It was not all censure: soothing, reasoning, and menace were mingled. My greatest effort was to convince him of the folly of such crimes; he had received some proof of the danger. He was in great pain, and did not think his life quite secure. He promised reformation with all the apparent fervour of sincerity. . . .
> I found he was poor, and, except a few shillings, left him the trifle of money which I had; endeavoring by every means to restore a lost wretch to virtue and society. (p. 17).

Frank even arranges for the highwayman to change lodgings so that neither the law nor the man's cronies can find him. As Frank sees it,

> I visited a man whose vices, that is whose errors and passions were so violent as to be dangerous to society, and still more dangerous to

himself. Was is not my duty? I thought myself certain of convincing
him of his folly, and of bringing back a lost individual to the paths
of utility and good sense. What should I have been, had I neglected
such an opportunity? I have really no patience to think that a thing,
which it would have been a crime to have left undone, should
possibly be supposed a work of supererogation! (p. 42)

These are rather remarkable passages. One is, perhaps,
tempted to notice first Frank's hubris—which of course is not at
all Holcroft's intention; the distance between Frank's, or
Holcroft's, perspective and our own is itself suggested by the
degree to which Frank's assurance of his own hold on right
seems overblown. Frank is certain that he knows what the paths
of utility and good sense are; further, he is sure that he can
bring back a man who has strayed from those paths and change
him from a menace to a contributor to society. He is absolutely
certain that it is his duty to make these efforts. Frank notices,
for example, that the highwayman "was in great pain, and did
not think his life quite secure," but that does not cause Frank to
temper his zeal to lecture, for pain or no pain, Frank has his
duty. We may smile at Holcroft's assurance here, but the tone
remains constant throughout the book. Holcroft loses this assurance completely within the following years. As obvious as
the paths of utility and good sense seem in *Anna St. Ives,* in
Hugh Trevor they seem just as uncertain.

The path of good sense, of course, is the path of reason. As I
suggested earlier, no relation is exempt from this rule of reason; all human relations must be based on it. Thus as Anna
explains to her father when they disagree, she must
"plainly . . . tell [him] the truth, because I believe it to be my
duty" (p. 24). The dialogue between them is amusing:

> Upon my word! A very dutiful daughter! I thought the duty of
> children was to obey the wills of their parents.
> Obedience—(Pardon my sincerity, sir.)—Obedience must have
> limits. Children should love and honour their parents for their
> virtues, and should cheerfully and zealously do whatever they re-
> quire of them, which is not in itself wrong.
> Of which *children* are to judge?

Yes, sir: of which children are to judge.

A fine system of obedience truly!

They cannot act without judging, more or less, be they obedient or disobedient: and the better they judge the better will they perform their duty. There may be and there have been mistaken parents, who have commanded their children to be guilty even of crimes.

And what is that to me? Upon my word, you are a very polite young lady. . . .

God forbid, my dear papa, that you should imagine I think you one of those parents.

I really don't know nor don't care, madam, what you think me. —My plans, indeed!—Disapproved by you!

If I saw any person under a dangerous mistake, misled, wronged, preyed upon by the self-interested, should I not be indolent or cowardly, nay should I not be criminal, if I did not endeavour to convince such a person of his error? And what should I be if this person were my father? (pp. 24–25)

As I noted in discussing Frank's attitude toward his own father, Holcroft strongly challenges the traditional ideal of the parent-child relationship and insists that the relationship must be based on reason rather than any form of blind trust. Anna has the same duty to point out error in her father as she does for any other human being. If Holcroft redefines even the usually sacred parent-child relationship, we may surely expect him to challenge other established relationships as well. He does.

Holcroft, like so many of these novelists of protest, finds the artificial distinctions that society imposes on men to be not only unreasonable but actively pernicious. Holcroft refuses to assign any validity to the conception of rank, insisting that if any distinctions must be made among men, they should be made on the basis of virtue and intelligence. The hero of his book is lowborn; the villain is an aristocrat. The heroine is an aristocrat, which poses an interesting question in terms of the hero and the heroine getting together; the question, obviously, is whether an aristocratic lady can marry a man of lesser rank without losing any of her social and moral influence? Holcroft's answer is yes, but even he considers that the "yes" indeed takes some explaining, hence, all those soul searchings in which

Anna indulges. Frank is sure that his rank is irrelevant to the potential social usefulness of their union, and he is sure that because Anna is always open to reasoned argument, he will be able to convince her that their marriage is not only personally appropriate but socially beneficial.

Holcroft's attack on the institution of rank continues throughout the book. Coke Clifton, a man so vile that he kidnaps Anna with the express intention of seducing her, has the effrontery to presume himself a better man than Frank just because of his rank. Frank realizes that rank forms but "ridiculous distinctions" (p. 7) and considers himself inferior to neither Clifton nor Anna. On the contrary, Frank finds it "absurd" to "suppos[e] there could be any superiority, of man over man, except that which genius and virtue g[i]ve" (p. 73). As Anna explains to her father when he notes that Frank "is a very extraordinary young gentleman," "Ah, sir! The word gentleman shews the bent of your thoughts. Can you not perceive it is a word without a meaning? Or, if it have a meaning, that he who is the best man is the most a gentleman?" (p. 344). Clifton, on the other hand, is impressed by rank, especially his own. He complains that "these fellows of obscure birth labour to pull down rank, and reduce all to their own level" (p. 178), Yet even he is forced to recognize "that a title is no sufficient passport for so much as common sense" (p. 178). His description of both his and Anna's family members suggests that some of the absurdities of rank are striking even to those who believe in the institution.

> I sincerely think there is not so foolish a fellow in the three kingdoms, as the noble blockhead to whom I have the honour to be related, Lord Evelyn: and, while I have tickled my fancy with the recollection of my own high descent, curse me if I have not blushed to acknowledge him, who is the head and representative of the race, as my kinsman! . . . by his medium I have been introduced to the uncle of [Anna], Lord Fitz-Allen, who has considerable influence in the family, and the very essence of whose character is pride. He is proud of himself, proud of his family, proud of his titles, proud of his gout, proud of his cat, proud of whatever can be called *his;* by which appellation in his opinion his very coach-horses are

dignified. I happen to please him, not by any qualities of mind or person, of which he is tolerably insensible, but because there is a possibility that I may one day be a peer of the realm, if my booby relations will but be so indulgent as to die fast enough." (pp. 178–79).

Clifton's ability to recognize absurdities such as these does not diminish his own pride in rank, and this pride is one of the faults Anna sets out to reform. The worship of rank is intimately connected with other social ills, and as we look at these passages in which Anna attempts to make Clifton understand why his belief in rank as a legitimate divider of men is wrong, we also begin to see an outline of Holcroft's vision of the ideal.

When Clifton importunes Anna with his love, she will have none of it—unless he can measure up to her ideal of what a husband must be. It may provide some humor, as well as perspective, if we keep in mind that Frank is the paragon who can satisfy all her conditions. She asks Clifton:

Dare you receive a blow, or suffer yourself falsely to be called liar, or coward, without seeking revenge, or what honour calls satisfaction? Dare you think the servant that cleans your shoes is your equal, unless not so wise or good a man; and your superior, if wiser and better? Dare you suppose mind has no sex, and that woman is not by nature the inferior of man?—

When poor Clifton tries to answer, she cuts him off:

Nay, nay, no compliments; I will not be interrupted—Dare you think that riches, rank, and power, are usurpations; and that wisdom and virtue only can claim distinction? Dare you make it the business of your whole life to overturn these prejudices, and to promote among mankind that spirit of universal benevolence which shall render them all equals, all brothers, all stripped of their artificial and false wants, all participating the labour requisite to produce the necessaries of life, and all combining in one universal effort of mind, for the progress of knowledge, the destruction of error, and the spreading of eternal truth? (p. 172)

There are many things to notice in this most interesting lover's lecture, but what must gall Clifton most would be the remarks on rank and equality. "The servant that cleans your shoes is your equal," unless he's a worse man? He's your superior, if he's a better man! All "riches, rank, and power are usurpations?" This is revolutionary stuff—and not just to Clifton. Holcroft is making very strong statements here which would have been much less than comfortable for many Englishmen only three years after the shock of the French Revolution.[6]

Anna St. Ives presents a utopian vision, much the same vision of a society based on mutual cooperation and goodwill that Godwin would present in *Political Justice*.[7] Moreover, the very excesses of *Political Justice* (Godwin's system so irritated some of his contemporaries that they satirized it and him in novels that played out Godwin's premises to their logical—and unworkable—conclusions)[8] make *Anna St. Ives* also seem out of touch with reality. Anna and Frank believe that there are no limits to their ability to change the world for the better and that, in fact, their own actions are only part of a larger social movement toward a benevolent, classless, and humanly sustaining society. "I live in an age when light begins to appear even in regions that have hitherto been thick darkness" (p. 383) Frank exclaims, and in *Anna St. Ives* Holcroft presents no evidence to contradict him.

Anna's lecture to Clifton about her requirements in a husband, then, is not the idle posturing of an inexperienced girl. These requirements are the catalog of the traits that any person must be expected to show; it is not the person with these attributes who is superior, but the person who lacks them who is not yet a fully functioning contributor to society. People like Anna and Frank, who have already reached this awareness, must help others to develop to the same level. Anna tries to explain her belief to Clifton, whose consciousness, to borrow a modern term, has not yet been raised. She tells him,

> You expect one kind of happiness, I another. . . . You imagine you have a right to attend to your appetites, and pursue your pleasures. I hope to see my husband forgetting himself, or rather placing self-gratification in the pursuit of universal good, deaf to the calls of

passion, willing to encounter adversity, reproof, nay death, the champion of truth, and the determined, the unrelenting enemy of error. (p. 171)

This requirement to be "the unrelenting enemy of error" demands that one know what error is. Anna and Frank would be more sympathetic as characters if they occasionally exhibited more humility along these lines; our sympathies, clearly against Holcroft's intention, begin to wear toward Clifton, who with some justification eventually grows tired of the constant pressure to reform. (But that is when he is still a villain. At the end of the book, he understands that it was all for his own good and the good of society; Holcroft leaves his reader no choice but to go along.)

Holcroft maps a number of likely areas for social improvement. Some of them I have already discussed, such as parent-child relations (the parent and the child must treat each other with precisely the same respect that they would have for any other person), rank as a social distinction (it is an absurd means of judging men), and the reform of the felon (the errant man must be firmly but kindly reeducated). Other areas for improvement, which Anna outlines here to Clifton, are the popular conceptions of honor, the "place" and potential of women, the proper social uses of wealth and power, and the social ideal of universal progress. Holcroft in one way or another manages to deal with most major social areas, and always does so within the context of the individual's responsibility and ability to change people and events.

Anna's requirements for a husband are precisely her requirements for any human being: integrity and benevolence. The sense of self must be secondary if a man, or woman, is to be socially useful; the opposite, self-absorption, leads not to social betterment but to social absurdity. Holcroft's examples abound: Anna's father's "improvement" mania; Clifton's obsession with rank and its supposed perquisites; the silly French count's ridiculous notions of honor, including his rather comic attempt to make a suicidal leap from a cliff because he'd seen it done by his contender in honor, Clifton. The placing of society's needs before one's own, on the other hand, creates harmony in society as well as contentment in the individual. If traditional conceptions of honor, class, and rank are no longer to provide distinctions among men, how are men to be separated? Holcroft's answer is that men are not to be arbitrarily classified at all. The only distinctions to be recognized are those of virtue and genius. All other distinctions are merely prejudices that need to be changed. Among the barriers that Holcroft attacks are prejudices about women; *Anna St. Ives* surely must rank among the earliest of the women's liberation tracts.

The individual must employ whatever means are available to him to promote human progress. Wealth and its power may be used to better the human condition, and this is their only legitimate purpose. Wealth and power not used in this cause are, to use Anna's word, "usurpations." Government, as we might expect, is one of the great usurpers, and Holcroft takes special delight in commenting on the *French* government. When Anna and her party arrive in France, for example, they are surprised to find that "the French innkeepers should not yet have discovered it to be their interest to keep carriages for travellers, as in England" (p. 68). Frank explains that in France the government "was in reality every where the innkeeper; and reserved to itself the profits of posting." Then comes the point. "The deepest thinkers," Frank notes, "inform us that everything in which governments interfere is spoiled." Holcroft has introduced the comment within the relatively safe context of a slap at the French, but the remark is clearly a jibe at English government as well. Frank, whose mind was "early turned . . . to the consideration of forms of government, and their effects upon the manners and morals of men" (p. 74), is to be taken as a serious critic of government, and he comments at length in several different contexts about the role of government and its (present) corollaries, wealth and power. He begins here, for example, by talking about the state of France, but quickly moves to a broader discussion; in 1792 it must have seemed safer at least to seem to talk of tyrannies abroad rather than those at home. This is Frank's analysis, in a letter to his friend Oliver, of some of the attributes of government:

How often has it been said of France, by various English philosophers, and by many of its own sages, What a happy country would this be, were it well governed! But, with equal truth, the same may be said of every country under heaven; England itself . . . in spite of our partialities, not excepted.

How false, how futile, how absurd is the remark that a despotic government, under a perfect monarch, would be the state of highest felicity! First an impossible thing is asked; and next impossible consequences deduced. One tyrant generates a nation of tyrants. His own mistakes communicate themselves east, west, north, and south; and what appeared to be but a spark becomes a conflagration.

How inconsistent are the demands and complaints of ignorance! It wishes to tyrannize, yet exclaims against tyranny! It grasps at wealth, and pants after power; yet clamours aloud, against the powerful and the wealthy! It hourly starts out into all the insolence of pride; yet hates and endeavors to spurn at the proud!

Among the many who have a vague kind of suspicion that things might be better, are mingled a few, who seem very desirous they should remain as they are. These are the rich; who, having by extortion and rapine plundered the defenceless, and heaped up choice of viands and the fat of the land, some sufficient to feed ten, some twenty, some a hundred, some a thousand, and others whole armies, and being themselves each only able to eat for one, say to the hungry, who have no food—'Come! Dance for my sport, and I will give you bread. Lick the dust off my shoes, and you shall be indulged with a morsel of meat. Flatter me, and you shall wear my livery. Labour for me, and I will return you a tenth of your gain. Shed your blood in my behalf, and, while you are young and robust, I will allow you just as much as will keep life and soul together; when you are old, and worn out, you may rob, hang, rot, or starve.'

Would not any one imagine, Oliver, that this were poetry? Alas! It is mere, literal, matter of fact.

Yet let us not complain. Men begin to reason, and to think aloud; and these things cannot always endure. (pp. 74–75)

Holcroft ends the letter by calling our attention to the fact that Frank indeed has broadened the target of his examination; he leaves it perhaps purposely ambiguous as to how much of the foregoing discussion applied to France and how much to other nations—that is England—as well:

> I intended to have made some observations on the people, the aspect of the country, and other trifles; I scarcely now know what: but I have wandered into a subject so vast, so interesting, so sublime, that all petty individual remarks sink before it. Nor will I for the present blur the majesty of the picture, by ill-placed, mean, and discordant objects. Therefore, farewell. (p. 75)

These are stinging indictments. We have met these complaints, stark as they are, in the work of Thomas Day, for example. A recurring theme in these novels is the injustice of the rich hoarding huge amounts of food and goods while the poor lack the most basic necessities, and the further, almost ludicrous injustice of the rich handing out a pittance to those same poor who have produced the wealth in the first place. As we shall see when we turn to Inchbald's *Nature and Art*, this problem is one of her primary concerns as well. Holcroft in *Anna St. Ives* presents the problem within an optimistic context. The disparities in society can be redressed: "men begin to reason and to think aloud; and these things cannot always endure." It is a firm vision in *Anna St. Ives*, but in his next novel, Holcroft is no longer convinced that reason can prevail; Godwin and Inchbald, writing within these same few years, similarly see their faith in improvement fail so rapidly that the process is more like explosion than erosion.

In *Anna St. Ives*, though, improvement is possible, even likely: it seems inevitable that reason will triumph and that men will learn to live benevolently with each other. Admittedly, the progress may be slow but the ends, at least, are in clear focus, as Anna explains:

> we do not perhaps make quite so swift a progress as we could wish: but we must be satisfied. The march of knowledge is slow, impeded as it is by the almost impenetrable forests and morasses of error. Ages have passed away, in labours to bring some of the most simple of moral truths to light, which still remain overclouded and obscure. How far is the world, at present, from being convinced that

it is not only possible, but perfectly practicable, and highly natural, for men to associate with most fraternal union, happiness, peace, and virtue, were but all distinction of rank and riches wholly abolished; were all the false wants of luxury, which are the necessary offspring of individual property, cut off; were all equally obliged to labour for the wants of nature, and for nothing more; and were they all afterward to unite, and to employ the remainder of their time, which would then be ample, in the promotion of art and science, and in the search of wisdom and truth! (p. 209)

It seems obvious to Anna that it is "perfectly practicable, and highly natural" for men to live together without distinctions of rank or wealth, pooling their resources and devoting their abundant free time to the study of truth; only lack of clear-sightedness, remediable by further education in the ways of men and morals, prevents the mass of mankind from enjoying such a state. It is the job of people like Frank and herself, then, to spread the light. Anna realizes that her vision seems for the moment to be utopian, but she insists that because hers is essentially the reasonable way of life, the progress of humanity must be in this direction. Almost chiding herself, she adds:

Is it not lamentable to be obliged to doubt whether there be a hundred people in all England, who, were they to read such a letter as this, would not immediately laugh, at the absurd reveries of the writer?—But let them look round, and deny, if they can, that the present wretched system, of each providing for himself instead of the whole for the whole, does not inspire suspicion, fear, disputes, quarrels, mutual contempt, and hatred. Instead of nations, or rather of the whole world, uniting to produce one great effect, the perfection and good of all, each family is itself a state; bound to the rest by interest and cunning, but separated by the very same passions, and a thousand others; living together under a kind of truce, but continually ready to break out into open war; continually jealous of each other; continually on the defensive, because continually dreading an attack; ever ready to usurp on the rights of others, and perpetually entangled in the most wretched contentions, concerning what all would neglect, if not despise, did not the errors of this selfish system give value to what is in itself worthless.
Well, well!—Another century, and then—!
In the meantime, let us live in hope; and, like our worthy hero,

Frank, not be silent when truth requires us to speak. We have but to arm ourselves with patience, fortitude, and universal benevolence. (pp. 209–10)

Although this perfect state of man where each works only to supply the needs of nature and then spends the remainder of his time contemplating truth (Godwin's *Political Justice* draws much the same ideal) is not to be immediately created, Anna and Frank both feel that they are actively working toward that end. Anna and Frank seem never to tire of intellectually exploring the potential within man for increasing his own social usefulness, and it seems to them that these explorations themselves are a step toward improvement or, indeed, are part of the improvement process. Anna, for example, recounts to her friend Louisa some inspiring moments with her wonderful Frank:

> The course of our enquiries has several times forced us upon that great question, "the progress of mind toward perfection, and the different order of things which must inevitably be the result." Yesterday this theme again occurred. Frank was present; and his imagination, warm with the sublimity of his subject, drew a bold and splendid picture of the felicity of that state of society when personal property no longer shall exist, when the whole torrent of mind shall unite in enquiry after the beautiful and the true, when it shall no longer be directed by those insignificant pursuits to which the absurd follies that originate in our false wants give birth, when individual selfishness shall be unknown, and when all shall labour for the good of all! (p. 278)

It makes a lovely picture, this Godwinian ideal of a society in which everyone rushes for the beautiful and the true, and each unselfishly labors for the good of all. Not only labor, but relationships will be released from the onus of ownership. Not only will there be no more servants, there will be no more children in the sense of saying, "This is my child." As Frank explains, "They will be the children of the state" (p. 279). It follows, as well, that the institution of marriage will not exist in its present form either, for "it is at least certain that in the sense in which we understand marriage and the affirmation—*This is my wife*—

neither the institution nor the claim can in such a state, or indeed in justice exist" (p. 279).

What comes next is one of the most interesting passages in the book, Holcroft's analysis of marriage. Like his friend Godwin, he does not find much to recommend the institution in its current state, but unlike Godwin, he still finds that, in some form, marriage is necessary in society. Ideally, the commitment would be spiritual (doing away with marriage would not be the same as countenancing promiscuity) rather than legal. But the current state is far from any ideal:

> Of all the regulations which were ever suggested to the mistaken tyranny of selfishness, none perhaps to this day have surpassed the despotism of those which undertake to bind not only body to body but soul to soul, to all futurity, in despite of every possible change which our vices and our virtues might effect, or however numerous the secret corporal or mental imperfections might prove which a more intimate acquaintance should bring to light! (p. 279)

Marriage should not be a matter of any bargain being struck, and in fact

> in the most virtuous ages the word bargain, like the word promise, will be unintelligible—We cannot bargain to do what is wrong, nor can we, though there should be no bargain, forbear to do what is just, without being unjust. . . . [Marriage] ought not to be a civil institution. It is the concern of the individuals who consent to this mutual association, and they ought not to be prevented from beginning, suspending, or terminating it as they please. (pp. 279–80)

Coke Clifton, who in the discussion of marriage is the foil to Frank, notes that there are few men indeed who are "fit to be trusted with so much power" (p. 280), to which Frank replies,

> You are imagining a society as perverse and vitiated as the present: I am supposing one wholly the contrary. I know too well that there are men who, because unjust laws and customs worthy of barbarians have condemned helpless women to infamy, for the loss of that which under better regulations and in ages of more wisdom has been and will again be guilt to keep, I know, sir, I say that the present world is infested by men, who make it the business and the

glory of their lives to bring this infamy upon the very beings for whom they feign the deepest affection!—If ever patience can forsake me it will be at the recollection of these demons in the human form, who come tricked out in all the smiles of love, the protestations of loyalty, and the arts of hell, unrelentingly and causelessly to prey upon confiding innocence! Nothing but the malverse selfishness of man could give being or countenance to such a monster! Whatever is good, exquisite, or precious, we are individually taught to grasp at, and if possible to secure; but we have each a latent sense that this principle has rendered us a society of detestable misers, and therefore to rob each other seems almost like the sports of justice. (pp. 280–81)

But just to be sure he has not been misunderstood, Frank earnestly cautions his listeners,

I would not teach any man's daughters so mad a doctrine as to indulge in sensual appetites, or foster a licentious imagination. I am not the apostle of depravity. While men shall be mad, foolish, and dishonest enough to be vain of bad principles, women may be allowed to seek such protection as bad laws can afford. . . ." (p. 281)

(It is hard not to be reminded of Godwin's fuming when *his* daughter ran off with Shelley.)

This was probably more shocking to the contemporary reader than anything we have seen so far. When Fielding criticized the legal and penal systems, a reader could nod in agreement without too much discomfort unless he happened personally to belong to one or the other of these professions. When Brooke and Day criticized the social irresponsibility of the rich, all their middle-class readers could applaud in recognition. But when Holcroft attacks the central institution of society—marriage— he attacks the cherished belief of every class and every sector of society; he attacks the foundation of society as it is constructed. His caveat, that the elimination of marriage will come only in the perfected state of society, reinforces his suggestion that then men will be so enlightened that they will no longer need legal restraints such as marriage to keep their institutions running smoothly.

The caveat serves another purpose as well, for it reminds us that Holcroft is presenting a reasoned vision; he is not suggesting an unprepared revolution in the relationships of men but a gradual education into enlightenment. The program that Frank and Anna are proposing for the improvement of mankind will not be implemented in a moment but shall be the product of the gradual reeducation of the mass of men by those, such as Anna and Frank, who already see the truth. Until the mass of men are so enlightened, the standing institutions of society do indeed have a function.

One of the most stimulating implications of the book, however, is that because those institutions are highly imperfect, the enlightened man must use his own judgment in deciding whether or not to conform to the requirements of society. I have discussed the rents Holcroft proposes in the fabric of filial obedience; similarly, the legal restrictions of society need be complied with only to the same limited extent. It should be Frank's duty to hand over the highwayman to the authorities, but Frank instead is instrumental in helping the man to avoid those authorities and, in fact, to avoid legal punishment for his crime. All those involved in the affair conspire to reform rather than punish the man: he is to be helped to move to the continent where he can work at his trade. Anna delightedly notes that "he is more than reconciled to labour, he is eager to begin. . . (p. 50). Neither she nor Frank even considers the idea of giving the man up to the authorities; for them society's punishment lies so far from their concept of reform that they do not even need to justify helping the man to evade the law.

Reform, for Anna and Frank, is accomplished by bringing the offender to an understanding of his behavior. There is no doubt that once a man understands the destructive nature of his actions, he will cease from the commission of any type of crime. The legal and penal systems make no provision for such reeducation, however, and seek to punish a man for crimes of which he has long since repented. Anna passionately insists that "whatever rooted prejudices or unjust laws may assert to the contrary, we are accountable only for what we do, not for what we have done" (p. 422). The inflexibility of the law in not mak-

ing allowance for reform is a major complaint not only for
Holcroft but for Godwin as well, as we shall see in *Caleb
Williams*. If the law makes no provision for human error and
repentence, the individual must. It is Frank's duty to help the
highwayman see his error, but once that error is recognized, it
is criminal of the state to require retribution. Coke Clifton's
actions against Anna and Frank, heinous as they were in fact
and, even more, in intention, must not be punished after he has
seen his error, for such punishment would be socially wasteful.
Anna and Frank, having foiled Clifton's plot to rape Anna, are
ecstatic not that she has been saved but that Clifton has been
saved. Clifton, Frank says when it is all over, is "a treasure, by
which [society] is to be enriched" (p. 481). Frank and Anna set
themselves a goal—there is "a mind of the first order to be
retrieved" (p. 118)—and only the good for society that such
retrieval implies is to be considered. Each person must be encouraged to develop to his greatest potential, for his own sake
but, still more, for the sake of that whole of which he is a part.

The whole is composed of both men and women, of course,
and Holcroft insists that the part women have to play is quite
equal to that of men. Not least among the fundamental ideas of
society that Holcroft challenges is the view of women that gives
them some special feminine character and on that basis assigns
them a special, and subservient, place in society. Holcroft
stridently insists that the responsibility for good in society is as
much woman's as man's and that essentially the same means of
promoting the advancement of truth are open to both sexes.
Holcroft is aware of the limitations that society places on the
activities of women. Anna disapprovingly notes that "few opportunities present themselves to a woman, educated and restrained as women unfortunately are, of performing any thing
eminently good" (p. 37). Holcroft emphasizes not any limita-
tion inherent in the female herself, but rather the limitations
that society imposes by its attitudes and by its education of
women. As we have seen, whenever Anna has the opportunity
to do good, whether by giving Frank Henley the means of
assisting his fellows or by reeducating and reforming a Coke

Clifton, she is indeed up to the mark. In fact, she herself notes that "restoring a . . . mind" is one of the "most . . . obvious tasks" (p. 37) society allows women. And as Clifton's constant self-conflicts and eventual reformation indicate, she is a powerful force when she focuses her efforts toward such a goal. Always against his will, Clifton is repeatedly forced to reassess his own actions in the light of Anna's arguments. But although moral reeducation is a task allowed women by society, it is not specifically a female task; Frank is just as active in such reclamation projects as Anna.

Holcroft repeatedly makes the point that such characteristics as intelligence, courage, benevolence, and even physical strength are not the province of one or the other sex. As Anna points out early in the book with regard to courage, for example, "it is a great mistake to suppose courage has any connection with sex; if we except, as we ought, the influence of education and habit. My dear mother had not the bodily strength of Sir Arthur; but, with respect to cool courage and active presence of mind . . . there was no comparison" (p. 12). And we may say the same of the daughter, Anna, who maintains a heroic composure during the kidnapping and the repeated threats of rape. Anna even manages to escape her captors by scaling a wall that her maid had assured her could only be climbed by a man. As she points out in looking back at the incident, she had often noted "the excellence of active courage, and the much greater efforts of which both sexes are capable than either of them imagine" (p. 465). She is convinced—and is an example to the reader that—"there is no such mighty difference [between the sexes] as prejudice supposes. Courage has neither sex nor form: it is an energy of mind . . ." (p. 423). Anna and Frank are to be considered equal in the energy of mind with which they meet their challenges. Anna learns from Frank, it is true, but Frank learns from Anna as well. Theirs is to be a partnership of idealism, which shall be focused to the great end of spreading the truth of benevolence and reason.

The limitations that society places on women are essentially learned limitations; in the new world that Anna and Frank foresee, these artificial restraints will no longer be operative, just as other barriers of rank and of personal relationships will fall. It is a human being who can say, "Shall I listen only to my fears; shrink into self; and shun that which duty bids me encounter? No. Though the prejudices of mankind were to overwhelm me with sorrows, for seeking to do good, I will still go on: I will persevere, will accomplish or die" (p. 146). The thoughts are not specifically male or female (although in this instance the speaker is Anna). Anna does not limit herself because she is a woman, and she never hides behind a feminine weakness. Perhaps too inflexibly, she refuses to submit to any emotion that she cannot rationally justify: "I could be a very woman—But I will not!—No, no!—It is passed—I have put my handkerchief to my eyes and it is gone—I have repressed an obstinate heaving of the heart . . ." (p. 122).

Anna is not perfect, but she is nearly so. She is a bit too insistent on following her reason to its logical conclusions, without adequately questioning her initial premises. But she is open to being disabused of any faults in her thinking and allows Frank to correct her few errors. Frank is not much more perfect than Anna—doesn't he need to be reasoned out of his reluctance to accept money from her so that he can improve himself and therefore add to his contribution to society? We are to see two excellent human beings who are actively engaged in the progress of mankind toward a better society. In *Anna St. Ives,* that progress is presented as a very real movement. The reader sees the proof in the reform of Coke Clifton, who at the end of the book waits to recover from his wounds in the hope that he "may now and then effect some trifling, pitiful good" (p. 479). In the last scene, Clifton is overcome by his own vileness, an evil that Anna and Frank assure him no longer exists, and by his vision of the incredibly good nature of these two he has tried to destroy. The repentence obliterates the crime; Clifton is ready to take his place as a contributor to humankind. He fears that he cannot live up to this new image of himself— "You would realize the fable of Pygmalion, and would infuse soul into marble," he cries to Frank, to which Frank replies,

"There is no need; you have a soul already; inventive, capacious, munificent, sublime" (p. 480). The scene builds to an ecstatic celebratory note, as Frank sums up:

> Ours is no common task! We are acting in behalf of society: we have found a treasure, by which it is to be enriched. Few indeed are those puissant and heavenly endowed spirits, that are capable of guiding, enlightening, and leading the human race onward to felicity! What is there precious but mind? And when mind, like a diamond of uncommon growth, exceeds a certain magnitude, calculation cannot find its value! (p. 481)

He leaves the room, he says, with a "glowing and hoping heart."

It is on this extraordinarily upbeat note that the novel ends. With Clifton's reformation, we seem to have proof that the society Anna and Frank envision is capable of realization. When earlier we read Anna's joyful vision of her future with Frank, we might have been skeptical of the good the two of them actually could do. The picture, although lovely, seemed perhaps a bit naive:

> [Frank] is anxiously studious to discover how he may apply the wealth that may revert to him most to benefit that society from which it first sprang. The best application of riches is one of our frequent themes; because it will be one of our first duties. The diffusion of knowledge, or more properly of truth, is the one great good to which wealth, genius, and existence ought all to be applied. This noble purpose gives birth to felicity which is in itself grand, inexhaustible, and eternal.
>
> How ineffable is the bliss of having discovered a friend like Frank Henley, who will not only pursue this best of purposes himself, but will through life conduct me in the same path. . . . (pp. 381–82)

Frank's vision in the next letter is even more enthusiastic:

> Oh, Oliver, how fair is the prospect before me! How fruitful of felicity, how abundant in bliss! Yes, my friend, jointly will we labour, your most worthy father, you, I, Anna, her friend, and all the converts we can make to truth, to promote the great end we seek!

We will form a little band which will daily increase, will swell to a multitude, ay till it embrace the whole human species!

Surely, Oliver, to be furnished with so many of the means of promulgating universal happiness is no small blessing. My feelings are all rapture! And yet if I know my heart, it is not because I have gained a selfish solitary good; but because I live in an age when light begins to appear even in regions that have hitherto been thick darkness; and that I myself am so highly fortunate as to be able to contribute to the great the universal cause; the progress of truth, the extirpation of error, and the general perfection of mind! (p. 383)

Clifton's reform shows us that these visions of Anna and Frank are indeed to be turned into realities, or rather, that such a perspective and the actions it implies is itself the foundation of an improved world. "Light," or the "spreading of truth," is the debunking of the traditional institutions of society. Anna and Frank challenge everything from the structure of the parent-child relationship to the structure of society itself. They see their time as an age of light because it seems to them that it is possible, through reason, to change society drastically. We have seen in their vision of an ideal society that "all distinctions of rank and riches" would be abolished and that all would labor "equally," in fact "that individual property is a general evil" (p. 284). Thus the complaint Holcroft is making against society in *Anna St. Ives* is across the board: all the relationships, individual and societal, are wrong because they are based on exclusivity. In giving us so detailed a vision of a better foundation for society, Holcroft is clearly criticizing the institutions as they exist. The changes he advocates are, indeed, revolutionary. And yet he would have us believe that because these changes are reasonable, they can come about through the spreading of truth from benevolent, rational human being to human being. The changes Holcroft sees as necessary in society, cataclysmic as they are, can be—should and will be—brought about peacefully through the influence of reason. It is all a matter, merely, of education. Indeed it is a lovely vision Holcroft presents in *Anna St. Ives;* the hopefulness collapses entirely in *Hugh Trevor.* In its place comes an all-pervasive disgust. In *Hugh Trevor,* the institutions of society are seen as so totally corrupt that reform seems impossible, and the only room left for applying reason is as a counsel to retreat.

1. Thomas Holcroft, *Anna St. Ives* (London: Oxford University Press, 1970), p. 2. All references are to this edition.

2. The improvement mania is of course a frequent subject of amused comment in the literature of this period; Holcroft's detailed explanation of how Abimelech nearly ruins Anna's father is, however, among the most biting of these references. The Baron St. Ives is totally engrossed by his hobby, and his wily steward cleverly feeds that passion. The baron not only has sunk a large proportion of his fortune into the rearranging and perfecting of his estates but has come near to destroying the beauty and utility of his lands. He is always ready to add another feature, another lake or hill. Meanwhile, the grasping Abimelech pockets large sums of the appropriated money, only to urge further improvements upon the improvements.

3. Evelina is raised without contact with her father, who totally neglects her; her entire upbringing and welfare depend on others. Yet when as a grown woman she finally meets her natural father, she is overcome with happiness and, far from feeling any antagonism, lovingly accepts him. (See my discussion in chapter three.) Evelina does not analyze her relationship with her father. His claim to her affection is assured, no matter what he does, by the fact that he is her parent.

4. The anecdote is used by Godwin to exemplify the primacy of reason over emotion in decision making: briefly, he says that if two people were drowning, and only one of them could be saved, it is the more socially valuable person who should be saved. Thus, if the two people were the Archbishop Fénelon and one's own mother, one would be obliged to save the Archbishop since he presumably is of more value to society as a whole. This is precisely the line of reasoning Anna pursues. If Anna's choice is between making a marriage that will bring her personal happiness and a marriage that will be socially useful, she must choose the latter. Although this particular anecdote appears in *Political Justice* (1793), published the year after *Anna St. Ives*, Godwin and Holcroft presumably would have been discussing such issues for some time. See note seven below.

5. Kenneth Neill Cameron in his sensitive essay on William Godwin in *Romantic Rebels: Essays on Shelley and his Circle* (Cambridge: Harvard University Press, 1973) rather gently puts Godwin's borrowing into a somewhat kinder light than it usually finds. He reminds us that although Godwin and his second wife, Mary Jane Clairmont, "earn [ed] a good deal of money by his books," the expenses of maintaining a household of five children, and their own "inexperience in business finally drove them to the wall." Nevertheless, as even the sympathetic critic must note, Godwin "did borrow; he did not always

pay back what he borrowed; he became both insistent and . . . not always completely frank in his borrowing" (pp. 25–26).

6. The years between the French Revolution and 1794, the year of the "Treason Trials," were years of both promise and fear. Dissenting societies flourished, and news from France was greeted by many with hope and enthusiasm. At the same time, of course, events in France were making many Englishmen very nervous, and the forces of repression were growing stronger—a reaction that would intimately affect Holcroft and his friends as they themselves were put on trial.

7. *Anna St. Ives* was published in 1792; *Political Justice* was published in 1793. But Godwin had been working on and presumably discussing *Political Justice* for at least a year and a half before its publication, so that the community of ideas between the two books is not surprising given the close intellectual relationship between Holcroft and Godwin.

8. For example, *The Vagabond, or Whatever is Just is Equal, but Equality is not always Just* (1799) by George Walker portrays a country that is run on the principles of *Political Justice*, where men starve while trying to determine how best to apportion that half day's work which Godwin had said would be sufficient in a society run according to reason.

5

HUGH TREVOR / *Thomas Holcroft*

Whenever I have undertaken to write a novel, I have proposed to myself a specific moral purpose. This purpose, in Anna St. Ives, was to teach fortitude to females: in Hugh Trevor, to induce Youth (or their parents) carefully to inquire into the morality of the profession which each might intend for himself. . . .

The precise scenes . . . or nearly the same, might have happened, and that is sufficient for the purposes of a novel.
Thomas Holcroft, *Memoirs of Bryan Perdue*

Walter Allen says that "the novelist must deal with men in a specific place at a specific time, and the novelists . . . have normally been acutely conscious of their time and the qualities in it that appear to distinguish it from other times."[1] This particular sense of time, that is, present as reality *and* past as reality, was not always part of the literary construct. His example is of course Elizabethan drama; no one would argue that Shakespeare's plays, *Hamlet, Lear, Henry IV,* to use Allen's examples, give us a "feel" for their respective historical periods: they give us human beings "outside history in our sense." The novels of social protest, perhaps even more than others, are precisely, acutely conscious of their time and its qualities, and this is true of the form for any period it witnesses. It is as true for Dickens, and still later for Gissing, as it is for the eighteenth-century novelists I discuss. All of them make direct, even strident, reference to their own day, and such references themselves serve as a form of historical document.

Holcroft's *Hugh Trevor* is a novel entirely of its time, chronicling the abuses to which each of the professions is liable; it is little more. In its bareness, however, it offers us a chance to see these corruptions almost as starkly as if we were contemporaries of Holcroft. For the historical feel of a period, sometimes a lesser novelist gives us a more accurate sense than a greater one, for while the greater writer shapes his material into art, he enforces his vision upon it. The lesser writer gives us more of a snapshot—a picture less posed but at the same time perhaps with more of the quality of the moment. *Hugh Trevor* is not a great novel, but it is a good chronicle of an age's peculiar corruptions.[2] It bears close relation to the early chronicles that Allen and other critics have seen as so vital in the formation of the novel (Defoe's debt to the travel books has been established, but the debt of other writers to the "soberly careful account of real life" tradition has not yet been adequately explored). *Hugh Trevor* shows an overwhelming sense of "now." *Anna St. Ives* is a more ambitious novel; Holcroft tries to do more with his characters and he tries to create a comprehensive system for social improvement. It is a richer novel for these reasons, but it is not as valuable as *Hugh Trevor* as a historical document just because *Anna St. Ives* is Holcroft's vision of what he would like to see, not of what is. *Hugh Trevor*, finally, rests on what is.

Hugh Trevor, like *Anna St. Ives*, is concerned with the role of a good man in a society that is largely corrupt. As in *Anna St. Ives*, the dominant feeling of the book is that benevolent rationalism can work wonderful improvements on the state of man and that man is essentially benevolent and rational. As in *Anna St. Ives*, we seem to be on the verge of an "age of light," although the evils of society are much more sharply defined in this later book. The happy ending is accomplished in *Hugh Trevor*—and the resident villain duly converted to a benevolent contributor to the community—but there remains a strong sense of all the uncorrected evils that Holcroft has shown in the course of the novel. Essentially, the tenor of *Hugh Trevor* is that, although man is good and for the most part educable to virtue, society as it stands is so corrupt that it will take enormous changes to clean it up. The book catalogs the necessary changes.

Holcroft ranges over law, politics, and even science in his survey of existing evils. His vehicle for the survey is the familiar eighteenth-century *bildungsroman*. As the inexperienced Hugh Trevor plunges from situation to situation and from career to career, he weighs all the philosophical and moral details of each circumstance (far be it from the idealistic Hugh to consider materialistic considerations—the only reason he can accept for needing money is that he may one day support his love, Olivia). The first evil of society is its miseducation of various classes. It teaches women to be fearful creatures, unable to hold their own in the contests of the world; it keeps the poor in ignorance; and it teaches the rich, among other things, to eat themselves to death! But of course the worst thing it teaches the rich—and Holcroft complains here in common with Inchbald, Bage, and Godwin—is to be gluttonous for themselves but unsparing for the poor. As part of this lifestyle, dishonesty and hypocrisy are so widespread as to be almost universal.

The novel is a chronicle of Hugh's education, both "formal" and "in the world," and although that of the world occupies most of Holcroft's attention, he does deal with school. As we might expect from what we know of the schools and universities of the time, his comments (like Godwin's in *Fleetwood* and *Mandeville*) are negative. Boarding schools for young ladies are places "where every thing is taught and nothing understood; where airs, graces, mouth primming, shoulder-setting and elbow-holding are studied, and affectation, formality, hypocrisy, and pride are acquired; and where children the most promising are presently transformed into vain, pert misses, who imagine that to perk up their heads, turn out their toes, and exhibit the ostentatious opulence of their relations, in a tawdry ball night dress, is the summit of perfection."[3] Young Hugh meets many such a miss in the course of the book.

What of the university for boys? It is a place of dissipation, stuporific drunkenness, and little learning. Like the boarding school for girls, it seems to exist primarily to prepare the rich idler for his later life. Hugh's introduction to the fabled Oxford is a speech of welcome from a friend, Hector, the words of which are mostly profanities, and an orgy with students and tutors that night, which ends in a drunken stupor:

> The night advanced, and they grew riotous. The lord and his tutor were for *sporting the door of a glum:* that is, breaking into the chamber of a gownsman who loves study. Hector vociferously seconded the motion, but the fellow and the master of arts cunningly endeavored to keep them quiet . . . by affirming the students they proposed to attack *sported oak:* in plain English, barred up their doors. Had they been without the walls of the college, there would have been a riot; but, having no other ventilator for their magnanimity, they fell with redoubled fury to drinking, and the jolly tutor proposed a rummer round—'D—n me,' said Hector, 'that's a famous thought! But you are a famous deep one, d—n me!'
>
> The rummers were seized, the wine poured out, and his lordship began with—'D-mn-t—n to the flincher.' Who should that be? I, the freshman? Oh, no! For that night, I was too far gone in good fellowship.
>
> This was the finishing blow to three of us. Hector fell on the floor; his lordship sunk in his chair; and I, after a hurrah and a hiccup, began to *cast the cat:* an Oxford phrase for what usually happens to a man after taking an emetic. Happily I had not far to go, and the fellow and the master of arts had just sense enough left to help me to my chamber, where at day light next morning I found myself, on the hearth, with my head resting against the fender, the pain of which awakened me. (p. 79)

Hugh gets his first taste of societal corruption at Oxford. Study is not rewarded, he learns, but dissipation is. The whole picture of Oxford is put before him by the exemplary Turl, who happens to reside there when Hugh does. Turl will be the rule by which Hugh can measure his values throughout the course of his maturation. Here they discuss the state of Oxford: "I am but just arrived," says Hugh, "will you be kind enough to give me such intelligence as may aid me to regulate my conduct? . . . I hoped for perfection which I begin to doubt I shall not find. What are the manners of the place?"

> —'Such as must be expected from a multitude of youths, who are ashamed to be thought boys, and who do not know how to behave like men.' —'But are there not people appointed to teach them?' —

'No.' 'What is the office of the proctors, heads of houses, deans, and other superintendants, of whom I have heard?' —'To watch and regulate the tufts of caps, the tying of bands, the stuff and tassels of which gowns are made. . . .'—'What are the public rewards for proficiency in learning?'—'Few, or in reality none.'— 'Beside numerous offices, are not exhibitions, fellowships, professors' chairs and presentations bestowed?'—'Yes, on those who have municipal or political influence; or who by servility and effrontery can court patronage.'—'Surely you have some men of worth and genius, who meet their due reward?'—'Few; very few, indeed. Sloth, inanity, and bloated pride are here too often the characteristics of office. Fastidiousness is virtue, and to keep the poor and unprotected in awe a duty. The rich indeed are indulged in all the licentious liberties they can desire.'—'Why do so many young men of family resort hither?'—-'Some to get what is to be given away; others are sent by their parents, who imagine the place to be the reverse of what it is; and a third set, intended for the church, are obliged to go to a university before they can be admitted into holy orders. . . .'—'Then you would not advise a young person to come to this city to complete his education?'—'If he possess extraordinary fortitude and virtue, yes; if not, I would have him avoid Oxford as he would contagion.' (p. 81)

Thus Turl, who is throughout the book a reliable witness, sees Oxford as a place where all the wrong things happen; where importance is given to form (wearing the right cap) rather than to substance; where tutors and housemasters join with students in degradation, idleness, and drunkenness. Oxford doesn't come in with high points. About the only thing Hugh picks up in the vicinity of Oxford is an attack of Methodism— "My teeth began to gnash, as if by irresistible impulse; my hair stood on end, and large drops of sweat fell from my face! The eternal damnation, of which I had read and heard so much, seemed inevitable; till at last, in a torrent of phrenzy which I had not the power to controul, I began to blaspheme, believing myself to be already a fiend! It is by such horrible imagery that so many of the disciples of methodism have become maniacs" (p. 94). Fortunately, he recovers.

Hugh's Methodism, however, comes to the attention of university officials, and he is suspended for two terms. Thus his formal education gives way to his worldly education, and he sets out for London. All sorts of accidents come upon him, most caused by his own naiveté. His pocket is picked on the street. This shock is almost immediately followed by another of a different sort, a great disillusionment when he goes to present a letter of introduction to a clergyman (Hugh at this point hopes that he himself will join the clergy) only to find that clergymen (!) lie: he is told that the Reverend Enoch is not at home, but when he presents the letter, he learns that the good Reverend really has been there all along. Hugh exclaims, "This was another phenomenon in morals! A clergyman suffer, nay encourage, or, as it must be, command, his servant to tell a lie? It was inconceivable!" (p. 102). But then Hugh continues, from the more sophisticated vantage of his current understanding, "I knew nothing of fashionable manners, and that being denied to people whom you do not wish to see, instead of being thought insolent or false, was the general practice of the well bred. At that time I understood no single point of good breeding: I had it all to learn!" He never does learn it well. "But indeed, so dull am I on such topics, that, to this hour, how it can be a clergyman's or any honest man's duty or interest to teach servants to lie is to me incomprehensible. The difficulty, as I have found it, is to teach both them and all classes of people to tell the truth. What the morality of the practice is cannot be a serious question" (p. 102). Hugh's—or Holcroft's—comment deserves notice. He calls to our attention a common, "civilized" practice, and says it is immoral. What in most other observers of the time would be at most a humorous characteristic of society is for Holcroft an evil. It is evil because it is not true and rational. Holcroft's stance on what is or is not moral is never less than forthright. What is sometimes striking, as here, is that he will often focus on something in society that, because it is so common, seems all right. Merely by commenting, he reminds his readers that the accepted is not necessarily the moral way to do things.

These shocks to young Hugh's moral system do not, however, upset his animal spirits; he is much too well-balanced—rational—for that. "My health, appetite, and spirits suffered no check, from this tide of novelty and tumult of accident. I eat heartily, slept soundly, and rose chearfully. It is true, I came up to London with propensities which, from my education, that is, from the course of former events, would not suffer me to be idle; and in the space of a few hours I had already received several important lessons, that considerably increased my stock of knowledge. Of these I did not fail to make an active use" (p. 108). His pockets have been picked, his moral system considerably abused, but it is all part of education. Not for him that unhealthy nineteenth and twentieth-century lamenting for the ideal. Hugh, in the midst of the tumult, is not discomfited; he sees it as learning and is content that he will be able to use this new knowledge. It is a marvelously optimistic view, and so the book goes. Each situation is an educational opportunity for Hugh; each situation is a chance for Holcroft to put before his reader the list of corruptions needing cures. These ills may be loosely grouped into two sets: social and political. To portray social ills, Holcroft simply surveys each social group. Like the gentleman he wasn't, he begins with ladies first.

Ladies, that is, women with pretensions, Holcroft finds quite ridiculous. He satirizes the whole class of women who are educated to be nothing but opinionated, useless, artificial counters in social games. One example shall have to suffice, Hugh's introduction to the Reverend Enoch's wife and daughter. The wife's mode of "making herself agreeable" is by "learning the private history of all her acquaintance, and retailing it in such a manner as might best gratify the humours, prejudices, and passions of her hearers. She . . . made great pretensions to musical and theatrical taste, and the belles lettres" (p. 113). But her daughter—her daughter is a refinement of the mother in this sort of thing:

> Eliza was mamma's own child. She had an *immense deal* of taste, no small share of vanity, and a tongue that could not tire. . . . she was a musical amateur of the first note. . . . her [music] master, Signor Gridarini, affirmed every time he came to give her a lesson, that, among all the dilettanti in Europe, there was not so great a singer as herself. The most famous of the public performers scarcely

could equal her. In the bravura she astonished! in the cantabile she charmed; her maëstoso was inimitable! and her adagios! Oh! they were ravishing! killing. . . .

Of personal beauty she herself was satisfied that the Gods had kindly granted her a full share. 'Tis true, her stature was dwarfish; but then, she had so genteel an air! Her staymaker was one of the ablest in town. Her complexion could not but be to her mind, for it was of her own making. The only thing that she could not correct to her perfect satisfaction was a something of a cast with her eyes; which especially when she imitated Enoch in making herself agreeable, was very like squinting. Not but that she thought squinting itself a pleasing kind of blemish. Nay there were instances in which she scarcely knew if it could be called a blemish.

They decide to put on a small entertainment: "Every body was sure, before any body heard, it would be *monstrous fine*. . . ."

We obeyed the composer's commands, and played with might and main during the first thirty or forty bars, till the *obligato* part came, in which Miss was to exhibit her powers. She then, with all the dignity of a *maëstro di capella* directed two intersecting rays full at Enoch, and called aloud, *piano!* After which casting a gracious smile to me, as much as to say I did not mean you, Sir; she heaved up an attitude with her elbows, gave a short cough to encourage herself, and proceeded.

Her fears give her no embarrassment, thought I, and all will be well. I could not have been more mistaken. The very first difficult passage she came to shewed me she was an ignorant pretender. Time, tune, and recollection were all lost. I was obliged to be silent in the accompaniment, for I knew as little what was become of her as she herself did. Enoch knew no more than either of us, but he kept strumming on. He was used to it, and his ears were not easily offended.

She certainly intended to have been very positive, but was at last obliged to come to a full stop; and, again casting an indignant squint at her father, she exclaimed 'Lord, Sir! I declare, there is no keeping with you!' 'No, nor with you neither!' said Enoch. 'Will you have the goodness to begin again, Mr. Trevor?' continued she. I saw no remedy: she was commander in chief, and I obeyed.

We might have begun again and again to eternity, had we stopped every time she failed: but as I partly perceived my silence in the accompaniment, instead of continuing to make a discordant noise with Enoch and herself, had chiefly disconcerted her, I determined to rattle away. My ears were never more completely flayed! But what could be done? Miss panted for fame, and the company wanted music!

We had the good luck to find one another out at the last bar, and gave a loud stroke to conclude with; which was followed by still louder applause. It was vastly fine! *excessive* charming! Miss was a ravishing performer, and every soul in the room was distractingly fond of music! 'There!' said Enoch, taking off his spectacles. 'There, ladies! Now you hear things done as they should be!" (pp. 113–16)

The ridiculousness of young Miss and the sickening flattery of her admirers is all very amusing, and Holcroft wants us to be amused. But we must remember, too, that these are the fashionable people, those with (at the least) the pretension to be leaders of society. Holcroft finds such behavior not simply ridiculous but symptomatic of a lack of seriousness, purpose, and commitment in these classes. It is only his first step in a series of delineations of social nauseas, and it is meant to get us, pleasantly enough, into the critical mood. On page 116 he chops down Miss. On page 117 Holcroft aims his shaft at "his lordship." Next he will attack bigger targets, such as the bishop.

"His lordship," the Earl of Idford, is an unscrupulous, ungenerous man. He has political pretensions and uses the idealism and the intelligence of Hugh to further his plans. While Hugh is anxious to remedy present ills of government—"The want of . . . parliamentary reform . . . extension of the excise laws . . . the enormous and accumulating national debt" (p. 117)—the earl is concerned solely with his own political maneuvering. The earl is antigovernment, and so seconds Hugh on all points, until the minister admits him to the party. At that juncture, he becomes a loyal advocate of the government. Holcroft is dealing here with several social and political issues. In prose as in practice, it is difficult to draw a line between the two. First, we should notice the explicit listing of governmental faults; Holcroft, as here, sometimes sounds more like a pamphleteer than a novelist.[4] His criticism of the morality that governs those who would pretend to leadership is a recurring theme in the book. Holcroft is not gentle in his delineation of those with pretensions to either political or religious power and their methods of gaining it. He sees the systems of religion and of secular government as corrupt. Lord Idford, for example, is a man with no scruples; he does very well within the system. He changes sides so quickly when it is expedient that poor Hugh cannot get his pamphlets out fast enough to keep pace. While Hugh is still writing his antigovernment tracts, Idford already has gained preferment from the incumbent prime minister and become a party man. Hugh is left with the now out-of-place antigovernment brochure.

But Holcroft is not content merely to complain of the rise of unprincipled men who gain power by exploiting their own lack of morality. Because we can assume that not all men in government would be as unpleasant as the Earl of Idford, it is logical to assume that the remainder would be empowered to do good. Holcroft, however, has a much more pessimistic view. Although part of what he sees wrong with the English government is that it attracts unscrupulous men like Idford, an even more serious problem is that the system itself is so corrupt that it corrupts even those men of idealism and firm moral principle who come to it. Holcroft's point is that even good men, in order to join the ranks of government, are in the very process of joining corrupted. For how does a newcomer enter the ranks? He must buy (or have bought for him) a borough. For the man without great wealth, this implies a patron, to whom the idealistic newcomer will then have certain obligations. But even the rich, once entered into the contest, can ruin themselves within the corruptions of the system. Holcroft shows us both possibilities: in either case, what emerges is bad for the participants and destructive to society.

First Holcroft gets Hugh into government. Hugh is fortunate in that, though he himself is poor, he has found a magnanimous and idealistic patron, Mr. Evelyn. Without making any demands in return, Evelyn supplies the necessary funding as well as political connections through his cousin the baronet. Hugh is thus provided with both money and influence. The baronet under whose tutelage Hugh finds himself is not a bad man. But he is part of the system and therefore somewhat corrupt—or, at the least, not entirely in touch with moral realities. However, he is a member of the opposition, and his rhetoric is, if somewhat strong, "on the right side":

> You know, cousin, how I hate corruption. It is undoing us all, it will undo the nation! The influence of the crown is monstrous. The aristocracy is degraded by annual batches of mundungus and parchment lords; and the constitution is tumbling about our ears. The old English spirit is dead. The nation has lost all sense and feeling. The people are so vile and selfish that they are bought and sold like swine; to which, for my part, I think they have been very properly compared. There is no such thing now as public virtue. No, no! That happy time is gone by! Every man is for all he can get; and as for the means, he cares nothing about them. There is absolutely no such thing as patriotism existing; and, to own the truth, damn me if I believe there is a man in the kingdom that cares one farthing for those rights and liberties, about which so many people that you and I know pretend to bawl!
>
> The Minister knows very well he could move the Monument sooner than me. I . . . love the people; and am half mad to see that they have no love for themselves. Why do not they meet? Why do not they petition? Why do not they besiege the throne with their clamors? They are no better than beasts of burthen! If they were any thing else, the whole kingdom would rise, as one man, and drive this arrogant upstart from the helm. I . . . love the people; I love my country; I love the constitution; and I hate the swarms of mushroom peers, and petty traders, that are daily pouring in upon us, to overturn it. (pp. 361–62)

Hugh can't help remarking that the baronet's antipathy to petty traders is somewhat misplaced in that the baronet's father had been "a common porter in a warehouse, had raised an immense fortune by trade, had purchased the boroughs which descended to his son, and had himself been bought with the title of Baronet by a former minister" (p. 362). But that is a small matter.

So Hugh enters politics already in debt to two men, Mr. Evelyn and the baronet. One is of spotless integrity; the other is more or less run-of-the-mill in virtue and motivation (the baronet's opposition to the incumbent government stems mainly from the fact that he had been denied a peerage). Hugh comes to the contest fresh and unsullied, a gentleman who "not only possesses a good education but a sense of justice which makes him regard every man as his brother; and which will neither suffer him to crouch to the haughty nor trample on the poor" (p. 363). But his purity is compromised simply by the acts necessary to get into government. In order to get votes, one must court not only patrons but voters. Hugh finds he must give so many "gifts" that he makes a return trip to Mr. Evelyn to ask for still more money. Of the baronet, Hugh laments that "he had purchased me as well as his borough; for he had made me his own member, and meant to profit by me in all possible ways" (p. 451). One of these ways is to use Hugh's now-proven electioneering talents to support one of the baronet's choices.

With Hugh, Holcroft shows us what it is to be poor and to get into government. But surely for the rich these inherent corruptions of patronage don't exist? Holcroft chronicles for his reader the contest for a borough between two men of fortune, the Earl of Idford and Hector Mowbray. Hector is the man favored by the baronet; fortunately, Hugh has no trouble supporting him because Hector is the brother of Hugh's love, Olivia. Hugh and Hector go off "to the field of battle" (p. 452). They enter into a scene of revelry, drunkenness, and gross bribery. The camps of the two rivals outdo each other in carousing and swearing. The scene is reminiscent of Oxford, and Hugh is as repulsed as he had been on his entry to the university. (One of Holcroft's points is that the boys who are taught dissolute ways in their youth grow up to be leaders with no better sense as adults than they had as students.) Hugh says, "I had been disgusted with the eating and drinking at the ready-bought borough of * * * * [his own constituency]: but that was abstinence itself, compared to [this] scene . . ." (p. 453). So drunk is Hector, the principle actor, that he throws his glass against the wall, inviting his comrades to do the same. When Hugh calls out that a waiter has been cut by the flying glass, "pointing to a man whose face was smeared with blood," Hector yells, "Put him down in the bill." Hugh finally finds himself alone, ruminating on "waiters who, being maimed or killed, are to be charged in the bill" (pp. 453–54).

Drinking gives way to equally serious pursuits, such as deliberating on the course of bribery necessary for winning the contest. Hugh is appalled at the idea of bribery and equally shocked at the extent of it:

> Meanwhile the waste that was committed, the bribes that were paid, and the money that was squandered in every way, as well in London, where voters were eagerly purchased and sent down by coach loads, as in distant parts of the county and kingdom, convinced me that the sums which this election would cost must be enormous. I even thought it my duty to take an opportunity, in one of Hector's half sober moments, to remonstrate with all the arguments and energy I could collect; and endeavored to persuade him to decline the poll. But my efforts were useless. He was equally vain of his wealth and his influence. His purse perhaps was as deep as that of the proud peer; his friends as numerous; and he would carry his election though he were to mortgage every foot of land he possessed. (p. 455)

The struggle builds on each side, with violence, scandal, and rancor increasing continually. By the end of the contest, it almost does not matter which man wins because both have been ruined. Thus it is in debauchery and waste that the seats of government are transferred. Hugh, disgusted with these and other corruptions, resigns his seat. He is no longer friends with the baronet (who switched sides when the king made him a baron) and cannot remain his man.[5]

No matter whether a man be rich or poor, entrance into the political arena is corrupting. Holcroft seems to be saying that under the existing political system, no amount of idealism can survive intact—except by retreating from politics. Clearly such retreat does not ameliorate the system. Moreover, although Holcroft makes many statements about the natural goodness of man and his natural instinct to do good, he does not seem to see any hope for reform from within the system as a result of that natural goodness, nor does he posit any method for revamping the entire edifice. Rather disappointingly, he has Hugh merely turn away from it all, leaving the reader with the sense that reform of the political system is simply hopeless. The reader might have expected more after Holcroft's lengthy exposition of political evils.

Holcroft seems to feel the same disillusionment with the state of religion in England. The case in point here is the bishop, whose main diversion in life is gluttony and whose talents are basically confined to signing his name to other men's work. He is a parody of a human being: "His legs were the pillars of Hercules, his body a brewer's butt, his face the sun rising in a red mist. We have been told that magnitude is a powerful cause of the sublime; and if this be true, the dimensions of his lordship certainly had a copious and indisputable claim to sublimity. . . . His mighty belly heaved and his cheeks swelled with the spiritual inflations of church power" (p. 129). The bishop is anything but spiritually minded. His dinners are gross affairs of gargantuan feasting, followed by table talk verging on the obscene: "Allusions that were evidently their [the bishop's and his friends'] common-place table talk, and that approached as nearly as they durst venture to obscenity, were their pastime. With these they tickled their fancy till it gurgled in their throats . . . and, while they hypocritically avoided words which the ear could not endure, they taxed their dull wit to conjure up their corresponding ideas." Hugh comments wryly, "I must own that, in my mind, poor mother church at that moment made but a pitiful appearance" (p. 148). When we remember that the bishop presents one of Hugh's sermons as his own and later publishes a tract written by Hugh under his own name, the purity of the church, as represented by the bishop, seeems curiously lacking. Among his lesser faults, we might add, the bishop is a panderer of sorts. When Hugh not only refuses to take the bishop's "cousin" off his hands but refuses also to allow the bishop to publish his tract (the bishop steals it anyway), they fall out; another door is closed to Hugh.

Hugh tries the political and the religious roads more or less at the same time; in fact, at one point he is turning out pamphlets for both his lordship and the bishop concurrently.

Among the other professions he explores are those of critic (he finds that in order to do enough reviewing to make a living one must review books without taking the time to read them) and law (which his friend Trottman explains to him has nothing to do with justice—only with statute). Holcroft has Hugh try or consider virtually every profession that is open to the man of limited means but decent education (even medicine—it seems science still has a long way to go). Each of them is so corrupted and corrupting that no man of principle can long remain in any one. Holcroft has thought out his complaints but not his solutions, for were we to judge by *Hugh Trevor,* virtually the only way a man of principle could earn a living without compromising his morals would be to inherit wealth (without plotting for that contingency, of course). Fortunately, in the concluding chapter, Hugh does just that. Clearly, the lack of any solution but the deus ex machina of a long-lost rich relative is a flaw in the moral framework of the novel itself. All through the book, we have been told that a man must be usefully employed in his society; the fact that many of those employments carry built-in moral risks does not excuse him for retreating into the womb of inherited livelihood.

The book has two basic premises: all of society's major institutions are corrupt, and men themselves are good. The structural problem of the book is that Holcroft does not manage to articulate these two concepts into a whole. Holcroft posits that men are essentially—naturally—good. His hero, Hugh, is always seeking for the upright way. Hugh has not only a natural predisposition for good but an intellectual commitment as well. The fact that he is constantly disappointed does not lessen his goodness; it merely points up the corruption in society. Natural goodness, of course, even accompanied by social corruption as in *Hugh Trevor,* is perhaps the staple of eighteenth-century fiction. Holcroft, however, draws a much more convincing case for corruption than for virtue.

Holcroft gives us a good protagonist; he gives us also the good wise man Turl, who is, again, only one in a series of wise-man figures in the novel of the time. Turl is so good that he refuses to engage in any of the corruptions which modern society requires; in order to keep himself from being corrupted, he opts to retire from the world and sets himself up as a small private craftsman. Hugh, in the world of action, is impotent to change its corruption and is continually frustrated. Turl, in retirement, is unsullied by the world but, at the same time, also has little power to effect improvements. The man of action and the philosopher, good men both, are both quite powerless. Then there is Mr. Evelyn, who is somewhere between the man of action and the retiring philosopher. He lives his life, a life devoted to science and good deeds, in a secluded spot where he can carry on his work but not be too much tempered by the world. He considers his large estate "a trust which I find it very difficult conscientiously to discharge" (p. 298), and his other sentiments are equally impeccable: "Happiness is the end of man: but it cannot be single. On the contrary, the more beings are happy the greater is the individual happiness of each: for each is a being of sympathies, and affections; which are increased by being called into action" (p. 299). He becomes Hugh's patron, and while Mr. Evelyn would not enter the political lists, he is ready to compete in the real world to the extent that he enthusiastically supports Hugh's efforts with both money and patronage. Although Mr. Evelyn is not fully engaged in the society around him, he is the closest Holcroft comes in *Hugh Trevor* to drawing a fully functioning man of the upper classes.

Perhaps the most interesting good man in the book is Hugh's plebian friend Clarke, a carpenter who embodies all the manly virtues in his untutored heart. Although he is a good Englishman, he is of course a near intellectual relation to Rousseau's noble savage—or, at least, he is as near as Holcroft can get. Hugh first meets Clarke when he mistakes Clarke for a pickpocket; by the time he discovers his mistake, Clarke has been enthusiastically trounced by a mob. Clarke demands the satisfaction of challenging Hugh, and all of Hugh's apologies fall on deaf ears. As much as Hugh does not want to fight this man he has already wronged, he finds he must. Without meaning to, Hugh almost kills him. The "satisfaction" accomplished,

Clarke accepts Hugh's obviously sincere apologies. Not only that, but overcome by Hugh's generous attitude (Hugh tries to repay Clarke's injury with money, and Hugh is at the time considerably more in want than Clarke), the even more generous Clarke insists on following Hugh in his travels. Hugh, not a bit the snob, is only too glad to have the company of this good fellow.

Clarke is not one of Holcroft's most convincing characters, and the relationship between Hugh and Clarke remains one-dimensional throughout. Clarke is in the book to show the value of the common man as human being, and he and Hugh together are to show the reader how wonderful relationships can be between human beings when they are able to forget about artificial distinctions of class and rank and are able to see each other simply as people. But here, as in *Anna St. Ives,* Holcroft is not quite capable of overcoming his own fascination with rank. Holcroft makes the relationship between Hugh and Clarke so chummy that Clarke keeps forgetting his place and addressing Hugh familiarly. Each time he realizes what he's done, Clarke apologizes. Holcroft, apparently, does not realize what this implies. If Clarke must keep apologizing, then Hugh is not democratic: he is merely exhibiting a form of class condescension. It is not that Hugh is a snob but that Holcroft is. When Hugh and Clarke ride together in the coach with Olivia and her aunt, for example, we are aware that it is a kindness in Hugh to allow Clarke to sit with him. Holcroft here, as in numerous passages in *Anna St. Ives,* thinks that he is writing one thing while he is really showing quite another.

At any rate, whatever the flaws in the relationship between Hugh and Clarke, Clarke himself represents human virtue unsullied either by institutions or philosophy. His instincts are toward kindness, compassion—and responsibility. It is not the upper classes who are to be envied, Holcroft suggests, but the solid working class. It is Hugh who is always at the mercy of changing currents and affiliations for his living; he cannot support himself simply by the work of his hands. Clarke, on the other side, is a truly independent man; wherever he is, he can set up shop and earn a living, secure in his own capabilities. Novels of several members of the Godwin circle repeat the sentiment that in order to be free, a man must be capable of supporting himself. Bage remarks to this effect in *Hermsprong;* Inchbald in *Nature and Art* makes a point of having Henry, the good character, put off his marriage for a year in order to learn a trade because "in this country, people of a certain class are so educated they cannot exist without the assistance, or what is called the patronage, of others . . ." and he does not want to join this class. He will defer his marriage for a year, he says, until he can "learn some occupation that shall raise [him] to the eminence of maintaining both [his wife and himself] without one obligation. . . ."[6]

Clarke is already in this enviable position. He thus has all the qualities that Holcroft would demand in a man, not the least of which is the ability to support himself and those for whom he is responsible. Additionally, he is brave, honorable, loyal, and so on. He would be the perfect gentleman, except that he is not a gentleman. Holcroft does his best to present to the reader "man as he should be," but still Clarke is a bit too simple for Holcroft's taste. Holcroft seems to be suggesting that, for the corrupt moment, all these sterling qualities are most likely to be found in simple folk such as Clarke. Yet Clarke cannot be a leader, and Holcroft is aware that England is sorely in need of leaders.

Unfortunately, those who are likely to lead are also most subjected to corrupting influences. That fact may be part of the reason for Holcroft's final evasion of the issue, in that Hugh does not become a leader nor, really, does he even figure out what to do with himself. He is merely saved by a graceful fall into fortune. Although Hugh himself never seems corrupt, because he is so angered by corruption, he does indeed find his ideals sullied at each step in his education. When he arrives at Oxford, he is dismayed to find everyone drinking and swearing; he too wakes up drunk. He goes to London and finds a temporary mentor in the Reverend Enoch; soon he finds himself copying Enoch in assiduously flattering the bishop. At the time, this behavior seems to him only the way of the world. Later he realizes it is a pollution of values. He allows the bishop to present his sermon as if it were the bishop's own; he is flattered. He gives his support to a politician of questionable moral integrity because it seems the way of advancement, and therefore of doing good, in the world. He runs for office from a pocket borough and gives "presents" to the voters:

> Disinterested as these worthy voters were, and purchased by wholesale as they had been when the family of the Brays bought the borough, they yet had wives and daughters; who wore watches, and rings, and gowns; and who would each of them think themselves so flattered, by a genteel present from me, that there was no describing the pleasure it would give them!
>
> Beside which, one lady had a great affection for a few pounds of the best green tea, bought in London. Another discovered that the loaf sugar in the country was abominable. A third could not but think that a few jars of India pickles . . . would be a very pretty present. It would always remind her of the giver. . . .
>
> The men too were troubled with their longings. With one it was London porter; with another it was Cheshire cheese and bottled beer. They would both drink to the donor. . . . (pp. 449–50)

Not until Hugh finishes his contest and goes on to another borough to campaign for someone else—only to find with shock that this Hector is bribing the voters—does all the "present" giving seem like bribery: "In what light could the presents that I had made be considered? In what were they different from and how much better than bribes?" (p. 454). Whatever Hugh attempts to do, he is forced into corruption. In the world Holcroft draws for us in *Hugh Trevor,* the only way to avoid corruption seems to be to refuse actively to participate in the institutions of society.

There is a nod at the idea of individual reform, but Holcroft's case is not convincing. All through the novel, the reader is aware of a terrible villain, one who seduces innocent women (always the worst crime in the eighteenth-century novel) and bilks widows of their fortunes (the widow happens to be Hugh's mother), one Wakefield. There is also a rather

interesting character named Belmont, who is somewhat myste-
rious but seems in general to be a worthwhile type. Belmont,
strangely enough, repeatedly insists to Hugh that Wakefield
might be a likely character to reform. Wakefield and Belmont
are the same; it is Wakefield's way of seeking reformation thus
actively to apply to Hugh. Hugh's mother conveniently dies,
and Wakefield marries Lydia Wilmot, the girl he had seduced
and abandoned but always loved. Nicely set with the fortune
Hugh should have inherited (but Hugh does not mind because
he has just inherited a different fortune), Wakefield lives a
reformed and virtuous life. Hugh graciously exults:

> Neither shall I be required to particularize the present happiness
> of Lydia, now Mrs. Wakefield; and of that man of brilliant and
> astonishing faculties who is her affectionate companion and friend,
> and from whose exertions, if I am not strangely mistaken, the
> world has so much to profit and so much to expect. Like me, he is
> in the enjoyment of affluence; and he enjoys it with a liberal and
> munificent spirit. Are there any who hate him, because he once was
> guilty of hateful crimes? I hope not. It is a spirit that would sweep
> away half the inhabitants of the 'peopled earth.' For my own part, I
> delight in his conversation, am enlivened by his wit, and prompted
> to enquiry by the acuteness of his remarks. He is a man whom I am
> proud to say I love. (p. 496)

But we have seen no reforming process worthy of our respect, and the reform remains unconvincing; Holcroft takes a
great deal more time and trouble with the characterization and
attempts at reform of Coke Clifton in *Anna St. Ives,* and there
we do come to believe that, perhaps, it is possible to precipitate
such change. But in this later book, the reform of Wakefield-
Belmont is unlikely in terms of what we know of the character;
in addition, there has been no concerted attempt at reform by
the positive characters. The reform is Holcroft's concession to
his own feeling that this is an age of light, but between *Anna St.
Ives* and *Hugh Trevor* the "is" has become "ought to be."
Holcroft has come to realize that his is not a particularly enlightened or idealistic age, and his attempt with Wakefield to
suggest a universal potential for good is not carefully executed.

In fact, the shallowness of Wakefield's reform only underscores the generally negative outlook of the book.

In *Anna St. Ives* Holcroft articulates the concepts of corrupt institutions and good human beings by positing that good people can reform both bad institutions and badly educated human beings (for there are no bad people). In the world of *Anna St. Ives,* everything is possible: benevolent intervention can do wonders. We remember Frank Henley, the hero of *Anna St. Ives,* saying with no irony at all that "my feelings are all rapture! . . . I live in an age when light begins to appear even in regions that have hitherto been thick darkness, and . . . I myself am so highly fortunate as to be able to contribute to the great the universal cause; the progress of truth, the extirpation of error, and the general perfection of mind."[7] But in *Hugh Trevor* such a statement would have to be ironic. We do not see an age of light in *Hugh Trevor;* we see an age in which men may perhaps be basically good but their institutions are definitely bad—and the good men do not seem to have much power. Turl, the most meritorious character in the book, advises Hugh in the paths of righteousness, but he himself takes no action in the arenas of power. Turl remains at his work, engraving. The philosopher-sage has chosen a clean way to make a living "by administering as little as he could to the false wants . . . of men" (p. 140). While Turl's distance from the tumult of the world seems proper for a sage, it hardly seems the way to go in terms of reforming the world. Holcroft in *Anna St. Ives* sees a direct road to reform: Frank wades into the thick of the fight. But in *Hugh Trevor* Holcroft has lost that focus. Hugh, we have seen, looks at the field—be it religious, political, or legal—and runs.

Godwin's *Caleb Williams* was published in the same year as the first part of *Hugh Trevor*. Both novels are highly critical of the state of "things as they are," to use Godwin's subtitle, and both can see little hope for improvement; although it is not usually stressed in critical interpretations of *Caleb Williams*, Godwin plots no course for the reforms he believes necessary in English society. Surprisingly, it is quite the opposite: when Caleb finally gets the justice he has fought for, that is, when his friend-turned-persecutor Falkland is brought before the bar on the charge of murder, Caleb himself is crushed and can only lament "that I am myself the basest and most odious of mankind! Never will I forgive myself the iniquity of this day. The memory will always haunt me, and embitter every hour of my existence. In thus acting [to bring Falkland to trial] I have been a murderer. . . ."[8] Thus, even justice, as Godwin draws the picture, does not satisfy the *human* need; none of the social institutions in *Caleb Williams* ever do satisfy human needs. If we backtrack in *Caleb Williams* a moment, it was the social institutions of honor and rank that initially pushed Falkland to commit murder, thus setting in motion the whole horrible chain of events that leads to the destruction of both protagonists.

As the eighteenth century turned into the nineteenth, men were conscious of an intense feeling of helplessness; things were simply not in their control. Among the causes of this unease, I have pointed to the enormous changes in English society wrought by the industrial revolution, with its displacement of large segments of the English peasantry and its creation of a newly powerful (but not yet assimilated) middle class, and, of course, the French Revolution. As Carl Woodring notes, "after the French Revolution it was in the nature of 'nature' to change. Suddenly in the late eighteenth century to look about was to see alteration, accelerated speed, and flux."[9] England herself at this time was undergoing frightening political convulsions, partially in reaction to the French Revolution, and Holcroft himself in 1794 was imprisoned on a charge of high treason.[10] Thinkers such as Holcroft and Godwin believed that man was inherently benevolent and rational, but it was hard to hold to that belief in the face of a world that more and more seemed not to have a satisfactory, nor even particularly discernible, order. In the work of a better novelist such as Godwin, the unease takes a psychological or symbolic form; the dislocations of man and society are symbolized in Caleb's and Falkland's flailings. As Caleb's would-be recanting at Falkland's trial shows, no amount of struggle gets one through the nightmare net of disorder. In the work of a lesser novelist such as

Holcroft, the parts of the picture simply do not fit. That which men cannot make sense of in life, small artists cannot bring together in art. And so Holcroft puts before us the two aspects of what he sees, the good of men and the evil of institutions, and leaves it there. He is not about to attempt to bring the two together in terms of what happens to the mind of man within such constructs—as Godwin does in all of his novels from *Caleb Williams* on. And since there is no societal grid for these two seemingly antithetical observations, no God as in the middle ages, no chain of being as in the early part of the eighteenth century, he cannot come to any but a hollow conclusion.

If, as in *Anna St. Ives,* one believes that benevolent intervention can make grand improvements, then the natural benevolence of man and the (temporary) evil of society can be reconciled. But if one recognizes that benevolent interaction is at best ineffectual and at worst harmful, there is no way to reconcile the two. That is where Holcroft left *Hugh Trevor.*

1. *The English Novel* (New York: E. P. Dutton, 1954), p. 6.

2. Gary Kelly, in *The English Jacobin Novel: 1780–1805* (Oxford: Clarendon Press, 1976), is one of the few critics who devotes significant attention to *Hugh Trevor;* although his discussion is very useful for its many historical identifications, his reading of the book as an English Jacobin tract sometimes leads to rather strained interpretations of particular incidents.

3. Thomas Holcroft, *The Adventures of Hugh Trevor* (London: Oxford University Press, 1973), p. 11. All references are to this edition.

4. Holcroft did of course do political pamphleteering of his own. See, for example, *A Plain and Succinct Narrative of the Gordon Riots* (London, 1780), ed. Garland Garvey Smith (Atlanta: The Library, Emory University, 1944).

5. In addition, he is in debt to the baron, and refuses to hide from prosecution behind his constitutionally privileged status as an MP.

6. Elizabeth Inchbald, *Nature and Art,* 2 vols., 2nd ed. (London: G. G. and J. Robinson, 1797), vol. II, pp. 31–32. An earlier exposition of the same theme is the tale of Mr. Clement in Henry Brooke's *The Fool of Quality* (see my discussion in chapter two).

7. Thomas Holcroft, *Anna St. Ives* (London: Oxford University Press, 1970), p. 383.

8. William Godwin, *The Adventures of Caleb Williams,* ed. David McCracken (London: Oxford University Press, 1970), p. 323. For a further discussion of

this theme in *Caleb Williams,* see my "From Mind to Society: *Caleb Williams* as a Psychological Novel," *Dutch Quarterly Review,* 7 (June 1977).

9. "Nature and Art in the Nineteenth Century," *PMLA,* 92 (March 1977), p. 193.

10. In chapter eight, I discuss the Treason Trials and their implications more fully in connection with the trial scene in Bage's *Hermsprong.*

6

CALEB WILLIAMS / *William Godwin*

Those gentlemen who, when they are told of the misery which our prisoners suffer, content themselves with saying, Let them take care to keep out . . . seem not duly sensible of the favour of Providence which distinguishes them from the sufferers . . . they also forget the vicissitudes of human affaires; the unexpected changes to which all men are liable: and that those whose circumstances are affluent, may in time be reduced to indigence, and become debtors and prisoners. And as to criminality, it is possible that a man who has often shuddered at hearing the account of a murder, may on a sudden temptation commit that very crime. Let him that thinks he standeth take heed lest he fall and commiserate those that are fallen.

John Howard, *The State of the Prisons*

As we near the end of the century, the tone of rebuke in the novel becomes increasingly sharp, and nowhere is this asperity more obvious than in Godwin's fiction, not only in *Caleb Williams* but in his later novels such as *Fleetwood* and *Mandeville*. From beginning to end, *Caleb Williams* cries out against tyranny and privilege. What is perhaps most remarkable about the book is that its nightmare sense of undeserved and inevitable disaster is based in fact, not fiction; that is, in its most horrifying scenes, in the prison for example, Godwin essentially reports on his society and its devices. The sense of danger in the novel, the apprehension that any mistake may be quite fatal, is built on the probability of such mischance that Godwin sees as he looks around him.

Caleb Williams is a very angry book. Godwin directs his anger at social institutions that misshape men, turning them against each other in the name of values that are meaningless or even destructive. Falkland's honor is the obvious example that comes to mind, and others abound in the book: Collins' hesitation to learn the truth about the revered Falkland, because it would destroy his scaffolding of good and evil, is as strong if not perhaps as obvious an example.[1] Second, and more specifically, Godwin's anger is directed against a social system that not only warps men but puts some men in such a position that they can offer no defense against injustices committed against them. Caleb, as a secretary or servant, simply has no recourse to the law. In the final confrontation, Falkland's confession establishes Caleb's innocence; Caleb's protestations would otherwise avail him nothing.[2] This defines the struggle as one of class. Godwin has introduced a new dimension to the novel of protest that did not exist before him but is very prominent in the protest novel after him.

Logically, none of the missteps in the novel seem serious enough to cause the disasters they precipitate. It is unfortunate that a boor like Tyrrel lives in Falkland's neighborhood, but that shouldn't result in Falkland's disgrace nor should disgrace result in murder. It is perhaps silly of Caleb to let his curiosity get the better of his judgment, but such a slip should not blight his whole life. At every step in the book, disastrous consequences always follow relatively unimportant acts. All of the opening encounters are innocuous enough. Falkland is a benevolent aristocrat who uses his wealth and influence to do good, as when he takes in the orphaned young Caleb Williams, the son of one of his tenants. Caleb is a bright, alert young man, full of energy and enthusiasm, who honestly wishes to serve his new master well. Squire Tyrrel is a boorish character, but even he has taken under his protection a helpless young relative, Emily, and a hardworking family named Hawkins. Emily and the Hawkinses are fine, moral people. Thus the main characters in the book, with the exception of Tyrrel, are all upstanding and likeable people, even beyond the ordinary in their humanity. From this set of morally ordinary, even above average people, so much horror and evil accrues. The essential question in *Caleb Williams* is why this happens. The ultimate answer Godwin gives is that the fault lies not in men but in the institutions that corrupt them.[3]

The main part of the book is given over to the series of petty and gross oppressions visited by Falkland, and by society, on an essentially helpless Caleb. The book has a nightmare quality, and yet the details of the nightmare come from an objective examination of contemporary society. Descriptions of the legal and (especially) the penal systems, which may seem to a reader to be gross exaggerations, are documentably accurate. A great deal of the social criticism in Godwin's book, in fact, comes from the piling up of detail of the tyrannies inflicted by men upon men, particularly by the more powerful upon the less powerful. The series of tyrannies Godwin sets before us constitutes a crushing indictment of his society. Godwin uses a double view to emphasize the pervasiveness of this tyranny, with first a series of unfair and oppressing actions committed by the brutal Tyrrel and then a series of equally vicious acts committed by his supposed antithesis, chivalrous Mr. Falkland. Godwin creates a sense of outrage in the reader through Tyrrel's devastating attacks on the Hawkinses and on Emily; the reader shares that outrage with Falkland. It is not shocking, although it is of course unpleasant, that a man like Tyrrel can wreak such havoc on innocent lives. The shock comes when the kind and responsible Falkland shows himself to be as tyrannical as Tyrrel. It is this second view of "things as they are" that is horrifying, because if the helpless innocent must fear the upstanding as well as the evil man, then there is no place to turn for help.

The situation of Emily, the young, impecunious cousin of Tyrrel, is a good case in point. Emily's mother had been disinherited because she had married against the family's wishes. With her father and mother dead, Emily goes to live in the Tyrrel house, where she enters into "a sort of equivocal situation, which was neither precisely that of a domestic, nor yet marked with the treatment that might seem due to one of the family" (p. 38). She is treated reasonably well, as long as she does not displease the master of the house. But her well-being is subject entirely to his whim, and it is this vulnerability that horrifies Godwin. Her situation is not unlike that of many a woman in Godwin's time who was by custom and by law at the mercy of any relative who would feed and clothe her. The nature of youth, its dependence on others for subsistence, makes us all at some time vulnerable to domestic tyranny, and this fact, although painful to Godwin, is to some degree accepted by him. But when that tyranny becomes acute, there must be recourse to outside arbitors, that is, to the law, and the fact that law protects tyrant rather than victim makes the situation intolerable. This is the case Godwin puts before us.

Tyrrel becomes set against Emily because she admires his rival, Falkland, and to punish her he tries to make her marry the repulsive Grimes. The normally compliant Emily sets herself in opposition to the plan, saying that she wants only to leave Tyrrel's protection and fend for herself; he responds, "Do you think, strumpet, that you shall get the better of me by sheer impudence. . . . So you want to know by what right you are here, do you? By the right of possession. This house is mine, and you are in my power. . . . When did you ever know any body resist my will without being made to repent? . . . Damn you, who brought you up? I will make you a bill for clothing and lodging. Do you not know that every creditor has a right to stop his runaway debtor? You may think as you please; but here you are till you marry Grimes" (p. 57). When Tyrrel says that she is in his power, he makes not an exaggerated claim but a statement of fact. Later on when Falkland contends with Caleb Williams, Falkland makes essentially the same statement, and the reader understands that the nature of the man does not change the frightening destructiveness of the power he wields. Tyrrel's threat to have Emily arrested for the debt of the money he has paid out over the years for her subsistence has the ring of an empty boast. What law would arrest a young girl for owing the price of her room and board to her cousin? The answer, of course, is that England's law would. When Tyrrel, having had Emily dragged to prison from her sick bed and having thus caused her death, is confronted as a murderer by her friends, his justification is that "I did nothing but what the law allows" (p. 91).

That law allows him, as the wealthy landowner, virtually complete sway over anyone within his circle who is not equally wealthy and powerful. A poor man's redress from the tyranny of an unfair landlord is only to be fortunate enough to put himself under the protection of another—who may be the same or worse. Thus Hawkins, a tenant farmer on the land of one of Tyrrel's neighbors, comes to Tyrrel when he angers his own landlord by refusing to vote for the landlord's man in an election. Godwin makes us aware of this corruption in English political life that in effect forces the less powerful to give up their franchise to the more powerful. This disenfranchisement is so taken for granted that it is Hawkins' refusal that is seen as criminal, a point reiterated to Tyrrel by the first landowner, Mr. Underwood, who says that harboring Hawkins would lead to "an end . . . to all regulation. . . . Any gentleman . . . would rather lose his election, than do a thing which, if once established into a practice, would deprive them for ever of the power of managing any election" (p. 68). Although he is in full agreement with the sentiments, this time Tyrrel protects Hawkins—both to show his own power and independence and because Hawkins is, in fact, supporting Tyrrel's candidate.

There is no benevolence in Tyrrel's helping Hawkins, however, as is clear when Hawkins quite innocently crosses his new master. Tyrrel gets the idea that Hawkins' son should be in his service, but Hawkins does not want his favorite son to "go to service" and has higher goals for him. For this offense, Tyrrel determines to ruin Hawkins. Sure of his power, he vows to Hawkins that "I will tread you into paste!", and he orders Hawkins immediately to quit the land he farms. Hawkins refuses to be cowed. He has a lease, he says, and he hopes that "there is some law for poor folk, as well as for rich" (p. 71). Hawkins believes that the law will protect him. Godwin's perspective on the matter is unequivocal, if ironic:

> Hawkins, to borrow the language of the world, was guilty in this affair of a double imprudence. He talked to his landlord in a more peremptory manner than the constitution and practices of this

country allow a dependent to assume. But above all, having been thus hurried away by his resentment, he ought to have foreseen the consequences. It was mere madness in him to think of contesting with a man of Mr. Tyrrel's eminence and fortune. It was a fawn contending with a lion. Nothing could have been more easy to predict, than that it was of no avail for him to have right on his side, when his adversary had influence and wealth, and therefore could so victoriously justify any extravagancies that he might think proper to commit. This maxim was completely illustrated in the sequel. Wealth and despotism easily know how to engage those laws as the coadjutors of their oppression which were perhaps at first intended (witless and miserable precaution!) for the safeguards of the poor. (p. 72)

As the sequel shows, Hawkins indeed is in error. All the power rests with those who have the wealth, if only because of the expense of any legal proceeding. If legal proceedings are expensive enough to deplete the reserves of the wealthy, then justice certainly lies beyond the financial means of the poor. Additionally, the judges themselves incline toward the side of the substantial landowner rather than the poorer man. Later in the novel, Caleb, pitted against Falkland, is in the same position as Hawkins is relative to Tyrrel: when the man of power sets out to destroy the powerless, the smaller man has no recourse and is destroyed.

Tyrrel persecutes Hawkins, among other ways, by causing his land to be flooded shortly before harvest. When Tyrrel has Hawkins' stock poisoned, Hawkins finally decides to seek legal redress, although he

had hitherto carefully avoided . . . the attempting to right himself by legal process, being of opinion that law was better adapted for a weapon of tyranny in the hands of the rich, than for a shield to protect the humbler part of the community against their usurpations. (p. 73)

But

in this last instance however he conceived that the offence was so atrocious as to make it impossible that any rank could protect the culprit against the severity of justice. (p. 73)

Tyrrel is delighted, realizing that right and wrong not entering into the matter at all, he can now even more thoroughly ruin Hawkins:

> This was the very point to which Mr. Tyrrel wanted to bring him, and he could scarcely credit his good fortune, when he was told that Hawkins had entered an action. His congratulation upon this occasion was immoderate, as he now conceived that the ruin of his late favourite was irretrievable. He consulted his attorney, and urged him by every motive he could devise to employ the whole series of his subterfuges in the present affair. The direct repelling of the charge exhibited against him was the least part of his care; the business was, by affidavits, motions, pleas, demurrers, flaws and appeals, to protract the question from term to term and from court to court. It would, as Mr. Tyrrel argued, be the disgrace of a civilized country, if a gentleman . . . could not convert the cause into a question of the longest purse, and stick in the skirts of his adversary till he had reduced him to beggary. (p. 73)

This dance through the courts does not exhaust Tyrrel's means of legal persecution. He has the road cut off which passes Hawkins' house; the son, unable to stand this additional burden, breaks down the barricade one night and is jailed under a law intended for poachers—which Tyrrel and a cooperating judge twist to meet the facts of this case. Godwin's allusion here to the Black Act, from which he quotes the relevant clause, is one more of those precise references that support the accuracy of the charges he makes against his society. Thus it is through entirely legal means that Hawkins, like Emily, can be ruined by Tyrrel simply because he had incurred his displeasure. Hawkins helps his son to escape and they both run away, only to be found after Tyrrel's death and tried and executed for his murder—the murder committed by the rich Falkland, whose standing in the community, of course, protects him.

Godwin's delineation early in the novel of the legal and social forces that militate against the poor and prevent them from redressing the tyrannies inflicted upon them by their "betters" serves to set in the reader's eye the image of an England in which tyranny and brutality are in no sense forces that exist only in bygone days or in foreign lands. Later, when Godwin is talking about the horrendous conditions in the prisons, he says that those who thank God that there is no Bastille in England speak only from ignorance. Before he can get on with his main story, that is, the depiction of the specific tyranny of mind and spirit that Falkland is empowered to exert over Caleb, Godwin must convince the reader that such an exertion of tyranny within the structure of his society is not a freakish accident but an everyday occurrence and that, further, this sort of tyranny is built into the structure of society itself.

Godwin is careful to show the inevitable steps by which innocents like the Hawkinses and Emily are ruined because his book is a protest against precisely these tyrannies. Godwin need not have gone into such detail about Tyrrel's depredations in order to give Falkland motive; actually, Falkland's motive for the murder has nothing to do with Tyrrel's actions upon anyone but himself. Godwin's details present a pattern of legal and social callousness that is itself a severe indictment of his society and which, as background to the depiction of the relationship between Falkland and Caleb, provides a powerful conviction that for men (especially the powerless in Godwin's England) almost any sort of misstep can be the cause of extraordinarily painful, even fatal, consequences. The precariousness of the balance that holds a man's affairs in order is a recurrent theme in the eighteenth-century novel, as in Fielding's tale of Amelia and Booth, in Brooke's story of Mr. Clement, and in Inchbald's story of Hannah. Because that precariousness stems largely from the corruption of social institutions, the resulting helplessness is extremely frightening, for one cannot look outside oneself for aid. It is from this source that the nightmarish quality of *Caleb Williams* proceeds—there is no recourse, no fallback apparent in any of the cases Godwin describes. To whom should Emily, or the Hawkinses, or Caleb turn? Like Amelia and Booth in Fielding's novel, they have no one who can help them; unlike Fielding, however, Godwin, forty years later, will not take the fairy-tale way out and invent a fall into fortune for characters who, without such intervention, could be expected to perish. And so they do. But Falkland is destroyed too; so deep are the traps of society that even the powerful are ensnared by them. These traps are not only legal and political; they are also psychological. And while he delineates the institutional abuses, Godwin also chooses to stress the psychological pressures in society that destroy the core of the benevolent interaction he assumes would otherwise operate between men. Thus Falkland, a man of undoubted intelligence, benevolence, and fine character, commits murder, allows innocent men to be executed for his act, and hounds Caleb virtually to the end of his bearing, all because of a narrow notion of honor that is simply a deteriorated concept of pride. Falkland's society destroys men not simply by its overt actions through legal, economic, or political institutions but through the mistaken codes it foists upon them. Godwin's attack is then twofold: society creates not only physical and institutional tyrannies but psychological ones as well. In Falkland's relationship with Caleb, the two areas of tyranny meet.

Godwin's delineation of his characters' psychological functioning is based on his view of society, for the ills of individuals reflect the conditions of their society. Falkland's initial conception of honor and chivalry is not a product solely of his own imagination but is a function of his upbringing and of social reinforcement. So, too, the largely irrational streak in men's relationships can be at least partially explained by referring to failings in the structure of society itself. As Burton Pollin suggests in the context of *Political Justice*, "The too frequent interference of the irrational, the subconscious, and the blindly habitual is admitted only as symptomatic of the bad training and the evil institutions that now prevail."[4] Society, in effect, creates the occasion for unhealthy human relationships because, as D. H. Monro points out in *Godwin's Moral Philosophy*, "society fosters certain attitudes that make men incapable of seeing things (and people) as they are."[5] Once we can no longer see reality, we cannot act in accord with reason but only in accord with our faulty perceptions. Godwin seems to be saying that most of the destruction man wreaks on man arises not from reason—given Godwin's views on the hand-in-hand nature of reason and benevolence this would be absurd—but from non-rational motivations. An action may seem to have a rational motivation although it in fact does not. Falkland's destruction of Caleb would seem to be caused by his fear that Caleb will discredit him: in fact, as Caleb points out and as Falkland might have been expected to notice, Caleb repeatedly indicates that he has no intention of informing on Falkland. The whole chase might have been avoided had Falkland seen Caleb as he is and had he realized that Caleb would not inform, as is made clear in the novel at so many points: "I would undertake that Mr. Falkland should never sustain injury through my means" (p. 144); or "so far as related to myself, I resolved, and this resolution has never been entirely forgotten by me, to hold myself disengaged from this odious scene, and never fill the part either of the oppressor or the sufferer" (p. 156); or "I determined never to prove an instrument of destruction to Mr. Falkland" (pp. 160–61).

Similarly, Caleb's picking at Falkland's scab is equally obsessive. Caleb, while protesting his good feelings toward Falkland, relentlessly breaks down his stability. He slowly works toward an intellectual intercourse with Falkland, of whom Caleb says, "He had long been a stranger to pleasure of every sort, and my artless and untaught remarks appeared to promise him some amusement. Could an amusement of this sort be dangerous?" (p. 108). But Caleb's own language, even while dwelling on his innocence, gives him away. Caleb, as he pulls Falkland into this intimacy, says that "Mr. Falkland's situation was like that of a fish that plays with the bait employed to entrap him" (p. 109), so that Caleb clearly sees not only the danger but his own less-than-innocent role as well. Caleb goads and sympathizes at the same time: "By my manner he was in a certain degree encouraged to lay aside his customary reserve, and relax his stateliness; till some abrupt observation or interrogatory stung him into recollection and brought back his alarm. Still it was evident that he bore about him a secret wound" (p. 109). Caleb allows Falkland to relax with him, then makes some "abrupt . . . interrogatory." To harrow and to sympathize is, in essence, the pattern of Caleb's response to Falkland, even in the last scenes when Caleb forces the magistrate to call Falkland before a tribunal only to decide that "there must have been some dreadful mistake in the train of argument that persuaded me to be the author of this hateful scene" (p. 320).

An evil society, such as the England that gives all power to an aristocrat like Falkland and none to a servant like Caleb, forces men into unnatural relationships that in turn produce more sickness. Part of Caleb's pleasure in goading Falkland, for example, is clearly derived from the sense of power it gives him. "I could never enough wonder at finding myself, humble as I was by my birth; obscure as I had hitherto been, thus suddenly become of so much importance to the happiness of one of the most enlightened and accomplished men in England" (p. 121). A healthy society, in which men were equal and could react to each other not in terms of social position or social advantage but in terms of individual merit, would not foster such feelings of pleasure in power. This feeling of pleasure is not confined to the underling. Falkland, as corrupted by the society as Caleb is, clearly enjoys his power when the time comes. For example, when Caleb strikes up a friendly relationship with Mr. Forester, which Falkland does not want, Falkland reacts violently: "Why do you trifle with me: You little suspect the extent of my power. . . . You might as well think of escaping from the power of the omnipresent God, as from mine!" (p. 144).

Falkland and Caleb are in many ways parts of each other, like Frankenstein and his monster in Mary Shelley's novel. The symbiotic relationship is so strong that when Falkland is destroyed, Caleb is also destroyed. While Caleb is hounded and lives the hard life of a fugitive, the marks of wear and destruction are visible on Falkland. And when one man ceases to exist, Godwin clearly indicates that the real life of the other is over. When Caleb describes the scene of his public humiliation of Falkland and Falkland's subsequent demise, it is in terms of

such unshakable guilt that his own future life becomes meaningless: "Meanwhile I endure the penalty of my crime [the
prosecution of Falkland]. His figure is ever in imagination before me. Waking or sleeping, I still behold him. . . . I live the
devoted victim of conscious reproach. . . . I thought that, if
Falkland were dead, I should return once again to all that
makes life worth possessing. I thought that, if the guilt of
Falkland were established, fortune and the world would smile
upon my efforts. Both these events are accomplished; and it is
now only that I am truly miserable" (p. 325).

It is part of the power of the book that the veil of misapplied
motivation never tears. Falkland and Caleb, Tyrrel and Emily,
all are caught up not only in institutional snares but in equally
crippling psychological ones. Caleb is unable to escape Falkland
physically throughout the book; only in the last scene is it obvious that he has not been able to separate himself psychologi-
cally either. Falkland has internalized society's conception of
honor so well that it has become his obsession, and that obsession makes Falkland, pillar of his community and protector of
the helpless, into a murderer and tyrant. The society that has so
distorted such a potentially useful individual then offers no
protection from his actions. That is why Caleb cannot escape:
society as it stands damages men and then encourages them to
do their worst. From the keeper in his prison to the squire on
his manor, societal controls are nightmarishly lacking.

The tensions between Falkland and Caleb come into the
open when Falkland discovers Caleb opening a secret trunk.
Their next interview establishes the sinister quality that hereafter will inform the relationship between the two men.
Falkland understands the nature of his own motivation, and
that understanding includes a certainty of his absolute inability
to change. Thus when he explains to Caleb that his own foolish
obsession with upholding his reputation has led him to commit
one murder and to allow the deaths of two innocent men, he
also says that he knows he will go on committing terrible acts in
the service of his honor:

This it is to be a gentleman! a man of honour! I was the fool of fame. My virtue, my honesty, my everlasting peace of mind were cheap sacrifices to be made at the shrine of this divinity. But, what is worse, there is nothing that has happened that has in any degree contributed to my cure. I am as much the fool of fame as ever. I cling to it to my last breath. Though I be the blackest of villains, I will leave behind me a spotless and illustrious name. There is no crime so malignant, no scene of blood so horrible, in which that object cannot engage me. It is no matter that I regard these things at a distance with aversion;—I am sure of it; bring me to the test, and I shall yield. I despise myself; but thus I am; things are gone too far to be recalled. (pp. 135–36)

Falkland holds out no hope to Caleb; there is no persuasion, rational or irrational, that will turn Falkland from the path he must follow. Caleb, having made the mistake of forcing himself into the circle of Falkland's desperation, is now irrevocably trapped.

And the tyrranical power available to Tyrrel is equally available to Falkland. Before the fatal series of incidents, Falkland had exercised his power in benevolent actions; afterwards, he uses it to thwart any discovery of his dishonor. Godwin has carefully built for the reader a picture of just how much power a rich man of his day has—we have already seen with what ease Tyrrel destroys Emily and the Hawkinses. The structural purpose of this early exposition is to set Falkland's control over Caleb in perspective; Falkland's persecution of Caleb is part of a pattern of tyranny. Without real legal limit, the rich take as their hereditary prerogative control over other people's lives. Thus when Caleb attempts to flee, Falkland tells him that he will crush him with "the same indifference" that he would "any other little insect that disturbed [his] serenity" (p. 153). He assures Caleb that no one will ever take Caleb's word against his. Had we not the example of Tyrrel in front of us, this unblushing assertion of power might seem exaggerated:

You write me here, that you are desirous to quit my service. To that I have a short answer, You never shall quit it with life. If you

attempt it, you shall never cease to rue your folly as long as you exist. That is my will; and I will not have it resisted. The very next time you disobey me in that or any other article, there is an end of your vagaries for ever. . . .
I have dug a pit for you; and, whichever way you move, backward or forward, to the right or to the left, it is ready to swallow you. . . .
If once you fall, call as loud as you will, no man on earth shall hear your cries; prepare a tale however plausible, or however true, the whole world shall execrate you for an impostor. Your innocence shall be of no service to you; I laugh at so feeble a defence. It is I that say it; you may believe what I tell you. . . . Begone, miscreant! reptile! and cease to contend with unsurmountable power! (pp. 153–54)

This is a frightening speech. It is obviously the speech of someone not in control of himself, but its terror lies not in its irrationality but in its accuracy. Falkland indeed does have the incredible power he claims. That he is obsessive, even insane, is irrelevant. He can and he does hereafter tailor Caleb's life to his own fit.

Caleb appeals to Mr. Forester, Falkland's brother, who earlier had shown him some kindness, and Mr. Forester attempts to give Caleb a fair hearing. Mr. Forester and some servants are to consider the case against Caleb. The informal "trial" is soon over. Falkland accuses Caleb of running away from his service because he had stolen some property, and when Caleb denies the charge, Falkland produces false evidence. Everyone, of course, believes Falkland. Caleb quickly is remanded to prison, there to await his real trial. Caleb, not yet having been tried or found guilty of any crime, nonetheless is subject to precisely the same prison conditions as the worst convicted felon. Those conditions are unspeakably awful, with dirt, disease, lack of food, lack of privacy, and various modes of brutality and torture all in order. The picture Caleb draws is so horrible that it defies our belief and suggests that he is grossly exaggerating, if not imagining, the conditions. It is, however, a precisely accurate picture of eighteenth-century prison conditions. The details in Godwin's descriptions are corroborated point by point in John Howard's *The State of the Prisons.*

When Caleb first walks into the prison, he is struck by the
"squalidness and filth with which these mansions are distinguished. . . . the dirt . . . appears to be already in a state of
putridity and infection" (p. 177). Far from exaggerating, Godwin here merely glosses over one of the most scandalous aspects
of the contemporary prison system, that incredible neglect of
the most elementary sanitary measures that made the prisons
breeding grounds for disease and death. According to Howard,
"many more prisoners were destroyed by [gaol fever], than
were put to death by all the public executions in the kingdom."
He goes on to suggest that the "mischief is not confined to
prisons. Not to mention now the number of sailors, and of
families in America, that have been infected by transports;—
multitudes caught the distemper by going to their relatives and
acquaintance in the gaols: many others from prisoners discharged; and not a few in the courts of judicature."[6] Conditions
are so bad in many prisons that even if a man is released, he
may never be physically fit for work again. Thus Caleb's tale of
his friend Brightwel, a man committed for no provable cause
who dies "of a disease the consequence of his confinement"
while awaiting trial, is an indictment not only of the unjust
system that keeps a man in prison without having tried him, but
also is an accurate assessment of the likely result of that
injustice.

Upon his admission to the prison, Caleb is put into the day
room with the other prisoners, where both convicted criminals
and men just awaiting trial are kept penned together: "I spent
the day in the midst of profligacy and execrations . . . I saw
reflected from every countenance agonies only inferior to my
own[.] He that would form a lively idea of the regions of the
damned, need only to witness for six hours a scene to which I
was confined for many months. Not for one hour could I with-
draw myself from this complexity of horrors, or take refuge in
the calmness of meditation. Air, exercise . . . I was . . . debarred
[from]" . . . (pp. 183–84). This practice of herding all prisoners, young and old (even male and female) together is corroborated by Howard, as I indicated earlier. He decries the lack

of privacy for meditation and the forcible keeping of bad company. He also carefully explains the inmate's physical need for fresh air[7] as well as his spiritual need for some form of occupation.[8]

If the day room with its noxious closeness and almost equally unsavory company is bad, the accommodations for night are worse. The cell in which Caleb spends fourteen or fifteen hours per day is a dungeon "7½ feet by 6½, below the surface of the ground, damp, without . . . light or air, except from a few holes worked for that purpose in the door" (p. 181). "Its only furniture was the straw that served me for my repose. It was narrow, damp, and unwholesome" (p. 184). A below ground dungeon with only straw for a bed in England in the eighteenth century? According to Howard: ". . . anyone may judge of the probability there is against the health, and life, of prisoners crowded in close rooms, cells, and subterraneous dungeons, for fourteen or fifteen hours out of the four and twenty. In some of those caverns the floor is very damp: in others there is sometimes an inch or two of water: and the straw, or bedding is laid on such floors; seldom on barracks-bedsteads. . . . In many gaols . . . there is no allowance of bedding or straw for prisoners to sleep on; and if by any means they get a little, it is not changed for months together, so that it is offensive and almost worn to dust. Some lie upon rags, others upon the bare floors."[9]

Thus the descriptions in the novel are conservative with respect to the real-life conditions that Howard found. Godwin could have given Caleb a dungeon with two inches of water and no straw—but perhaps he thought that might strain credibility. Along these lines, one wonders how many of Godwin's readers have assumed that Godwin was using artistic license in having the jailor attach iron fetters to Caleb's swelling ankle as punishment for his attempted escape. In fact, we learn from Howard that the use of fetters for hands, feet, or both was quite common in English prisons, and he even pleads that doctors, when attending sick prisoners, should have their irons removed.[10] Generally, Howard notes, he must condemn the "loading prisoners with heavy irons, which make their walking and even lying down to sleep, difficult and painful . . . ."[11] Thus, Godwin's descriptions of Caleb—left in fetters with an increasingly swollen leg (until he bribes the jailor to get him a doctor); or unable to move more than eighteen inches from the staple in the ground to which his chain is attached (p. 199); or incarcerated in the "strong room," the door of which "had not been opened for years; the air was putrid; and the walls hung round with damps and mildew," for the awful crime of having loosened his fetter so that he could sleep; or further punished in the strong room by "the fetters, padlock and the staple . . . as in the former case, in addition to which they put on . . . a pair of hand cuffs" and sent "nothing but a bit of bread, mouldy and black, and some dirty and stinking water" (pp. 200–201)— are factual if we judge by Howard's descriptions in *The State of the Prisons*. The details of moldy bread and putrid water are not poetic either; Howard notes that many prisoners get little or no food and, as for water, "many prisons have no water . . . in some places where there is water, prisoners are always locked up within doors, and have no more than the keeper . . . think[s] fit to bring them."[12] Godwin's prison scenes then, horrible as they are, accurately describe contemporary prison life. In some cases, as I have noted with the description of the dungeon, Godwin did not even use the worst examples, perhaps feeling that the reader might reject these darkest truths as unlikely imaginings. Once we are aware of the truth of Godwin's descriptions, we perhaps should look more closely at the rhetoric that accompanies them.

Caleb Williams is written in rather flamboyant style, with many exclamation points and an even greater number of grand oratorical declarative statements: "No man that has not felt in his own most momentous concerns justice, eternal truth, unalterable equity engaged in his behalf, and on the other side brute force, impenetrable obstinacy and unfeeling insolence, can imagine the sensations that then passed through my mind" (p. 183). The style, however, should not disguise for a modern reader the validity of the complaints Godwin lodges against his government and the society that allows that government to maintain its policies. Godwin sees those policies as highly repressive and destructive. When we consider the factual truthfulness of his descriptions, the appeals to the reader to recognize the injustices and barbarities endemic in his society become statements of necessity rather than of political rhetoric:

> We talk of instruments of torture; Englishmen take credit to themselves for having banished the use of them from their happy shore! Alas, he that has observed the secrets of a prison, well knows that there is more torture in the lingering existence of a criminal . . . than in the tangible misery of whips and racks. (p. 180)
>
> Thank God, exclaims the Englishman, we have no Bastille! Thank God, with us no man can be punished without a crime! Unthinking wretch! Is that a country of liberty where thousands languish in dungeons and fetters? Go, go, ignorant fool! and visit the scenes of our prisons! witness their unwholesomeness, their filth, the tyranny of their governors, the misery of their inmates! After that show me the man shameless enough to triumph, and say, England has no Bastille! Is there any charge so frivolous upon which men are not consigned to those detested abodes? Is there any villainy that is not practised by justices and prosecutors? But against all this, perhaps you have been told, there is redress. Yes, a redress, that it is the consummation of insult so much as to name! Where shall the poor wretch, reduced to the last despair, and to whom acquittal perhaps comes just time enough to save him from perishing,—where shall this man find leisure, and much less money, to see counsel and officers, and purchase the tedious, dear bought remedy of the law? No, he is too happy to leave his dungeon and the memory of his dungeon behind him; and the same tyranny and wanton oppression become the inheritance of his successor. . . .
>
> I consulted my own heart that whispered nothing but innocence; and I said, This is society. This is the object, the distribution of justice, which is the end of human reason. For this sages have toiled, and the midnight oil has been wasted. . . .
>
> The language which these institutions hold out to the unfortunate is, Come, and be shut out from the light of day, be the associate of those whom society has marked out for her abhorrence, be the slave of jailers, be loaded with fetters; thus shall you be cleared from every unworthy aspersion, and restored to reputation and honour! This is the consolation she affords to those whom malignity or folly, private pique or unfounded positiveness have without

the smallest foundation loaded with calumny. For myself I felt my own innocence, and I soon found upon enquiry that three fourths of those who are regularly subjected to a similar treatment are persons whom even with all the superciliousness and precipitation of our courts of justice no evidence can be found sufficient to convict. How slender then must be that man's portion of information and discernment, who is willing to commit his character and welfare to such guardianship! (pp. 181–83)

   During [this] period . . . the assizes, which were held twice a year in the town in which I was a prisoner, came on. Upon this occasion my case was not brought forward, but was suffered to stand over six months longer. It would have been just the same, if I had had as strong reason to expect acquittal, as I had conviction. If I had been apprehended upon the most frivolous reasons upon which any justice of the peace ever thought proper to commit a naked beggar for trial, I must still have waited about two hundred and seventeen days, before my innocence could be cleared. So imperfect are the effects of the boasted laws of a country whose legislators hold their assembly from four to six months in every year! I could never discover with certainty, whether this delay were owing to any interference on the part of my prosecutor, or whether it fell out in the regular administration of justice, which is too solemn and dignified to accommodate itself to the rights or benefit of an insignificant individual. (p. 189)

The appeal to his countrymen to recognize that, indeed, only ignorance allows Englishmen to be sanguine about their own institutions is well taken. John Howard's works were specifically addressed to that ignorant complacence, and obviously the publication of his findings had made only the smallest improvement in a situation that was still, as Godwin wrote, the stuff of which nightmares are made. The bitterness of Godwin's plaints, within this context, seems almost restrained. When Godwin, toward the close of the prison scenes, recapitulates what the reader has already seen of imprisonment and due process—including the fact that the order *is* long imprisonment and *then* legal process—the dialogue is as much educational as polemical. This summation comes in an exchange between Caleb and Thomas, Mr. Falkland's old servant, as Thomas visits Caleb in prison:

Lord bless us! said he, in a voice in which commiseration was sufficiently perceptible, is this you?

Why not, Thomas? You knew I was sent to prison, did not you?

Prison! and must people in prison be shackled and bound of that fashion?—And where do you lay of nights?

Here.

Here? Why there is no bed!

No, Thomas, I am not allowed a bed. I had straw formerly, but that is taken away.

And do they take off them there things of nights?

No; I am expected to sleep just as you see.

Sleep? Why I thought this was a Christian country; but this usage is too bad for a dog.

You must not say so, Thomas. It is what the wisdom of government has thought fit to provide.

Zounds, how I have been deceived! They told me what a fine thing it was to be an Englishman, and about liberty and property, and all that there; and I find it is all a flam. Lord, what fools we be! Things are done under our very noses, and we know nothing of the matter; and a parcel of fellows with grave faces swear to us that such things never happen but in France, and other countries the like of that. Why, you han't been tried, ha'you?

No.

And what signifies being tried, when they do worse than hang a man, and all beforehand? Well, master Williams, you have been very wicked to be sure, and I thought it would have done me good to see you hanged. But, I do not know how it is, one's heart melts, and pity comes over one, if we take time to cool. I know that ought not to be; but, damn it, when I talked of your being hanged, I did not think of your suffering all this into the bargain. (p. 202–3)

Godwin's horror at the destruction that the legal system wreaks on men, and his view of that system as a tool of the powerful ("[Mr. Falkland] exhibited . . . a copy of what monarchs are . . . who reckon among the instruments of their power prisons of state" [p. 177]) leads him to consider briefly the alternative to legality, the existence of the criminal outside the law. Although he finds that there are some good arguments to be made for existing outside such a thoroughly corrupt system, he finally rejects that alternative. Godwin, although he has been called the father of anarchy, is not ready to espouse it in *Caleb Williams*, and after a brief flirtation he turns away.

The servant Thomas, who had wished to see Caleb hanged until he saw him suffering in imprisonment, manages to slip Caleb some tools and Caleb escapes. Half starved and totally exhausted, Caleb is found by a group of robbers. When they discover that he has no money, they demand his clothes! Caleb sees them as fellow fighters against oppression, and as such he appeals to them not to take what little he possesses: "The same hatred of oppression that arms you against the insolence of wealth, will teach you to relieve those who are perishing like me" (p. 211). His protestations are wasted upon the foremost assailant, Gines, who attacks him and leaves him to die. Mr. Raymond, the leader of the band, accidentally finds Caleb and takes him back to their hideaway. Caleb's mistreatment by members of Raymond's band results in the expulsion of Gines for not being up to the level of humanity demanded by the robber leader. A man of high principle, Raymond explains to his followers that "our profession is the profession of justice" and "we, who are thieves without a licence, are at open war with another set of men, who are thieves according to law." Each of them is "a man living among his equals" (p. 216). The principles espoused by Mr. Raymond seem higher than those we have seen operating throughout the book: justice, open statements of purpose as opposed to hypocritical posturings, and equality seem to be the rules governing the robber band. When Caleb tells his tale, Mr. Raymond sees it as "only one fresh instance of the tyranny and perfidiousness exercised by the powerful members of the community against those who were less privileged than themselves" (p. 220). Because society is so corrupt, men are forced into a stance like his, for

who that saw the situation in its true light would wait till their oppressors thought fit to decree their destruction, and not take arms in their defence while it was yet in their power? Which was most meritorious, the unresisting and dastardly submission of a slave, or the enterprise and gallantry of the man who dared to assert his claims? Since by the partial administration of our laws innocence, when power was armed against it, had nothing better to hope for than guilt, what man of true courage would fail to set these laws at defiance, and, if he must suffer by their injustice, at least take care that he had first shown his contempt of their yoke? For himself he should certainly never have embraced his present calling, had he not been stimulated to it by these cogent and irresistible reasons. . . . (p. 220)

Godwin is clearly sympathetic to Mr. Raymond, although he carefully has Caleb disprove these arguments: the essential criticism of the robber life is that it is not socially productive, and if Godwin is angry at the social waste aristocratic corruption implies, he must also warn against the destructive potential of life outside the law. He notes that these outlaws have great funds of imagination and energy and laments that the corrupt nature of the political system forces so much of its human potential into destructive channels. Caleb's arguments against viewing the outlaw as avenger are so strong that Mr. Raymond is convinced—but, the final irony in the laws of the country, he has no choice but to continue in his path. The laws of England, he reminds Caleb, "leave no room for amendment" (p. 227), and so a man's earliest mistake dooms him to a life of crime. Once more Godwin has returned to the theme of the one false step.

Caleb stays with the robbers long enough to recuperate, but he is not a criminal and his abhorrence of their way of life and its damaging effect on their humanity forces him to leave their protection and set off on his own. He wishes to find some small place where he can quietly live until Falkland's pursuit ends, through death or simply disinterest, and he is free of Falkland's curse. Falkland's ability to tyrannize Caleb is virtually unlimited, however, and wherever Caleb goes Falkland thwarts his attempts to reinstate himself in society. Each time Caleb establishes a new identity and begins to make friends, Falkland has his agent make it known in the village that Caleb is an outlaw, a thief, a liar—whatever is detestable. By this means, Caleb is effectively cut off from any social bonds, for he is never left in peace long enough to form them. Falkland's scheme makes Caleb helpless. Whatever Caleb tries, wherever he goes, at the crucial moment of reentering society, he finds that Falkland's insinuations of his supposed crimes have deprived him not only of his livelihood but of the sustenance of human contact. This, finally, is what is unbearable. Caleb, who even during the tortures of prison had kept silent, now forces the authorities to call Falkland before them and publicly accuses him of Tyrrel's murder.

The published ending of the novel allows Caleb to find a justice of sorts: the much weakened Falkland, once again publicly brought face to face with the charge of murder, confesses all. Caleb's innocence of any crime is established; however, he feels that he has destroyed Falkland by forcing this public avowal, and his guilt and repentance for that act make his own acquittal unimportant. He laments of Falkland that "a nobler spirit lived not among the sons of men" (p. 325). The fault is society's. Of himself, Caleb insists, "Where is the man that has suffered more from the injustice of society than I have done?" (p. 321). With regard to Falkland, he wonders "of what use are talents and sentiments in the corrupt wilderness of human society?" (p. 325). Caleb and Falkland, as the book stands in its published version, are both victims of the society that has molded them and deformed their relations with each other. This ending is fascinating from a psychological point of view, emphasizing as it does the essential "doubleness" of Caleb and Falkland that Godwin has suggested at many points. It insists on the genuine value of Falkland as a human being and presents him finally as an unwilling oppressor, at once a tool and a victim of a society whose corrupt institutions destroy the sound and just relations between men. At the end, both Caleb and Falkland are destroyed; Caleb survives only to mourn, and Falkland, we are told, dies a few weeks after the hearing.

This is the published ending. But it is Godwin's second thought, and a departure from the original ending. In the first ending, Caleb does succeed in bringing Falkland to a new hearing, where he makes a passionate plea of his innocence. Falkland coolly answers the plea by referring to his own reputation and standing in society and opposing them to Caleb's "known" status as a thief and a liar. The court once again believes the aristocrat against the poor man, and Caleb is denounced by the court for even daring to attempt to sully the name of such a pillar of the community. Caleb is remanded to prison where, tortured and alone, he sinks into madness. Even the news of Falkland's death some time later does not mean anything to him, for he has so far retreated into madness that he cannot remember who Falkland was. The account of the vibrant, energetic, ambitious young man who was Caleb ends with him completely broken: "True happiness lies in being like a stone—Nobody can complain of me—all day long I do nothing—am a stone—a GRAVE-STONE!—an obelisk to tell you, HERE LIES WHAT WAS ONCE A MAN!" (p. 334). Falkland in this original ending is not co-victim with Caleb; in fact, after Caleb is safely locked away, Falkland's health improves!

The earlier ending downplays the psychological closeness between Falkland and Caleb, emphasizing only the destructiveness of the social hierarchy itself. It is a weaker ending than the second, published one because it simplifies the human issues Godwin had raised. In the first ending, Falkland finds respite from Caleb, but the novel all along has shown that society misshaped both men so badly that neither is fit to function. Godwin's revised ending, with both men destroyed, insists that society's distortion of human relations creates a horror that no amount of human maneuvering can avoid. Even foreseeing danger and trying to elude it cannot ward off terrible consequences—thus Hawkins does not want his son to go into service because he might learn bad habits from fellow servants, but instead the boy is jailed and later hanged, all effects somehow resulting from this initial step. Caleb decides to find out what happened to Falkland . . . and having made that rather unconsidered (as opposed to ill-considered) decision, his life is permanently blighted. The book is colored by a sense of imminent, unavoidable danger. And this is not Godwin's vision alone, but rather, I think, a reflection of his time. It is interesting, for example, that John Howard twice in *The State of the Prisons* makes the point that the most prosperous, respected man can suddenly tumble into poverty or commit a murder and that no one of us can thus assume that he is safe, that what happens to other men is not his concern.[13]

Caleb Williams inveighs against the abuses of power to which society subjects its members. Godwin's attack on the class system marks a new and essential direction for the protest novel; he is not suggesting that there is a need for a more egalitarian view of men, with less emphasis on rank, as had Brooke and even Holcroft, but that the abuses inherent in the class system itself are explosively and unavoidably destructive. Godwin's protest is informed by that intuition Howard describes that the step from social health to social catastrophe is often an insignificant one. Men have failings: they can be over-curious, they can have too much pride, they can have too much respect for the importance of their own reputations. Society itself is responsible for the most part of these misperceptions. And society itself stands ready, once a man has erred, to compound and compound that error until he is beyond the reach of any help. Godwin leaves us no hope that there is any way out.

1. William Godwin, *The Adventures of Caleb Williams*, ed. David McCracken (London: Oxford University Press, 1970), p. 310. All references are to this edition.

2. Caleb's own helplessness before the law is even more obvious in the unpublished ending: in Godwin's first version of the conclusion, Falkland simply refutes Caleb's accusations, and Caleb is sent to prison, there to be tortured into insanity by Gynes.

3. This had been his point in *Political Justice* as well, but there he had arrived at a rather more optimistic conclusion than he does in *Caleb Williams*.

4. *Education and Enlightenment in the Works of William Godwin* (New York: Las Americas Publishing Co., 1962), p. 2.

5. *Godwin's Moral Philosophy* (London: Oxford University Press, 1953), p. 68.

6. *The State of the Prisons*, ed. Kenneth Ruck (London: J. M. Dent; New York: E. P. Dutton, 1929), p. 6. All references are to this edition.

7. Howard, p. 4.

8. Howard, p. 1.

9. Howard, p. 5.

10. Howard, p. 29.

11. Howard, p. 12.

12. Howard, p. 4.

13. In addition to the epigraph for this chapter, note Howard, p. 14, "My mind reverts to an admirable thought of Mr. Eden's, *Principles of Penal Law,* p. 330. 'A very slight reflection, on the numberless unforeseen events which a day might bring forth, will be sufficient to show that we are all liable to the imputation of guilt; and consequently all interested, not only in the protection of innocence, but in the assignment to every particular offense, of the smallest punishment compatible with the safety of society.'"

7

NATURE AND ART / *Elizabeth Inchbald*

It is a relief to turn from the unremitting horror of Godwin's *Caleb Williams* to Mrs. Inchbald's *Nature and Art*. *Nature and Art* is a book of great charm, but the quickness of Inchbald's satire does not obscure the bitterness of her portrait of English society. Like Holcroft and Godwin, she sees much that needs reform, and like them she decries the corruption in all walks of English life. She too is shocked at the callousness and injustice manifested by a society that proclaims itself humane but that acts only according to self-interest and pride. Rather than using Holcroft's method of enumerating faults, or Godwin's of piling dramatic detail upon detail to create a suffocating atmosphere of dismay, Inchbald cuts down the pretensions of her society with wit. *Nature and Art* is a revolutionary novel, but it dresses the strength of its statement in a tone of good-humored irony.

The good humor is deceptive. Inchbald did not find it easy to support herself and her yet poorer sisters, and in the struggle to make ends meet, she was forced to see a good deal of the less pleasant side of her society. Her novel in large part pleads against individual and societal callousness, much of which she had seen at firsthand.

She finds that society does not provide a supportive structure for its members. On the contrary, as soon as a person attains a position of any power, he is corrupted by it, and those who are born to wealth and position are educated to callousness and irresponsibility. We have seen the complaint against the education of the rich in many of these novels, *The Fool of Quality* and *Sandford and Merton* especially. Inchbald's criticism is even more far reaching, for she shows that the corruption is not a matter only of class education but of the attainment of high position.

Nature and Art is the story of two generations, the elder brothers William and Henry, and the younger cousins William and Henry. We meet the brothers as they leave their village to make their way in the world after the death of their father. The elder William and Henry have no resources or friends but each other. The only negotiable talent they have between them is the younger brother's ability to play the fiddle, a talent that enables Henry not only to support himself but to see William educated and placed as a clergyman. Once he has become a clergyman, William is ashamed of Henry's fiddling, not to mention Henry's unpretentious wife, and they separate. While William rises ever higher in the church, Henry goes to sea and is shipwrecked among savages. Years later, Henry manages to send his son, also Henry, to the care of his brother, and for the remainder of the novel we watch William from the older generation and the two children, young Henry and William's son William, as they act in and react to society.

The two young brothers start out essentially equals. They are ready to work to make their way, but society provides no useful employment for them. As Inchbald observes, "To obtain a permanent livelihood, is the good fortune but of a part of those who are in want of it."[1] This is a criticism we have not often seen in these novels (except perhaps by implication in *Amelia*), which for the most part seem to assume that if one wants to work, employment is available—even Caleb, hounded from town to town, always manages to find something. At worst, the problem of employment is seen, as in the story of Mr. Clement in *The Fool of Quality*, as that of the individual who simply is not educated to any useful occupation; it is a matter of individual lack of foresight rather than social fault. Inchbald makes a quite different point. William and Henry can only find chance employment, an errand to run or such, for regular employment depends on the caprice of the employer rather than the qualification of the employee. Without influence or means, even the lowest occupations are closed:

If they applied for the place even of a menial servant, they were too clownish and awkward for the presence of the lady of the house;—and once, when William (who had been educated at the free grammar-school of the town in which he was born, and was an excellent scholar) hoping to obtain the good opinion of a young clergyman whom he solicited for the favour of waiting upon him, acquainted him "That he understood Greek and Latin," he was rejected by the divine, "because he could not dress hair." (vol. I, pp. 6–7)

The only service society does find useful from the two brothers is Henry's ability to "play upon the fiddle." His fiddle playing opens all doors, not only for himself, but through the contacts he makes, for William as well. Inchbald devotes a paragraph to Henry's sudden rise—the last sentence points to Henry's having achieved the ultimate goal in society:

No sooner was it publicly known that Henry could play most enchantingly upon the violin, than he was invited into many companies where no other accomplishment could have introduced him. His performance was so much admired, that he had the honour of being admitted to several tavern feasts, of which he had also the honour to partake without partaking of the expence. He was soon addressed by persons of the very first rank and fashion, and was once seen walking side by side with a peer. (vol. I, p. 9)

Inchbald's insistence on Henry's ability to "play upon the fiddle" suggests that Henry was not an accomplished artist but rather an entertainer, one who could play at a tavern supper. Such is the sort of talent society respects, an entertaining spectacle, a diversion, and for this it dispenses its rewards. Henry can enter circles that any other—and greater—talents could not gain him, and he becomes acquainted with "persons of the very first rank and fashion" (vol. I, p. 12), finally attaining that great honor of being seen "walking side by side with a peer." Inchbald mocks the distorted values represented by Henry's success when she notes that "yet, in the midst of this powerful occasion for rejoicing, Henry . . . had one grief which eclipsed all the happiness of his new life:—his brother William could *not* play on the fiddle! consequently, his brother William . . . could not share in his good fortune" (vol. I, p. 10).

William refuses to let Henry teach him to play; he does, however, accept Henry's offer to "go down to Oxford, or to Cambridge" (vol. I, p. 13). Inchbald equates Henry's accomplishment in music with that of William in learning, suggesting that what William will bring back from the university will be no more valuable than Henry's fiddling. At the university, says Henry, "no doubt they are as fond of learning, as in this gay town they are of music" (vol. I, pp. 13–14). Henry's following increases, and as he becomes more popular he continues to help William. Finally, "in return for the entertainment that Henry had just afforded him," a "great man" (vol. I, p. 17) promises him a living for his brother as soon as its present incumbent, then on his death bed, vacates it. William passes his examinations, takes his orders, and becomes the incumbent in his turn. After a number of years, Henry with his fiddle procures a deanship for William.

Inchbald creates an incisive portrait of William the churchman. These early scenes, in which we see how William comes to his vocation and by what means he rises in his profession, lay the groundwork for the later descriptions of William's remarkably uncharitable career. William becomes a churchman because it is one of the few ways a man of his interests, that is, the classics and literature, can make a living, and such virtues as kindness, compassion and devoutness are not even relevant. As Inchbald comments, Henry, "possess[ed] the virtues of humility and charity, far above William, who was the professed teacher of these virtues" (vol. I, p. 22). Because these requisites do not affect the choice of profession or the entrance to it, we should not expect them to affect advancement in it, and indeed they do not. William rises in the church simply through influence, his brother's influence at that. Inchbald's phrasing is exact: Henry "had the gratification of procuring for [William] the appointment to a deanery" (vol. I, p. 23). Once he has been placed, William advances his own career. He becomes intimately friendly with his bishop, the two men of religion "passing their time in attending levees and in talking politics," the dean's wife, "passing hers in attending routs and in talking of herself . . ." (vol. I, p. 44). There is no suggestion in their talk or their actions that these curates are men whose responsibilities extend to care of their spiritual charges; rather, they are concerned with living fashionably and well. The dean and the bishop, whether deliberately or as a result of their manner of living, are entirely out of touch with the realities of life that the poor experience. Whenever young Henry and the dean converse, this remarkable perspective is apparent. Inchbald uses these conversations to expose the institutionalized selfishness of the churchman and to catalog many of the injustices and distortions of English society.

For example, young Henry overhears his uncle, in a fit of rage, telling the coachman that he will never drive again. Henry is very confused, not understanding how the man will be punished by not being allowed to do what seems to him an unpleasant job. His uncle decides that he had better instruct the child, and calls Henry to him:

"There are in society rich and poor; the poor are born to serve the rich."

"And what are the rich born for?"

"To be served by the poor."

"But suppose the poor would not serve them?"

"Then they must starve."

"And so poor people are permitted to live, only upon condition that they wait upon the rich?"

"Is that a hard condition? or if it were, they will be rewarded in a better world than this."

"Is there a better world than this?"

"Is it possible you do not know there is?"

"I heard my father once say something about a world to come; but he stopt short, and said I was too young to understand what he meant."

"The world to come,"(returned the dean) "is where we shall go after death; and there no distinction will be made between rich and poor—all persons there will be equal."

"Aye, now I see what makes it a better world than this. But cannot this world try to be as good as that?"

"In respect to placing all persons on a level, it is utterly impossible. God has ordained it otherwise."

"How! has God ordained a distinction to be made, and will not make any himself?" (vol. I, p. 78)

William is so accustomed to the concept of privilege that he is sure "God has ordained it." His role as a churchman, then, is not to interfere in any way with the relations between rich and poor, and further, it is no part of his duty to help the poor. Young Henry's puzzlement that God would ordain a distinction to be made on earth that is not to be maintained in heaven remains unanswered.

Although the criticism in the book is blunt, Inchbald avoids sermonizing, as Holcroft in *Anna St. Ives* does not. She manages to walk the fine line between blunt commentary and preaching partially by resorting frequently to the device I have just examined, a dialogue between Henry and his uncle, in which Henry's simple logic demolishes the careful complexity his uncle builds to mask the unfairness and brutality of society. Inchbald implies that the failings of society should be apparent to anyone who looks at the institutions with eyes undimmed by prospects of the convenient, the self-serving, the traditional, and the simply avaricious.

William is hardly used to his new role as cleric before he begins to draw lines between himself and those "less worthy." When he first becomes a churchman, he immediately develops a dislike for Henry's fiddle—a first step toward separating himself from a brother whose occupation is no longer sufficiently dignified. When he becomes dean, he distances himself from Henry still further. As Inchbald says, Henry's procurement of a deanship for William "at once placed between them an insurmountable barrier to all friendship, that was not the effect of condescension on the part of the dean" (vol. I, p. 23). The dean marries for prestige; Henry marries for love. The dean and Lady Clementina refuse to associate with Henry's simple and virtuous wife, and the break finally becomes complete. The last comment on this aspect of William's snobbery and the distortion of perspective it entails comes when William hears of the death of Henry's wife. William thinks to himself that "had he known she had been so near her dissolution, she might have been introduced to Lady Clementina. . . . They would have had no objection to have met this poor woman for the *last time,* and would have descended to the familiarity of kindred, in order to have wished her a good journey to the other world" (vol. I, p. 30).

Inchbald exposes the pretension of people like the dean and his wife. Little Henry bows to his uncle's wig and his aunt's earrings because aunt and uncle put so much stock in these adornments; as the dean explains, wigs are worn "as a distinction between us and inferior people: they are worn to give an importance to the wearer" (vol. I, pp. 64–65). Henry dutifully respects the wigs, although he does mention that this wearing of things to give a person importance is "just as the savages do; they hang brass nails, wire, buttons, and entrails of beasts all over them, to give them importance" (vol. I, p. 65). Either through Inchbald's observations in her own voice or through Henry's comments, every aspect of William's family life is ridiculed. William marries his wife "merely that he might be proud of her family; and, in return, suffer that family to be ashamed of *his* (vol. I, p. 29). She is everything he could want in a wife—snobbish in the extreme and motivated only by vanity. Her interests precisely match her husband's for "that, which in a weak woman is called vanity, in a man of sense is termed pride—make one a degree stronger, or the other a degree weaker, and the dean and his wife were infected with the self-same folly" (vol. I, p. 36). Their son, young William, in every respect satisfies his parents. As a child, he is precocious but not kind; as a man, he is successful but callous. It is this younger William who, as a judge on the bench, sentences to death the very woman he had seduced and betrayed.

The dean himself exemplifies distorted values rather than evil. After the death of his wife, when Henry leaves the country, William sincerely repents their angry parting and wishes to see his brother again, but as time passes and that event grows less likely, the desire cools. Inchbald rather ironically notes that "the avocations of an elevated life erase the deepest impressions" (vol. I, p. 42). Somewhat along the same lines, Inchbald remarks that although William was in general a "man of integrity," in certain instances, as when he wants to please those above him in the church, "he was a liar" (vol. I, p. 89).

Inchbald, like Holcroft in *Hugh Trevor,* is disgusted by the practices she sees in the upper echelons of the church, among them men signing their names to other men's work. William cheerfully prostitutes himself for the bishop, giving him his own writings and, even in the case of those few things he brings out under his own name, attributing the best parts of the work to his superior. From the context of the discussion, it is clear that the corruption in the church is only one of the series of corruptions that permeate the upper level of society. In both the religious and the secular world, truth is of little import. William's friend the bishop has "the desire of fame, and [the] dread of being thought a man receiving large emolument for unimportant service." (vol. I, p. 87). William, on the other hand, would do anything to gain "noble acquaintance" and giving his work away seems small price to pay for having important friends. Inchbald puts it most uncharitably:

> The elder William was to his negligent or ignorant superiors in the church, such as an apt boy at school is to the rich dunces— William performed the prelates' tasks for them, and they rewarded him—not indeed with toys or money, but with their countenance, their company, their praise.—And scarcely was there a sermon preached from the patrician part of the bench, in which the dean did not fashion some periods, blot out some uncouth phrases, render some obscure sentiments intelligible, and was the certain person, when the work was printed, to correct the press.

In particular, "the Honourable and Right Reverend Bishop of * * * * delighted in printing and publishing his works: or rather the entire works of the dean, which passed for his. . . ." Inchbald is furious that William sacrifices his integrity: "So degradingly did William, the shopkeeper's son, think of his own honest extraction, that he was blinded, even to the loss of honour, by the lustre of this noble acquaintance . . ." (vol. I, pp. 87–89).

Holcroft in *Hugh Trevor* attacks the same corrupt practices in the church. Hugh, like William, gives his writing to his superiors for publication under their names. The implications of this particular kind of corruption are particularly damaging to the perception of church as somehow separate from the failings of the world, for the inability of the great men of the church to produce anything by themselves points to a bankruptcy of thought within the body. The church, with its dealing, hypocrisy, and outright lies, is no different from the secular world, except that it is doubly disgusting to find these corruptions in the church. Both Holcroft and Inchbald make a major point of examining accepted customs like these, and neither has much taste for the polite deceptions that damage the essential honesty not only of the institution but of the individual. Inchbald sees such games as yet another perversion of the relationships between men that corrupt social institutions foster, for William's willingness to prostitute his talents for the bishop is not conditioned solely by the desire to rise in his profession but is in at least equal degree a product of his pleasure—his wonder—at finding himself the intimate of those socially superior to himself.

Although Inchbald essentially is using the established church as an example of a typical upper-class institution, some comment must be made here about perspectives on the church in the late 1700s as well as about the role Inchbald's own Catholicism might play in shaping her viewpoint. The Catholicism can be dealt with briefly. As a Catholic, she would have had reason to resent the establishment that ran the Church of England. Catholics, of course, had long been discriminated against in England, both in the private and public spheres; in 1796 she would still have been victim to some degree of that discrimination. The discomfort Inchbald evidences in her view of the Anglican hierarchy was not confined to Catholics, however. Much of the suspicion she and many of her contemporaries show can be attributed to the position the church had long held in society. The Anglican church was the established church, and it was, indeed, very established. It was, and certainly appeared to be, very comfortable; its clergy would draw little sympathy—and perhaps a certain amount of suspicion—for the sacrifices they might claim to make for mother church. It had been a good while, after all, since the Anglicans had had any martyrs. Also, because of its long-standing relationship with the ruling structures of the society, the church would inevitably be viewed with whatever suspicions were entertained about government and governors. The appraising eye Inchbald casts on the church, then, might be shared by many of her contemporaries, Catholic or not.

With respect to the particulars in the portrait of the church and its clergymen that we have seen in *Nature and Art,* Inchbald seems in her broad outlines to be reflecting long established prototypes. The steps in William's career follow what seems to have been a quite common pattern. D. R. Hirschberg in his work on "Social Mobility in Early Modern England"[2] describes some of the trends in church service and advancement for the years 1660 to 1760, trends which, if we judge from *Nature and Art,* had not much changed by the end of the century. What he finds, first of all, is that most of the bishops do not come from the aristocracy; the majority of successful churchmen come from the less exalted ranks of the population.[3] Thus William's rise from undistinguished beginnings is not unusual. The first step in the evolution of a churchman is his education, and Hirschberg's research supports Inchbald's portrait, for he finds that the most important element in providing for the education of a cleric is what he calls "seed money," that is, money to get to the university and begin. Once there, as he notes, "the talented might find ways to survive."[4] Again, William's career follows just this pattern: it is Henry's "seed money" that allows William to go to the university; once he has begun, he manages to complete his studies.

We remember that William's decision to be a clergyman is the result not of calling but of calculation: the church seems to be a good choice of livelihood for one who likes to study and not to do much else. Hirschberg notes that "for many [joining the church] was a calculated decision;" a decision that considered the fact that the church offered a decent (or better) income for moderate investment.

> Once in a church post the incumbent was fairly secure. If not overly well paid, at least he need not fear losing his livelihood with the fall of a patron. University and church officials were readier

than most courtiers or politicians to promote talented outsiders to patronage in their gift. The cost of a university education was at least comparable to the sums necessary to purchase office in other fields, and there were greater prospects of quick returns through college fellowships. Even if the typical rewards of a clerical career might be moderate, so too were the stakes required.

Churchmen knew full well that fellowships and livings served to entice young men, and in fact valued them as a way to convince the worthy to join the church.[5]

When Hirschberg summarizes his findings on patterns of careers in the church, he might be describing William's rise:

> What was the nature of bishops' social mobility? Surely the bishops themselves are proof that occupational and vertical social mobility were possible in this period. The majority were of undistinguished birth, yet rose to become princes of the church. Even if the rewards of episcopal service were not so great as many believed, men who had talents but few other resources were able to turn their abilities into professional success and a more substantial social position than their fathers'. Future bishops sought mobility consciously, to take advantage of one part of the occupational/social system that appeared relatively accessible to newcomers.[6]

Just so, William rises from obscurity and poverty to substantial social position and financial security. Whatever the truth of the personal characteristics Inchbald gives William, her portrait of social mobility via the church seems accurate. Some of the implications of this relatively exposed social position—the observation of private, domestic matters to which men in public positions are vulnerable—seem also to have been accurately recorded by Inchbald. William's wife is a common type; the wives of clergy seem fairly frequently to have drawn a good deal of negative comment.

Finally, we come to the matter of William's writing assignment for his bishop. Inchbald and Holcroft, as I have noted, complain that it is an established and somehow immoral custom for younger churchmen to write sermons and other works to be presented under the signature of the bishop. It is difficult to determine just how frequently this type of work was required, and perhaps more interestingly, we might also ask how it was viewed by both the younger clergymen and their bishops. Taken from the clergy's perspective, this preparation of texts may simply have been part of the younger clergyman's work, not to be viewed as anything dishonest at all. If, as Hirschberg suggests, it was the rule for the higher level churchman to be interested in fostering the successful flowering of the younger cleric's talent, such writing chores may simply have been among his assignments, perhaps even viewed as special opportunities to prove his talents. The extent of the practice and its place in the relations between the clergyman and his superior have not been adequately documented, and present a fruitful area for further study.

Although it is easy to see Inchbald's delineation of William, his family, and his bishop as an attack on the corruption of the church, it is an attack on the church as only one of many corrupt social institutions. Inchbald insists on that perspective by making William and his lady so clearly part of the world. Thus, Inchbald juxtaposes to this discussion of the practices of men in the church the practices of men in the secular world. Discussion of lies in the church is followed by discussion of libel in high society.

Inchbald explicitly links the two by using the dean's wife as the connecting device. While the dean is being a churchman, she is out being a lady, with the inevitable result that her name, having become "known," becomes an object of gossip. "The dean's wife being a fine lady—while her husband and his friend pored over books or their own manuscripts at home, she ran from house to house, from public amusement to public amusement; but much less for the pleasure of *seeing* than for that of being *seen*" (vol. I, p. 89). One day she came home from her visits in tears; "three ladies accompanied her home, entreating her to be patient under a misfortune to which even kings are liable,—namely, defamation" (vol. I, p. 90). The delicious conversation goes on with innocent little Henry trying to comfort the vain, silly woman, who, it seems, has been accused in print of gambling.

> "[I]f only one believe it, I shall call my reputation lost. . . ."
> The dean, with the bishop (to whom he had been reading a treatise just going to the press, which was to be published in the name of the latter, though written by the former) now entered, to enquire why they had been sent for in such haste.
> "My reputation is destroyed—a public print has accused me of playing deep at my own house, and winning all the money."
> "The world will never reform," said the bishop: "all our labour, my friend, is thrown away."
> "Here it is in print," said she, holding out a newspaper.
> "The dean read the paragraph, and then exclaimed "I can forgive a falsehood *spoken*—the warmth of conversation may excuse it—but to *write* and *print* an untruth is unpardonable.—and I will prosecute this publisher."
> "Still the falsehood will go down to posterity," (said Lady Clementina) "and after ages will think I was a gambler."
> "Comfort yourself, dear madam," said young Henry, wishing to console her: "perhaps after ages may not hear of you; nor even the present age think much about you." (vol. I, pp. 91–93)

This conversation is a commentary on the passages that precede it about William's writing for the bishop. William and the bishop come running in together, and Inchbald emphasizes that William had just been reading the bishop his newest treatise—to be published under the bishop's name. William's indignant assertion that spoken falsehoods may be excused as the product of the moment but "to *write* and *print* an untruth is unpardonable" underscores his blindness towards his own actions.

Lady Clementina is a lady of fashion. Her interests and her problems are those of the social world, and her husband, like her, is also very much involved with reputation and rank. Not only are the dean and his wife part of this society that is the subject of the scandal sheets and gossip mongers, but the lady's actions do not protect her from the attacks such organs might make. Inchbald's taunt about those who have to make much ado about guarding their reputations—because the reputations are open to some mockery—not only calls attention to the failure of the dean's wife to maintain a fitting decorum but to the view she and the dean have of themselves: they are figures of society, and their place in the church hierarchy assures their rank in that society.

This identity between the church and the secular world is apparent in the pamphlets the dean writes, his own "state of the union" essays. They are pegged directly to his satisfaction with his own advancement in the church. He writes of a joyous, productive, happy land but reserves the intention, should he not be promoted, to reverse his position. The dean's pamphlet

> glowed with [his] love for his country; and such a country as he described, it was impossible *not* to love. "Salubrious air, fertile fields, wood, water, corn, grass, sheep, oxen, fish, fowl, fruit, and vegetables," were dispersed with the most prodigal hand,— "valiant men, virtuous women; statesmen wise and just; tradesmen abounding in merchandise and money; husbandmen possessing peace, ease, plenty; and all ranks, liberty." (vol. I, pp. 99–100)

When Henry overhears his uncle talking about people who have only a bit of bread to eat, he is shocked to hear that such poor people live in England, for he doesn't remember them being mentioned in his uncle's pamphlet. When he looks again at the "luxurious details" of the riches talked of in the pamphlet, it seems to him that there must be enough for all:

> "Why do not they go and take some of these things?"
> "They must not," said the dean, "unless they were their own."
> "What! uncle, does not part of the earth, nor any thing which the earth produces, belong to the poor?"
> "Certainly not."
> "Why did not you say so, then, in your pamphlet?"
> "Because it is what every body knows." (vol. I, pp. 101–2)

The dean's answer reflects no sense of responsibility and, even further, no awareness that anything could be wrong in this division of the wealth of the nation. Clearly William sees his pamphlets as political rather than spiritual commitments; they bring him literary reputation and success. William and his church are comfortable in the service of the powerful. The poor, having no power, are of no interest. Inchbald sees the dean's callousness as part of a social pattern. The rich are generally insensitive to the poor, and she makes that point even more forcefully in the second half of the book. Her sympathies are with those worthy and very human poor. One of the most effective moments in the book is when the returning elder Henry meets some of William's parishioners. They inform him that William is dead, and it is terribly obvious that they have never been fooled by his show of dignity. They had always understood that he did not care for them, and they clearly express the reciprocity of their own feelings.

The rich in *Nature and Art* are almost entirely unpleasant characters, with the exception of the older William, who, occasionally, exhibits a degree of decency. Most typical of these characters are such people as Clementina or another charming lady we meet, the wife of Lord Bendham, who

> took her hue, like the chameleon, from surrounding objects. . . . At court, humble, resigned, patient, attentive—At balls, gaming-tables, and routs, gay, sprightly, and flippant—At her country seat, reserved, austere, arrogant, and gloomy.
>
> Though in town her timid eye, in presence of certain persons, would scarcely uplift its trembling lid, so much she felt her own insignificance; yet, in the country, till Lady Clementina arrived, there was not one being of consequence enough to share in her acquaintance; and she paid back to her inferiors there, all the humiliating slights, all the mortifications, which in London she received from those to whom *she* was inferior. (vol. I, pp. 120–21)

Inchbald has a marvelous time with the lady's hypocrisies. When she is in town, she admits to her house "the acknowledged mistresses of a man in elevated life" (vol. I, p. 123), although in the country she sees to it that a fall from chastity of any parish girl is publicly and severely punished. Inchbald explains that

> it was not . . . the crime, but the rank which the criminal held in

society, that drew down Lady Bendham's vengeance: she even carried her distinction of classes in female error to such a very nice
point, that the adulterous concubine of an elder brother was her
most intimate acquaintance, whilst the less guilty unmarried mistress of the younger, she would not sully her lips to exchange a
word with. (vol. I, p. 123)

Such a woman has the pretension because of her rank to set
herself up as the arbiter of morality in the village. Even more,
Lord and Lady Bendham pass not only on the morals but the
economics of the poor. The lord and lady are indifferent to the
suffering they see around them because that suffering affects
the poor and not themselves. The rich simply do not accept the
idea that the poor can have the same needs and feelings that
they have, a point to which Inchbald returns with increasing
anger as William sacrifices the innocent Agnes to his own feelings. Such episodes as this with Lord and Lady Bendham are
used by Inchbald to show that the insensitivity and hypocrisy of
the dean's family are typical of members of their class.

Inchbald notes that "one single day of feasting" in the castle
"would have nourished for a month all the poor inhabitants of
the parish," but the plenty is not shared. The lord and lady
have "ample fortune" but, somehow, "had never yet the oecon-
omy to be exempt from debts." Although they are not able to
live within their means, they do "contrive and plan excellent
schemes 'how the poor might live most comfortably with a little
better management.'" Lady Bendham notes that, after all,
"those people never want to dress—shoes and stockings, a coat
and waist coat, a gown and a cap, a petticoat and a handkerchief, are all they want—fire, to be sure, in winter—then all
the rest is merely for provision." And she does give them presents in addition: "last year, during the frost, a hundred
pounds" (vol. I, pp. 125–26). Young Henry, listening to all this
at dinner one evening, is not impressed by Lady Bendham's
generosity, although, as we might expect, his uncle the dean is
moved to exclaim, "how benevolent." Henry's reaction is "how
prudent." When pressed, he elaborates that "it was prudent in
you to give a little; lest the poor, driven to despair, should take

all" (vol. I, p. 127). That is an inflammatory, even revolutionary, statement. *Nature and Art* was published only seven years
after the French Revolution, and one can guess which poor
Inchbald might have had in mind.

The remainder of the discussion is as heavily ironic. Lord
Bendham retorts that such actions by the poor would be
punished by hanging, and Henry replies that "hanging . . . was
formerly adopted as a mild punishment, in place of starving"
(vol. I, p. 127). That the poor, to escape starvation, must accept
charity from the rich instead of being able to earn a subsistence
for themselves is for Inchbald an almost insupportable injustice. When Lady Bendham insists that the poor should consider themselves "much obliged" to the rich for charity, Henry
considers that "that is the greatest hardship of all." As he sees it,
it is most unjust that "what the poor receive to keep them from
perishing, should pass under the name of *gifts* and *bounty*.
Health, strength, and the will to earn a moderate subsistence,
ought to be every man's security from obligation" (vol. I, p.
128). This was one of the first criticisms Inchbald had enunci-
ated in *Nature and Art;* remember that it was only the accident
of Henry's luck with the fiddle that had kept Henry and
William from starving. Inchbald finds such a lottery for the
primary necessities of life horrifying, and she suggests that
these conditions could be ameliorated by governmental intervention. Henry notes that if Lord Bendham "would only be so
good as to speak a few words for the poor as a senator, he might
possibly for the future keep his hundred pounds, and yet they
never want it" (vol. I, p. 129). But Inchbald is sure that such
help, logical as it seems, will not come from men like Lord
Bendham.

People like the dean and his wife, like the Bendhams, are in
control of society. Inchbald is dismayed at the quality of the life
to which they condemn the poor, and she is saddened by the
emptiness of their lives as well. Further, the evils of the system
perpetuate themselves generation after generation, for
William's son is even more callous and unfair than William, and
the son's life is even emptier. Much of the problem is that the

rich are educated to respect the wrong values. Inchbald does not develop the elder William's character very carefully, although it is clear that he does not become distanced from his brother Henry until after he has gone away to the university. She is explicit, however, about the role of education in shaping the younger William and Henry; Inchbald attributes the difference in the characters of the younger generation directly to the differences in their education.

When he first sees him, young Henry is angered by his cousin William, for William seems to Henry to be a little man. William has been brought up with great care, but the care is all to the wrong ends. William has been taught always to be clever, and never natural. His upbringing has everything of art and nothing of nature, and the result is a child who is a little man, and a man who has no moral measure except self-interest. Such a prodigy takes much work in the making. Inchbald details for us the process employed by William's parents:

> Young William passed *his* time, from morning till night, with persons who taught him to walk, to ride, to talk, to think like a man—a foolish man, instead of a wise child, as nature designed him to be.
>
> This unfortunate youth was never permitted to have one conception of his own—all were taught him—he was never once asked, "What he thought?" but men were paid to tell him "how to think." He was taught to revere such and such persons, however unworthy of his reverence; to believe such and such things, however unworthy of his credit; and to act so and so, on such and such occasions, however unworthy of his feelings.
>
> Such were the lessons of the tutors assigned him by his father— Those masters whom his mother gave him, did him less mischief; for though they distorted his limbs and made his manners effeminate, they did not interfere beyond the body. (vol. I, pp. 44–46)

Inchbald's conclusion is that "considering the labour that was taken to spoil him . . . it was some credit to him that he was not an ideot, or a brute" (vol. I, p. 47). William grows up to be just the sort of man his education should make him: he does not think for himself but he accepts the empty judgments of society. As a child he is taught to "revere such and such persons," and in his adult life he lives by the rules of rank and favor.

Young Henry's education is the opposite of William's. The elder Henry and his child had been shipwrecked on an island inhabited only by savages, and in the years there he educated his son as well as he could. Little Henry's education essentially consists of informal lessons in morality and the value of inquiry; his father omits specifics of rank and society in the belief that should young Henry need to know them, he could learn them at that point. The elder Henry describes the education he has given his son in a letter to William:

> "Pray, my dear brother, do not think it the child's fault, but mine, that you will find him so ignorant—he has always shown a quickness and a willingness to learn, and would, I dare say, if he had been brought up under your care, have been by this time a good scholar—but you know I am no scholar myself. Besides, not having any books here, I have only been able to teach my child by talking to him, and in all my conversations with him, I have never taken much pains to instruct him in the manners of my own country; thinking, that if ever he went over, he would learn them soon enough; and if he never *did* go over, that it would be as well he knew nothing about them.
>
> "I have kept him also from the knowledge of everything which I have thought pernicious in the conduct of the savages, except that I have now and then pointed out a few of their faults, in order to give him a true conception and a proper horror of them. At the same time I have taught him to love, and to do good to his neighbour, whoever that neighbour may be, and whatever may be his failings. Falsehood of every kind I included in this precept as forbidden, for no one can love his neighbour and deceive him.
>
> "I have instructed him too, to hold in contempt all frivolous vanity, and all those indulgences which he was never likely to obtain. He has learnt all that I have undertaken to teach him; but I am afraid you will think he has learned too little." (vol. I, pp. 54–56)

The character of young Henry is precisely what we would expect from his education: he is spontaneous, honest, sensitive, and open-minded. His conception of worth is based not on the rank but on the humanity of a person. Unlike his cousin

William, as a child he has the freshness of childhood, and as a man the depth of maturity. Henry is far the better human being. The presumption is that had young William been removed from the pernicious influence of his vain parents, he would have grown up a better person. In Brooke's *The Fool of Quality* and Day's *Sandford and Merton,* we have already seen these assumptions: Brooke and Day indeed do remove the children from such parents for their education, and in each case the child develops into a fine, caring human being.

In *Nature and Art* young William receives just the education to be expected from the dean and Lady Clementina, and he fits perfectly into society, for he is a prodigy of reflection. Even as a child, his is a voice in echo of his father's, and indeed, he has been so educated that he can see nothing wrong with this kind of unthinking acceptance. Henry, his cousin, questions the assumptions of society and finds much to puzzle over in the relations between rich and poor, rank and worth, honor and truth:

> Their different characters, when boys, were preserved when they became men: Henry still retained that natural simplicity which his early destiny had given him; he wondered still at many things he saw and heard, and at times would venture to give his opinion, contradict, and even act in opposition to persons, whom long experience and the approbation of the world had placed in situations which claimed his implicit reverence and submission.
>
> Unchanged in all his boyish graces, young William, now a man, was never known to infringe upon the statutes of good-breeding; even though sincerity, his own free will, duty to his neighbour, with many other plebeian virtues and privileges, were the sacrifice. (vol. I, pp. 114–15)

The difference in character is of vital importance not only to the individual but to the larger society. William's actions toward the young girl he seduces and abandons cause her death; Henry's compassion and generosity save the life of the girl's infant.

The criticism in the first half of the book is directed at general targets: pretension, vanity, lack of discrimination, ambiguous morality. It is a pleasant irony in that the reader laughs comfortably with Inchbald at the foibles of the society described.

The second part of the novel shows the human consequences of this skewed moral vision in the upper classes, and Inchbald's tone is harsh and tragic as she describes the set of parallel relationships between William and Hannah and Henry and Rebecca. William seduces and destroys the innocent Hannah, while Henry cherishes and protects his Rebecca. William's carefully detailed destruction of Hannah becomes a symbol of the callousness, cruelty, and stupidity with which the upper class acts in relation to those less powerful than themselves.

During a summer which the dean and his family are spending in the country, both William and Henry fall in love with lower-class girls of the neighborhood, William with Hannah Primrose and Henry with Rebecca Rymer. William immediately sets out to make Hannah his mistress. He is quite open about the limit of his relationship both to Henry and to Hannah, but Inchbald makes the point that William only assures Hannah he "could never make her his wife" after it was obvious that "he had obtained her heart, her whole soul entire—so that loss of innocence would be less terrifying than separation from him . . ." (vol. I, p. 145). Henry cannot understand William's actions. To William's complaint that Hannah still holds back from having sexual intercourse with him and so treats him with "unkind moderation," Henry asks, "You design to marry her then?" William asks how Henry can "degrade [him] by the supposition?" As the dialogue goes on, Henry tries to suggest that marrying a woman you love is not degrading but that seducing her is. William is unshakeable: Hannah, the daughter of simple cottage folk, is not of sufficient rank to be considered for his wife. All of the prejudices of his education come pouring from him as he debates with Henry:

> "Would it degrade you more to marry her than to make her your companion? To talk with her for hours in preference to all other company? To wish to be endeared to her by still closer ties?"
> "But all this is not raising her to the rank of my wife."
> "It is still raising her to that rank for which wives alone were allotted."

"You talk wildly!—I tell you I love her; but not enough, I hope, to marry her."

"But too much, I hope, to undo her?"

"That must be her own free choice—I make use of no unwarrantable methods." (vol. I, pp. 147–48)

William is not to be moved; his education has taught him that he has the right to whatever he wants and that considerations of rank take precedence over human considerations when responsibility must be taken. Although he "loves" Hannah, William does not see her as a suffering human being; rather, he is aware that she causes him frustration. This is the same callousness and lack of responsibility that we have already seen, for example, in the discussions at Lord Bendham's table. But in the episodes with Hannah such lack of simple humanity is even more horrifying, for we are concerned not with general discussion of the poor but with the destruction of one particular young woman. What in a summary of the plot sounds like soap opera does not in the book read that way, for Inchbald has so well prepared the ground for something like this that Hannah's destruction by William has poignancy and dignity.

Part of Inchbald's point, although clearly not the center of her sympathy, is that the rich harm themselves by confining themselves behind these barriers. William is truly fond of Hannah and would have a happy home life with her as his wife. But he marries for "connections, interest, honours" a woman in whom he has no personal interest. Their life together from its inception is devoid of any meaning, and Inchbald suggests that this sort of arrangement is a commonplace of marriage in the upper classes. William marries the niece of Lord Bendham, Miss Sedgely. He "had never seen in her whole person, or manners, the least attraction to excite his love. He pictures to himself an unpleasant home with a companion so little suited to his taste . . ." but nevertheless agrees when the dean explains "what great connections, and what great patronage" (vol. I, pp. 165–66) the marriage would bring. The bride-to-be feels quite as William does and consoles herself that "I shall not care a pin for my husband . . . and so I will dress and visit, and do just as I like—he dare not be unkind because of my aunt . . ." (vol. I, pp. 167–68). This is the bargain William makes in place of marrying Hannah. As for any worry he might have had for Hannah, "business, pleasures, new occupations, and new schemes of future success, crowded to dissipate all unwelcome reflections" (vol. II, p. 10).

Hannah tries to murder the child she bore William, but faltering at the last moment, she leaves the infant uncared for but alive in the forest. Henry accidentally finds the infant and brings the baby to Rebecca to be cared for. The infant is discovered; Rebecca is accused of being the mother, and several very ironic scenes take place in which the dean and his son William with great moral indignation examine the supposed unwed mother. Only Henry notes that he finds the unknown father much more culpable than the mother.

When Henry later discovers that the infant is the child of Hannah and William, he asks Hannah to clear Rebecca's reputation. She is brought before the dean and forced to name the father. Inchbald describes the scene:

> While Mr. and Mrs. Norwynne, just entered on the honey-moon, were sitting side by side enjoying with peace and with honour conjugal society; poor Hannah, threatened, reviled, and sinking to the dust, was hearing from the mouth of William's father the enormity of those crimes to which his son had been accessary.—She saw the mittimus written that was to convey her into a prison—saw herself delivered once more into the hands of constables, before her resolution left her, of concealing the name of William in her story. (vol. II, p. 62)

The dean insists that she publicly name the father of her child; overcome by his relentless questioning, she admits that "one of your family is my child's father." When he has ascertained that the culprit is not one of his servants nor his nephew, he holds the rest of the talk in private, for

> in all particulars of refined or coarse treatment, he would alleviate or aggravate according to the rank of the offender. He could not feel that a secret was of equal importance to a poor, as to a rich

person—and while Hannah gave no intimation but that her delicacy rose from fears for herself, she did not so forcibly impress him
with an opinion that it was a case which had weighty cause for a
private conference, as when she boldly said, "a part of *his* family,
very near to him, was concerned in her tale. (vol. II, pp. 64–65)

Hannah refuses the dean's order to give up her child, and
because she had disobeyed him, the dean refuses to help her.
The dean, as Inchbald puts it, "candidly" tells the few witnesses
to Hannah's questioning that it was

an affair of some little gallantry, in which, he was extremely sorry
to say, his son was rather too nearly involved, requir[ing], in consideration of his recent marriage, and an excellent young woman's
(his bride's) happiness, that what had occurred should not be publicly talked of. . . .
    The clerk and the two constables most properly said—"His hon-
our was a gentleman, and of course must know better how to act
than they. (vol. II, pp. 69–70)

And so the affair is hushed up. It is of no import to anyone in
the dean's family. Certainly William is untouched by Hannah's
plight; indeed, even his name is not dirtied. Because of their
position, the dean and his family are immune from the effects
of their actions.

William goes off in honor and comfort with his new bride;
Hannah goes home in shame to her parents and watches them
suffer and die because of her dishonor. Forced from her home,
she seeks employment in the city and, because of the stigma of
her illegitimate child, is thrown out of even the worst servant
positions. The only place she is not an outcast is in a
whorehouse, and from serving there she eventually learns to
steal. Jailed for theft, she is brought before the successful and
respected judge William, who not recognizing the wretched
woman before him, sentences her to death. She leaves behind a
note, pleading not only for her life but for the care of her son;
it is delivered to William after her execution and after the
demise from grief of their son. Finally, Inchbald notes with
some asperity, William is subject to Remorse. Inchbald clearly
finds William's punishment less than satisfying.

In the characters of the younger and the elder Williams, Inchbald has drawn bitter portraits of those who have the "appearance of moral excellence" rather than "moral excellence itself" (vol. II, p. 108). They are conscious only of externals, and although they stand in society as arbiters of morality, they are themselves essentially amoral. The dean waits cheerfully, if perhaps impatiently, for his good friend the bishop to die so that he can move up into his position; the son William, putting all his energies into study to avoid "that domestic encumbrance called his wife," joins his application "to the influence of the potent relations of the woman he hated" (vol. II, p. 128) and rises quickly in his profession. Their personal lives are empty of love and friendship; their professional lives are devoid of commitment to morality and compassion. We have seen the dean dispensing justice; the son acts in the same way. Judge William speaks to Hannah as she stands before his bench in a voice that "was mild, was soft, compassionate, encouraging." But, Inchbald notes, "this gentleness was the effect of practice, the art of his occupation. . . . In the present judge, tenderness was not designed for the consolation of the culprit, but for the approbation of the auditors" (vol. II, p. 139). William pronounces Hannah's sentence—death—and "adjourn[s] the court to go to dinner" (vol. II, p. 142).[7] Inchbald, like many of her contemporaries, is horrified that the social system can be so cruel in its workings. Once Hannah has been victimized by William, she seems not to have any recourse from continuing victimization. William's private vice is hurtful, but it alone does not cause Hannah's destruction. Rather, William is a part of a powerful social machine, and it is the machine in its entirety that crushes. Like Caleb in Godwin's novel, once Hannah is caught in the machine she can expect no escape from its grinding gears. In a sentimental novel Hannah's letter of appeal to her judge and lover would reach him and effect a pardon, but in this novel, rather more realistically, her appeal is considered the delirious delusion of a lost woman; what possible connection, her jailors reason, could there be between the destroyed wreck of a poor woman they hold for her death and the successful, respected judge who had pronounced her sentence? Hannah is executed on schedule.

The death of Hannah gives increased weight to a novel that might otherwise rest simply as a satire on the manners of the English upper classes. Her death is a real tragedy, and the origins of that tragedy lie unmistakably with William and with the social and legal institutions that protect the powerful and destroy the helpless. Inchbald sees Hannah's tragedy as a man-made disaster, and as such she can have no pity for the perpetrator. Hannah is destroyed because she trusts William, but William's entire education, socially dictated as we have seen, explicitly has taught him to be lacking in the elements of character that would make him trustworthy. It is true that perhaps Hannah should have known better, but Inchbald makes it clear that every element is against Hannah being able to defend herself from the older, better educated, more worldly William's seduction. She is not equipped to reason against William, and he uses his advantage deliberately. William's seduction of Hannah is not, as he and his family would have it, merely a youthful indiscretion; it is a murder.

William, finally made aware of his crime, is left to suffer the rest of his days in remorse. For once Inchbald writes with understatement: "[William] envied [Hannah] even the life she struggled through from his neglect—and felt that his future days would be far less happy than her former existence. He calculated with precision" (vol. II, p. 157). The remainder of the book, unfortunately, is anything but an understatement. Inchbald thumps her reader with a simplistic, moralizing summing up that pulls together all the strings of the plot, accounts for the last days of each of the main characters, and even supplies the almost obligatory eighteenth-century happy ending: after an absence of nineteen years, Henry returns and marries the unchanged Rebecca! The moralizing becomes syrupy, and Inchbald's moral perspective dissolves into a totally unconvincing statement that what is wrong with the way the Williams of the world live their lives is that they are removed from nature.

The solution to human problems is for everyone to return, as do both Henrys, to the simple life:

> Each morning wakes the father and the son to cheerful labour in fishing, or the tending of a garden, the produce of which they carry to the next market town. The evening sends them back to their home in joy; where Rebecca meets them at the door, affectionately boasts of the warm meal that is ready, and heightens the charm of conversation with her taste and judgment.
> [They then partake of] a supper of roots from their garden, poultry that Rebecca's hand had reared, and a jug brewed by young Henry. . . . (vol. II, pp. 196–97)

Clearly this return to a "hut, placed on the borders of the sea" (vol. II, p. 196) and a simple, self-sufficient existence complete within the family unit is neither practical nor desirable for everyone; as a solution to the problems Inchbald had exposed in *Nature and Art,* it is simplistic. The moral vision of the book collapses in the last chapters. Henry and his family merely retreat from society and leave the world to its own devices. They live their quiet, comfortable existence and philosophize that the poor are really much better off than the rich—the rich are to be pitied, not the poor—for the poor just need to be educated to esteem poverty instead of wealth and then they would be perfectly happy! Inchbald obviously is espousing the doctrine that nature is better than art, that simplicity is more wholesome than artifice. Throughout the book, the Williams represent the excesses of the artificial and the Henrys are the types of wholesome simplicity. Inchbald's dichotomy works well in most of the book when she uses the Henrys as foils for the Williams. Young Henry's different perspective from his uncle and cousin William, as we have seen, affords Inchbald ample scope to examine the pretensions of society. But when she describes "nature" rather than "art" at the end of the book, Inchbald does so without any hint of irony. She commits herself to absurd statements. If the poor "have not always enough," Henry equates that with the fact that his uncle William was always striving for "more" also. It seems to escape Henry that the poor man's "enough" implies necessities such as food and shelter while uncle William's "more" is on a clearly less basic level. After one of their cheerful days of fishing and gardening, the two Henrys and Rebecca sit together contentedly and philosophize about the poor.

"My son," said the elder Henry, "where under heaven, shall three persons be met together, happy as we three are? It is the want of industry, or the want of reflection, which makes the poor dissatisfied."

"I once," replied the younger Henry, "considered poverty a curse—but after my thoughts became enlarged, and I had associated for years with the rich, and now mix with the poor, my opinion has undergone a total change—for I have seen, and have enjoyed, more real pleasure at work with my fellow-labourers, and in this cottage, than ever I beheld, or experienced, during my abode at my uncle's; during all my intercourse with the fashionable and the powerful of this world."

"The worst is," said Rebecca, "the poor have not always enough."

"Who has enough?" asked her husband. "Had my uncle? No— he hoped for more—and in all his writings sacrificed his duty to his avarice. Had his son enough, when he yielded up his honour, his domestic peace, to gratify his ambition? Had Lady Bendham enough, when she staked all she had, in the hope of becoming richer? Were we, my Rebecca, of discontented minds, we have now too little. But conscious, from observation and experience, that the rich are not so happy as ourselves, we rejoice in our lot."

He continued: "I remember, when I first came a boy to England, the poor excited my compassion; but now that my judgment is matured, I pity the rich. I know that in this opulent kingdom, there are nearly as many persons perishing through intemperance as starving with hunger—there are as many miserable in the lassitude of having nothing to do, as there are bowed down to the earth with hard labour—there are more persons who draw upon themselves calamity by following their own will, than there are, who experience it by obeying the will of another. Add to this, that the rich are so much afraid of dying, they have no comfort in living."

"There the poor have another advantage," said Rebecca, "for they may defy not only death, but every loss by sea or land, as they have nothing to lose."

"Besides," added the elder Henry, "there is a certain joy, of the most gratifying kind that the human mind is capable of tasting, peculiar to the poor, and of which the rich can but seldom experience the delight."

"What can that be?" cried Rebecca.

"A kind word, a benevolent smile, one token of esteem from the person whom we consider as our superior."

To which Rebecca replied, "And the rarity of obtaining such a token, is what increases the honour."

"Certainly," returned young Henry: "and yet those in poverty, ungrateful as they are, murmur against that Government from which they receive the blessing."

"But this is the fault of education, of early prejudice," said the elder Henry:—"our children observe us pay respect, even reverence to the wealthy, while we slight or despise the poor. The impression thus made on their minds in youth, they indelibly retain during the more advanced periods of life. . . ."

"Let the poor, then" (cried the younger Henry) "no more be their own persecutors—no longer pay homage to wealth—instantaneously the whole idolatrous worship will cease—the idol will be broken." (vol. II, pp. 197–202)

And so ends the book.

The absurdity of these remarks is manifest. It is only "the want of industry, or the want of reflection" that makes the poor unhappy. They need only work and reflect on their good fortune, and they will be content; this from the same Inchbald who had opened her book with the complaint that "a permanent livelihood is the good fortune but of a part of those who are in want of it."

The absurdities mount as Inchbald goes on. Why should we pity the poor for starving when, "in this opulent kingdom there are nearly as many persons perishing through intemperance as starving with hunger?" Henry fails to recognize that starvation is not by choice but that gluttony is. Similarly, he equates the hardships of "being bowed down to the earth with hard labour" with "being miserable in the lassitude of having nothing to do"—hardly, one would think, in the same category. But, of course, even if the poor die from their labor or from starvation, they are still better off than the rich, since "they may defy death . . . as they have nothing to lose." And, finally, that last "most gratifying kind" of pleasure that only the poor can taste: "a benevolent smile . . . from the person we consider our superior." Pity the rich who never can taste of this most exquisite of human pleasures.

It is tempting to assume that Inchbald is being ironic in these last passages and that she must see the falseness of such arguments, but there is no hint that she is not serious. The last chapters build almost poetically to her conclusion. According to Inchbald it is only because everyone, rich and poor, has been educated to revere wealth that the poor are unhappy; indeed, it is an intellectual unhappiness the poor experience. If the poor could rid themselves of this false estimation of value, they would be happy. Inchbald is really serious: it is not starvation or brutal labor which makes men miserable, it is lack of perspective.

The collapse of Inchbald's witty satire into this silly panegyric on poverty is difficult to explain. Inchbald is very clever at exposing the pretensions of the rich, and her bitterness against the distortions in personal relationships, and in the structure of society that they create, gives her criticism an incisive edge. Her sympathy is as heavily on the side of the poor as her ire weighs against the rich, but her critical vision does not extend so far as to see that the fact that the rich can be gluttonous and unhappy does not make poverty a positive state. She loses her perspective entirely and fails to realize that one may respect the poor without praising their poverty. Where earlier in the book she had insisted that if the rich would but share some of their wealth the poor would not need to go hungry, at the end she loses that critical, reforming perspective and says, instead, that hunger is really not a bad state—it isn't, after all, any worse than gluttony. If earlier in the book she had hinted at the changes necessary to make society more equitable and to help the poor to a more decent life, at the end, in her revulsion at the excesses of the rich, she praises poverty itself. But while she glorifies poverty, she does not really image it, for although she says that hunger isn't worse than gluttony, she does not draw any picture of starvation. Henry and his family are quite comfortable. It is from the safety of their "enjoyment of every [simple] comfort which such distinguished minds knew how to taste" (vol. II, p. 195) that they discuss poverty. Simplicity of lifestyle and poverty are not the same, but Inchbald confounds them in her last scenes.

We ought not to fault Inchbald too severely for her failure of perspective in these last pages.[8] She lives in a time when many, and sometimes conflicting, social theories vie with each other for the humanitarian's attention. Inchbald reflects the most important of them, but she does not assimilate them into a unified vision. Nearest at hand are the revolutionary ideas of the Godwin circle, and these fuel her dismay at the hypocrisies and inequities she sees in society. The Rousseauean ideal of the noble savage, of course, informs her central distinction between nature and art. She is aware of and sympathetic to other reform movements of the time; the prison reformer John Howard, for example, shows up as Mr. Haswell in her play *Such Things Are*. Indeed, *In Such Things Are* the lines of nature versus art are even more emphatically drawn than in the novel. But Mrs. Inchbald is, at the same time, influenced by much more conservative thinkers as well, in particular, it would seem, that great apologist for "things as they are," Soame Jenyns. The last pages of *Nature and Art* essentially restate Jenyns's explanation of the advantages of poverty in *A Free Inquiry into the Nature and Origin of Evil:*

> Poverty, or the want of riches, is generally compensated by having more hopes and fewer fears, by a greater share of health, and a more exquisite relish of the smallest enjoyments, than those who possess them are usually bless'd with. The want of taste and genius, with all the pleasures that arise from them, are commonly recompensed by a more useful kind of common sense, together with a wonderful delight, as well as success, in the busy pursuits of a scrambling world. The sufferings of the sick are greatly relieved by many trifling gratifications imperceptible to others, and sometimes almost repaid by the inconceivable transports occasioned by the return of health and vigour. Folly cannot be very grievous, because imperceptible; and I doubt not but there is some truth in that rant of a mad poet, that there is a pleasure in being mad, which none

but madmen know. Ignorance, or the want of knowledge and literature, the appointed lot of all born to poverty . . . is the only opiate
capable of infusing that insensibility which can enable them to
endure the miseries of the one, and the fatigues of the other. It is a
cordial administered by the gracious hand of providence; of which
they ought never to be deprived by an ill-judged and improper
education. It is the basis of all subordination, the support of society,
and the privilege of individuals: and I have ever thought it a most
remarkable instance of divine wisdom, that whereas in all animals,
whose individuals rise little above the rest of their species, knowledge is instinctive; in man, whose individuals are so widely different, it is acquired by education; by which means the prince and the
labourer, the philosopher and peasant, are in some measure fitted
for their respective situations.[9]

Inchbald contradicts much of her own criticism of society earlier in the book; note that she even restated Jenyns' argument
that it is only the faulty education to value wealth that makes
the poor unhappy. This is quite different from her earlier discussion of education, in which she had argued for an education
in such humane values as honesty, simplicity, lack of pride, and
so on. Earlier she spoke of educating the young to despise
artifice and hypocrisy and to value simplicity and truth; at the
end of the book she, like Jenyns, thinks that education must
simply teach people not to aspire to more than they have. It is a
most unrevolutionary ending to an otherwise very critical book.

It is tempting to explain Inchbald's last chapters as a withdrawal from political confrontation, as a "blind" designed to
protect her from any prosecution her criticism might draw,
similar to Godwin's revised last chapter of *Caleb Williams;* this is
not, I think, the case. To tone down her criticism, Inchbald did
not have to commit herself to such a panegyric on poverty.
Rather, her turn in these last chapters seems simply to mark the
influence on Inchbald's writing of some of the most conservative thought of her time. She does not seem to feel the need
to reconcile the different schemes of thought she reflects; indeed, she seems unaware that her statement in these last chapters of *Nature and Art* does not fit with what came before. Her
ending indicates a failure not only of social but of artistic vision.

In the history of ideas, though, the confusion that Inchbald evidences here is itself of interest, for it reflects clearly the conflicting forces on a benevolent person's view of society as the end of the century approaches. Inchbald is not a careful thinker, and her humane instincts lead her to espouse, in the hope of alleviating misery, sentiments that are—simply—contradictory.

1. Elizabeth Inchbald, *Nature and Art*, 2 vols. 2nd ed. (London: G. G. and J. Robinson, 1797), vol. I, p. 5. All further references in the text are to this edition.

2. "Social Mobility in Early Modern England: The Anglican Episcopate, 1660–1760." Unpublished paper. Department of History, University of Pennsylvania, 1979. These findings will appear in the forthcoming D. R. Hirschberg, *Patronage, Professionalization, and Social Mobility: The Anglican Episcopate, 1660–1760* (New Brunswick: Rutgers University Press). The following discussion owes much not only to Professor Hirschberg's excellent article, but to several long conversations as well. It should be noted that his research ends at the year 1760; I have not discovered any studies of this subject that deal with the last part of the century.

3. Hirschberg, p. 3.

4. Hirschberg, p. 7.

5. Hirschberg, p. 11.

6. Hirschberg, p. 30.

7. Inchbald's comment recalls Pope's famous couplet from the *Rape of the Lock*, "The hungry Judges soon the Sentence sign,/And Wretches hang that Jury-men may Dine" (Canto III, ll. 21–22).

8. Inchbald's argument recalls the debate about luxury that had been so prominent in the early part of the eighteenth century. Addison, for example, wrote in *Spectator* 574 that "All the real Pleasures and Conveniencies of Life lie in a narrow Compass; but it is the Humour of Mankind to be always looking forward, and straining after one who has got the Start of them in Wealth and Honour. For this Reason, as there are none can properly be called rich, who have not more than they want; there are few rich Men in any of the politer Nations but among the middle Sort of People, who keep their Wishes within their Fortunes, and have more Wealth than they know how to enjoy. Persons of a higher Rank live in a kind of splendid Poverty, and are perpetually wanting, because instead of acquiescing in the solid Pleasures of Life, they endeavour to outvie one another in Shadows and Appearances. Men of Sense have at all times beheld with a great deal of Mirth this silly Game that is playing over their Heads, and by contracting their Desires, enjoy all that secret Satisfaction which others are always in quest of" (*The Spectator*,

ed. Donald F. Bond [Oxford: The Clarendon Press, 1965], p. 563). But Addison does not advertise poverty. His point is that men should be satisfied with what they have rather than constantly goading themselves with ideas of more. This is not the same as suggesting that poverty itself is a positive value or that to be hungry is merely the reverse of being a glutton. Within this context too, then, Inchbald's conclusion must still be viewed as a failure of perspective.

9. In his famous review of *A Free Inquiry*, Samuel Johnson quoted this passage and answered it: "*Poverty* is very gently paraphrased by *want of riches*. In that sense almost every man may in his own opinion be poor. But there is another poverty which is *want of competence*, of all that can soften the miseries of life, of all that diversify attention, or delight imagination. There is yet another poverty which is *want of necessaries*, a species of poverty which no care of the publick, no charity of particulars, can preserve many from feeling openly, and many secretly.

"That hope and fear are inseparably or very frequently connected with poverty, and riches, my surveys of life have not informed me. The milder degrees of poverty are sometimes supported by hope, but the more severe often sink down in motionless despondence. Life must be seen before it can be known. This author [Soame Jenyns] and *Pope* perhaps never saw the miseries which they imagine thus easy to be born. The poor indeed are insensible of many little vexations which sometimes imbitter the possessions and pollute the enjoyments of the rich. They are not pained by casual incivility, or mortified by the mutilation of a compliment; but this happiness is like that of a malefactor who ceases to feel the cords that bind him when the pincers are tearing his flesh." Richard B. Schwartz's *Samuel Johnson and the Problem of Evil* (Madison: The University of Wisconsin Press, 1975) provides a full discussion of the Jenyns review as well as a facsimile of the whole of the original printing of it.

8

HERMSPRONG / *Robert Bage*

By the end of the eighteenth century, rationalism had not made men reasonable, commerce had not redistributed enough of the wealth, and the French Revolution had not created the awaited political égalité. If it had seemed for a while that it was only necessary to point the way toward progress, by the 1790s, especially after the Treason Trials, it was difficult so much as to decide on a direction. Holcroft in *Hugh Trevor* and Godwin in *Caleb Williams* give up even the suggestion that things can be made better, and Inchbald opts for nature, with the absurd results we have seen. Robert Bage in *Hermsprong* manages to leave us with a cheerful catalog of all the faults in his society. Like his contemporaries, he has no broad social program to propose, and like them he presents an impressive list of problems. But his tone, finally, is different from theirs because he scrupulously balances good and bad points. On an individual level, the ridiculous Lord Grondale is an aristocrat, but so is the admirable Hermsprong; Dr. Blick is a cleric, but so is Mr. Woodcock. The institutions of society have very serious faults, yet they still often manage to function appropriately, as in Hermsprong's jury trial. Bage, like Inchbald, uses wit to attack corruption, but unlike her he never diminishes the ironic perspective between his view of society and its own perception of itself. Tragedy is potential in *Hermsprong*, but it never actually develops as it does in *Nature and Art* and in *Caleb Williams*. Caroline does escape marriage to the odious Sir Philip, and she even lives happily ever after; Hermsprong does incur the enmity of the powerful Lord Grondale, but he lives happily ever after too. Bage puts a fairy tale ending on a very critical book and it fits, for the book all along has told us to regard the issues with Bage's detachment—to keep in mind "man as he is not."

"Man as he is," Bage suggests, is unfortunately often closer to Lord Grondale than to Hermsprong. Lord Grondale is ridiculous not because he is an aristocrat but because he conducts himself like a caricature of an aristocrat at his worst: a man with no responsibility except to amuse himself. He is morally and physically corrupt, but that corruption is not an inevitable concomitant of his rank. He is an evil person—the pity of it is that his position in society allows him so much leeway to gorge his corruption. The major complaint of *Hermsprong*, as it is of the majority of these novels, is that too much power is given to men who, except for their accidental (i.e., hereditary) position, should be the least likely to wield it. Lord Grondale is conceited, arrogant, vain, selfish, and stupid; he is part of the government; he has vast power at home.

From his youth, Lord Grondale has been readying himself for a life of uselessness. As Bage ironically tells us, the young Lord Grondale had "acknowledged no superior in matters of gallantry," and by forty he had already drunk himself into gout. With this preparation, Lord Grondale briefly but effectively applies himself to the traditional political career. Politics has nothing to do with ethical positions, philosophy, or benevolence but is simply the means to a title. "He beg[ins] with opposition," but does not get much response; on the other hand, "he was not addicted to scruples, and had, besides, several Cornish boroughs." He finds, therefore, that the incumbent government can offer him an office and is "like many of his predecessors, instantly illumined, and [feels] the error of his former perceptions."[1] But he does not get the preferment he wants, and he reverts to the opposition, finally managing to barter his boroughs for a title and become Lord Grondale.[2] Principle plays no part in any of these dealings. Holcroft in *Hugh Trevor* remarks on precisely the same corruption in the political process: remember how shocked Hugh had been when Lord Idford changed sides after being offered government preferment, leaving poor Hugh with a stack of unwanted opposition pamphlets. Similarly, I have already noted several complaints against the custom of owning boroughs. Lord Grondale's success in politics has nothing to do with his personal characteristics—unless we count the lack of scruple as a plus. One of the repeated laments in this and other novels is that the English political system is geared to power without capability. The most ridiculous character in the book, Sir Philip Chestrum, insists to Miss Campinet that he too would be a welcome addition to government; he adds (without understanding the implication of his own statement) that no one is interested in his personal attributes: "I have been amongst the courtiers, I assure you; but they never asked after my learning; but whether I was church and king; and if I had any boroughs? And why not? Every man to his trade. I should have been amongst them before now, for my talents lie that way . . ." (vol. II, p. 145). And Bage makes it clear that Sir Philip, despite a temperament and a lack of education that make him clearly unsuited to hold any sort of power ("he found himself possessed of great wealth . . . of unbounded pride, without the necessary judgment to correct it; of literature, not quite none; and of the smallest possible quantity of human kindness" [vol. II, p. 138]), could indeed be part of the power structure if he chose to be.

The church is equally corrupt; there, too, merit plays little role although hypocrisy, lack of morals, and a broadly sycophantic nature are of use. Bage juxtaposes his portrait of clerical corruption, Dr. Blick, with that of Lord Grondale. The two are variations on a single theme. Dr. Blick's most important clerical attribute is his "agreeable art of assentation" (vol. I, p. 42). He knows how to make himself useful to Lord Grondale, "whose peculiar merit he conceived to be such, that even a bishopric, could he be induced to ask it for a friend, would scarce be refused him by administration" (vol. I, p. 42). Dr. Blick perceives advancement to be tied solely to patronage rather than to performance of any religious duties, and a man like Lord Grondale is presumed to have the power to secure such a bishopric—such a favor "would scarce be refused him by administration." The threads of corruption are tightly woven;

because Dr. Blick wants advancement from Lord Grondale, he is willing to do whatever Lord Grondale asks. Lord Grondale, who as we have seen is in no way suited for power, covets more of it, so he has his agent Dr. Blick become justice of the peace. Later in the novel, when Lord Grondale wants to get rid of Hermsprong, he turns to Dr. Blick in his role of justice to find a trumped up charge he can apply. Thus the corruption seeps from institution to institution.

Bage analyzes Dr. Blick's shortcomings in some detail. Dr. Blick "united pride with meanness; . . . he was as haughty to his inferiors, as cringing to superiors. An eternal flatterer of Lord Grondale, he did not even presume to preach against a vice, if it happened to be a vice of his patron" (vol. I, p. 107). Dr. Blick even justifies Lord Grondale's living with a woman to whom he is not married: "the learned divine, having . . . explained how marriage and consuetudinage existed together in patriarchal times, proved that what was right then could not be wrong now; and that it was scarce possible a lord should be wrong at any time" (vol. II, p. 9).

It is not only Dr. Blick's pandering that diminishes his morality, for even on issues in which there is no question of advancement he takes a worldly, even an immoral, point of view. The closest he comes to the morality we would expect from a clergyman is a kind of knee-jerk proclamation that is merely half-digested dogma. For example, in a discussion about man's perception of death, Dr. Blick says that "the love of life is so strong, that scarcely any calamity can weaken it" (vol. I, p. 122). Hermsprong insists that "death is privation of sense," an attitude that

> appeared to the Doctor to border on infidelity; a thing so execrable, root and branch, that it ought to be burnt out of the world by fire and faggot.
> "Sir," said he, "are you an atheist? Death, privation of sensation! . . . It is renovation—it is the gate of life—it is a passport to eternal joys."
> "Then surely," said Hermsprong, "it is not an evil." (vol. I, p. 125)

Thus the spiritual reminder comes not from the clergyman but

from Hermsprong. Dr. Blick is full of speeches on what constitutes morality, but in fact he shows little understanding of
even the positions he defends. His practice of his duties as a
clergyman is as slipshod as his understanding of them. On the
morning after a disastrous storm, for example, Hermsprong
and Miss Campinet go among the villagers as early as possible
to lend what assistance they can. However, "The Reverend Dr.
Blick, having been disturbed in the night, lay an hour longer
than usual" (vol. I, p. 209), so that by the time he goes out
Hermsprong and Miss Campinet have already long been at
work. Dr. Blick is not impressed with Hermsprong's efforts, for
he assures Miss Campinet that Hermsprong

> "is an infidel; and . . . without faith, our best works are splendid
> sins."
> "So this profusion of benevolence is with you, Doctor, only a splen-
> did sin?"
> "Nothing more, Miss Campinet. A pure stream cannot flow from a
> corrupt fountain."
> "You prefer faith, then, to charity."
> "Certainly, Miss Campinet,—to every thing: So, I hope, do you?"
> "I hope I believe as I ought; but I own, Doctor, I feel a biass in
> favour of such splendid sins." (vol. 1, p. 210)

Dr. Blick, in charge of three parishes, with ambition to be a
bishop, has no spiritual, benevolent, or humane instincts and
cannot recognize such qualities in others. Dr. Blick, the successful clergyman, is clearly unfit to be a clergyman at all. He is
to be contrasted with Mr. Woodcock, his curate,

> a man of learning; of high probity; simple in his manners; attentive
> to his duties; and so attached to his studies, that he may be said to
> be almost unacquainted with mankind. . . . and from the bountiful
> rector of Grondale [Dr. Blick] has forty-five pounds per annum,
> for doing half the duties of Grondale, and the whole of Sithin. . . .
> (vol. I, p. 108)

Dr. Blick, on the other hand,

> has furnished himself with a prudent quantity of adulation, which

has answered his purpose well; he has church preferment to near 1000£. per annum. . . . (vol. I, p. 132)

(Dr. Blick earned his lucrative position, Bage assures us, by throwing a contested political election to Lord Grondale's candidate—although the means "trenched a little upon moral honesty" [vol. I, p. 135].) Mr. Woodcock, for his forty pounds, does almost all of Dr. Blick's duties, and he does them, as befits a clergyman, with sensitivity and generosity. Bage contrasts Mr. Woodcock's ways with his parishioners with Dr. Blick's:

> taking care not to lose any thing of his dues, by a foolish lenity, or by a love of peace, the Doctor knows it his duty rather to govern than to teach his flock; and he governs *à la royale*, with imperious airs, and imperious commands. Woodcock, on the contrary, is one of the mildest of the sons of men. It is true, he preaches humility, but he practices it also; and takes pains, by example, as well as precept, to make his parishioners good, in all their offices, their duties, and relations. To the poor, he is indeed a blessing; for he gives comfort, when he has nothing else to give. To him they apply when sick; he gives them simple medicines; when they are in doubt, he gives them wholesome counsels. . . . (vol. I, pp. 132–33)

Mr. Woodcock considers himself a teacher rather than a governor, and he practices the virtues he teaches. He functions in relation to Dr. Blick, as Hermsprong does to Lord Grondale, as the example of what man should and can be when he is not corrupted by society.

The simplicity, sincerity, and honesty that Hermsprong and Mr. Woodcock manifest are unfortunately not the rule in civilized lands, and Hermsprong repeatedly points out that he learned his strange manners from the savages among whom he was educated. Bage does not suggest that Englishmen adopt the customs he describes, but rather he uses savage customs as a contrast to civilized life. Bage's emphasis is not on the ideal of the noble savage but on the degeneracy of the European concepts of civilization and pleasure. Hermsprong finds that the progress of human civilization has not resulted in the overall improvement of human happiness, but that, on the contrary,

civilization has created unnatural desires that leave civilized
men forever dissatisfied. He argues against the assumption
"that we have been in a progressive state of improvement for
some centuries," insisting that "you have built cities, no doubt,
and filled them full of improvement, if magnificence be improvement; and of poverty also, if poverty be improvement.
But our question . . . is happiness, comparative happiness, and
until you can trace its dependence upon wealth, it will be in vain
for you to boast your riches" (vol. II, pp. 19–20).[3]

Hermsprong points out that those supposed boons of civilization, science and art, really mean very little even to Western
man in terms of his happiness: the common people, when not
oppressed by poverty or labor, seem happy with little knowledge of them. It is the rich who are always unhappy, who are
oppressed by boredom that they unsuccessfully try to appease
with useless belongings. The Indians, on the other hand, having satisfied their material and security needs, "can rest in
peace." Hermsprong finds their happiness "more continued,
and more uninterrupted."

Hermsprong has not much more trouble explaining away the
pleasures derived from intellectual pursuits. First of all, the
Indians do have intellectual outlet in their daily lives, in pursuing their hunting and their defense, not to mention the com-
posing of their songs. And beyond that, he implies, the Western
pleasure in sedentary, solitary pursuits is not as wholesome as
the savage's pleasures. While Hermsprong spent his evenings
in reading, the savages spent theirs in sport. Hermsprong end-
ed with a headache, the savage, "with a salutary weariness" (vol.
II, p. 22). Reading, Hermsprong suggests, is often just another
outlet for that boredom he sees in the upper classes.

Bage argues that the artificiality of upper class life affects the
basic structure of society itself. Commerce largely has been developed to satisfy wants that are artificial rather than natural.
The limited needs of the savages show how necessity can take a
definition different from the European's. When Hermsprong
is asked if he has ever been in any country where happiness is
more widespread than in England, he suggests that En-

glishmen confuse money with happiness. His banker, Mr. Sumelin, counters that:

> "Money produces the conveniencies of life, and its comforts; these produce happiness."
> "It produces also the pride, the vanity, the parade of life; and these, if I mistake not, produce in their consequences, a tolerable quantity of the anxieties; and anxiety is not happiness."
> "To depreciate money, is to depreciate commerce, its mother; this the English will not bear."
> "I know it well; but I suppose there may be too much even of good things."
> "We say, the more commerce, the more prosperity."
> "This is changing the idea. Individual happiness was the question; not national prosperity. Your debts and other blessings flowing from the best of all possible governments, impose upon you the necessity of being the first workshop of the world. You labor incessantly for happiness. . . ."
> "[T]hose [savages] I . . . know, have not seemed too abundant in felicity. . . ."
> "They have . . . no inconsiderable portion of positive happiness; and a still greater of what may be called negative; they want the far greater part of your moral causes of misery."
> "And one physical—food."
> "There are improvident characters among them . . . but they have in general enough, though not what you would call plenty. . . . Keep your splendid abundance, and its diseases. Give them simple plenty, strength, and health. Give them to multiply the objects of their reflection; and to extend the powers of their mind. That, to me, should seem the happiest state of society. . . ." (vol. II, pp. 161–63)

A new complaint has entered the list of those with which we have by now become familiar, for while almost all of these novels have complained of corrupt social institutions and frivolous aristocrats, these faults in the social system were not tied to the basic economic motive of trade. Commerce was the positive value against which these frivolities could be seen in all their emptiness. We remember Brooke's praise of the merchant, or producer, and his denigration of the aristocrat, or consumer. When the issue of trade has been raised at all, it has been discussed in a positive context; otherwise, it simply has not come up—which is to say that commerce and its abuses has not been seen as a problem in society.[4] Even in *Hugh Trevor*, where Holcroft seems to take every occupation to task for its corruptions, the professions associated with trade are not satirized. Partially this is so because Hugh essentially is trying out the various possibilities open to a "gentleman," but, remember, the merchant brother of Richard Moreland in *The Fool of Quality* was also a gentleman.

So coming upon this complaint here in *Hermsprong* we may note, for these protest novels at least, the beginning of an awareness that commerce may not be worthy of quite so much approval as eighteenth-century Englishmen had been in the habit of giving it. When Mr. Sumelin insists that "to depreciate money, is to depreciate commerce, its mother; this the English will not bear," he expresses, albeit perhaps with some irony, a common view of the matter. Certainly for the eighteenth-century English, the prevailing opinion seemed to be, as Mr. Sumelin suggests, "the more commerce, the more prosperity." Bage questions this view, which to him seems to force man into a continuing cycle of working to produce ever more goods to satisfy ever growing demands. It leads, as well, to an increasingly powerful, and therefore corrupting, government. English society provokes its members into elevating to necessity that which is mere vanity.

The English have become "a people who will do nothing til they are bought. . . . Which of [its] patriots would prefer a civic crown, to a bank note or a purse of guineas?" Hermsprong's indictment is severe: "I impute to you nothing worse than the having followed the usual course of things. You are rich; and addicted to pleasure, to luxury. . . . a consequence . . . of this addiction [is] political carelessness; the immediate precursor of political corruption" (vol. II,164–65). The corruption is basic and pervasive: it cannot be reformed because it is not a growth from the political system but is part of the system itself. Hermsprong's analysis of political corruption is typical of the response to corruption at the end of the century: a clear vision of a fault with no vision of a reform. This is partially so because,

Bage notes, in England "at the moment," with regard to politics "the order of the day . . . [is] determined ignorance" (vol. I, p. 150). The corrupt government the English have is only what they deserve because no serious efforts are made to improve it. Lord Grondale, corrupt in every personal and professional aspect, is not the exception but the rule of the politician. Convenience, Bage charges, is the central motivation of rich Englishmen; the addiction to luxury produces carelessness that leads to corruption.

Bage shows us from several angles that self-gratification is the consuming passion of such men as Lord Grondale and that it misshapes not only the politics of the nation but, through the politics, the law as well. Law exists to satisfy the desires of the rich, or so it seems to Lord Grondale. That "purse of guineas" Hermsprong mentions buys not only a seat in Parliament but a legal proceeding as well. When Lord Grondale wants to get rid of Hermsprong, he calls in Dr. Blick and tells him to find some legal pretense for forcing Hermsprong from the country. Bage's view is not so negative that he assumes such a proceeding will be successful, but his point is that Lord Grondale (like Godwin's Falkland or Inchbald's Dean William) would assume that the law was at his disposal. Bage remarks that at Grondalehall "it was not of justice they talked; it was of law" (vol. III, p. 174). Lord Grondale decides that "Hermsprong should be summoned by Dr. Blick and another justice, before the whole bench, at the next quarter sessions; that the most able counsel should be retained, and amply paid for his utmost exertion. That the whole force of their artillery should be brought down at once, to obtain a commitment to prison. Once there, they might easily find means to retain him, till he would be sick of his confinement, and consent to exchange it for another kingdom" (vol. III, pp. 176–77).

Earlier, Lord Grondale had suggested that Hermsprong be committed by Dr. Blick for assault and battery on Sir Philip Chestrum. Lord Grondale is sure that "[his] interest, joined to Lady Chestrum's, [will] make this county no longer a desirable residence for the fellow" (vol. III, p. 45). Lord Grondale's conviction that the laws operate for his convenience is reinforced by the sycophants with whom he surrounds himself, like Mr. Corrow, his lawyer, who suggests that Hermsprong be prosecuted for sedition. Hermsprong and several friends once had discussed the possibility that if things could not be worked out in England, they might simply retire to Hermsprong's land in America and essentially form their own society (a scheme Coleridge and Southey seriously considered in real life under the name of Pantisocracy). Lord Grondale's lawyer turns this into proof that Hermsprong had endeavored to entice Wigley to America, which in the present temper of the times, might be made something of (vol. III, p. 124). Then he gets to the really damning evidence against Hermsprong:

> "He has read the Rights of Man; this I can almost prove; and also that he has lent it to one friend, if not more; which you know, my lord, is circulation, though to no great extent. I know also where he said that the French constitution, though not perfect, had good things in it, and that ours was not so good, but it might be mended. Now, you know, my lord, the bench of justices will not bear such things now; and if your lordship will exert your influence, I dare say they will make the country too hot to hold him." (vol. III, p. 125)

To have "almost" been proven to have read the *Rights of Man,* to have lent it to one friend, and—even—to have suggested that there are good things in the French constitution as well as things that could be improved in the English one—these are silly accusations indeed. And yet, given the paranoia that raged in England at the time, this list of complaints could have been used to cast suspicion on a man. Bage, for example, might have been familiar with the events of the trial of Thomas Muir in August 1793 for treason. There was no evidence of conspiracy or preparations for violence, but that was not important to the Lord Justice Clerk, Robert M'Queen, Lord Braxfield, who told the jury that "two things must be attended to that require no proof. First, that the British Constitution is the best that ever was since the creation of the world and it is not possible to make it better." He apparently never got to the second thing.[5]

Finally, in addition to his dangerous reading, Hermsprong is also observed engaged in questionable enterprises. Dr. Blick and Mr. Corrow, reasoning ingeniously from the fact that Hermsprong had been seen among rioting miners, even had been observed to give them money, decide that Hermsprong must be a French spy. Given the English hysteria against the French, which had been mounting steadily in the years after the French Revolution and which had peaked after February 1793 when Britain and France had gone to war,[6] such an allegation would not have been so unusual. All of these goings-on are added together, along with some other suspicious actions of Hermsprong (he has never shown the proper respect to Lord Grondale's rank, for example), and Hermsprong is put on trial.

Bage has made it obvious that the charges against Hermsprong are ridiculous, but the trial itself, rather uncharacteristically for this book, is presented in a serious tone. Bage has made light of all society's failings, but when he comes to grips with evaluating the judicial system of England, which he presents as the real safeguard of individual liberty, he is serious in proportion to the gravity of his subject. In the face of whatever else is corrupt in society, the judicial system is the final safeguard. Bage pronounces in a long and triumphant scene that that safeguard still stands. Lord Grondale and his friends can bring Hermsprong to a hearing, but justice still is more powerful than their corruption. In this very important area, at least, the system still works. The trial is in marked contrast to the trial scenes in *Caleb Williams*, where Caleb is at the mercy of Falkland.[7] The scene in *Hermsprong* runs for twenty-three pages (vol. III, pp. 182–204) and is central to the novel.

Lord Grondale's advocate begins by trying to stir up the justices and the crowd:

> "At a time when the nation is so greatly, excessively, and alarmingly alarmed, agitated, and convulsed; when danger is so clearly and evidently to be feared, dreaded, and apprehended, from enemies both exterior and interior, it behoves the magistrates of the several counties to be wakeful and vigilant in detecting, discover-

ing, and bringing to condign punishment, all traitors who are working and hatching their wicked and diabolical plans in secret."

He notes that in these "alarming" times an "alarming" riot has taken place and presents the court with the "alarming" news that this Hermsprong not only has been seen in the crowd but was seen dispursing money among them. Also,

"this person is not well disposed towards this government, in church and state . . . "

and has "counselled and advised" people on going to America, so that

"although there may be other particulars of a public nature, tending to criminate this person, I do not think a larger and more copious catalogue is necessary. . . . "

Then he gets to the second series of suspicious actions:

"the whole tenor of his conduct to Lord Grondale, a nobleman of the first consequence, whose numerous virtues it is not in my power to praise as they deserve."

Hermsprong, against this noble lord's express wishes, had bought at auction a piece of property Lord Grondale had wanted; it was well known that no one was to bid against his lordship. And even worse, in this house Hermsprong had installed Mrs. Garnet, Lord Grondale's innocent but rejected sister. And beyond that—Hermsprong had seduced Lord Grondale's daughter. . . .

Hermsprong, quiet until now, cannot allow this allegation to go unanswered:

"Seduction, Sir!" said Hermsprong. But recovering himself, and bowing to the bench, he said, "I ask pardon of the court," then casting an indignant glance at the advocate, sat down.

Dr. Blick attempts to make Hermsprong's outcry into a major issue, and in the court's reaction to this attempt, Bage makes his first suggestion that the judicial process has not joined the list of social corruptions. Dr. Blick jumps up to demand that

> "to interrupt a gentleman in the midst of his pleading, is a high contempt of this court, and ought to be punished by commitment."

Hermsprong

> looked full in the worthy magistrate's face. It was a look which seemed to say, can this be possible? and it ended with a smile of such superlative contempt, that the doctor felt his cholor rise to an invincible height.

The justices seem about to go along with Dr. Blick, when the respected justice Mr. Saxby protests.

> "I blush," said he, "when I see this court attend to the passions of any of its members, or of its own. What may be the nature of the particular offence given to our reverend brother, I know not; it was contained in a look; and this court, I think, has not cognizance of looks. As to the offence against the court itself, it was the smallest possible.It was an instant, perhaps a laudable impulse, and instantly and genteelly atoned for. I request there may be no farther delay of our proper business."

Mr. Saxby's dismissal of Dr. Blick's protest sets the tone of the proceedings: this is to be a fair attempt to judge the truth and importance of the allegations against Hermsprong, and he will get an unprejudiced hearing. Lord Grondale's power, then, will not carry the day.

Hermsprong answers each charge separately, explaining in each instance that the acts of which he is accused were indeed committed but that the interpretations put on them are inaccurate. He bid for the house in order to have an appropriate place for the worthy Mrs. Garnet; he possesses the affections of Lord Grondale's daughter, but this hardly constitutes seduction. As to his disrespect for Lord Grondale's person, he says that

> "to this I plead guilty, and freely confess I have no respect for his person. If this be a crime in the English jurisprudence, I must be content to suffer the penalty."

Hermsprong answers the public charges with equal ease and forthrightness. He indeed gave advice about America—in response to a request for such information. With regard to being a spy, he simply notes that no suggestion of proof has been made; the lack of evidence of incriminating behavior is also his defense to the charge of giving money to the rioters. A junior justice who had been at the riots, finding that Hermsprong is not about to give more details, fills in the information. Hermsprong, he tells the court, had incited the mob only to reason and moderation and had dispensed money among them in the hope of quelling some of their most pressing hungers. He did, however, strike one of the rioters—when the king's name was insulted. Hermsprong is acquitted.

The seriousness with which Bage treats the legal process and the outcome that he draws underscore the gravity of the issues at stake. Bage would have been well aware of the Treason Trials of 1793 and 1794 that had brought Thomas Hardy, Horne Tooke, John Thelwall, and Thomas Holcroft to trial. After a series of trials in 1793 and early 1794 a "spotty record of prosecutions" in the English courts had been achieved, as Carl B. Cone notes in his excellent account of the events.[8] But as 1794 went on, the government became, to use Cone's word, more "extreme," and on October 6 a Middlesex grand jury returned indictments against twelve men—this was the charge William Godwin answered in his *Cursory Strictures.* Thomas Hardy, the first man to be tried, was acquitted after nine incredibly long days (usually from eight in the morning to after midnight) of proceedings. G. D. H. Cole tells the story so well: "The trial was an obstinate and long-drawn-out struggle; it lasted nine days, and the evidence fills four printed volumes. When at last the jury retired, to be absent three hours, there was 'an awful silence and suspense.' The tension so affected the foreman of the jury, a Mr. Buck of Acton, that on their return he delivered the verdict in a whisper scarcely to be heard in court, and fell down in a faint the moment he had spoken. But stronger voices than his were there to pick up his 'Not Guilty' and shout it triumphantly through the court and to the waiting crowd outside."[9]

The relief that the legal system could stand against even governmental attempts at repression would have been as profound for Bage and his friends as it was for those in the courtroom, but it also would have been measured in an awareness that these attempts at repression were in no way a closed affair. Following the trials, in 1795 and 1796, the government passed the "Two Acts" which "made writing and speaking as much treason as overt acts, made inciting to hatred of the government a 'high misdemeanor,' and made public meetings illegal except when licensed...."[10] Thus the court scene in *Hermsprong* is both an affirmation of the value of the English legal system and a reminder of the active need for the safeguards it represents. The obvious innocence of Hermsprong makes the attempt to prosecute him all the more sinister. Hermpsrong's triumph is complete, but although his innocence of any wrongdoing should have made his acquittal a foregone conclusion, that result was not inevitable. If Justice Saxby had not been among the justices, if the junior justice who spoke for Hermsprong had not done so, the outcome could well have been different. The system does work, but the safety afforded by it is in fact tenuous, as recent events had demonstrated.

Hermsprong is totally exonerated from any wrongdoing, and further it becomes known that he is the real Lord Grondale; all of Lord Grondale's wealth rightfully belongs to him. It is a delicious denouement that the unpretentious, simple-mannered, decent Hermsprong should be the true aristocrat, and the blustering and gross Lord Grondale the pretender. But if Hermsprong is himself an aristocrat, then the customs of society which he has been mocking are not aristocratic only, but are more broadly current. A large area of the social criticism in the book in fact relates to what we might call vice by assumption, that is, vices that the middle classes take on because they think that such pretensions will make them aristocratic. When Hermsprong remarks that he never dines because he finds it rather melancholy to sit at table for several hours making inane conversation while unhealthily stuffing himself ("if to dine . . . were only to eat, twenty minutes would be ample" [vol. II, p. 155]), he remarks not simply on an aristocratic vice but on a middle-class one as well. The most wonderful put-down of the assumption of aristocratic vices by the middle classes must be, however, Hermsprong's refusal to duel with the ridiculous young Fillygrove: "'I think, Mr. Fillygrove,' said Hermsprong with a smile, 'we had better leave this species of folly to gentlemen born; if it gets among gentlemen by assumption, where will it stop?'" (vol. I, p. 182).

Perhaps Hermsprong's most salient attribute is his passion for truth. He will not, to borrow a phrase, say the thing which is not. English society, as Bage draws it, is dominated by a constant necessity to do just that in the name of good manners, in the hope of gaining advancement, and, eventually, simply from habit. This politeness, hypocrisy, and artificiality is the opening for corruption. Hermsprong feels it a duty to speak the truth:

> "It was imposed on me as a duty by my father . . . to speak . . . with the spirit of conscious truth; and to act . . . with the spirit of conscious justice. I have obeyed my father; and hope I have been rewarded, as he promised me I should, by a proper portion of firmness and intrepidity. If this . . . has the appearance of boasting, I answer, that to the weak and enervating humility of thinking, or pretending to think, worse of myself than I deserve, I am, and desire to be, a stranger. That I am not the first of men, I know. I know also that I am not the last. I see not the difficulty of man's becoming a judge, tolerably just, of the temper of his mind . . . and learning the lesson, conceived so hard to be learned, of thinking himself, what he is. I have energies and I feel them; as a man, I have rights, and will support them; and in acting according to principles I believe to be just, I have not yet learned to fear." (vol. II, pp. 53–54)

He has been taught, he later adds, "to attend to the truth of things only, and to reject all prejudices that lead to injustice" (vol. II, p. 62). Truth, understanding, realization for the self, and justice for others are intimately related. Only by the reactions of the other characters in the book do we remark the eccentricity of such guiding principles.

The application of this standard to the relations among men has an important corollary in its implication for women. Women, like men, have the duty to uphold the measure of truth, but they first must be allowed the education that will allow them to use their minds. Bage finds, with Mary Wollstonecraft, that English society is far from giving women that freedom. Miss Fluart (who is close to Bage's ideal of a thinking woman), Mr. Sumelin, and Miss Campinet discuss the issue of women's education at some length. Their conversation grows out of a discussion on politics in which the ladies have taken little part. Hermsprong notes that he has been told it is a breach of politeness to talk politics in front of ladies, but that he thinks "no subject improper for ladies, which ladies are qualified to discuss; nor any subject they would not be qualified to discuss, if their fathers first, and then themselves, so pleased" (vol. II, pp. 165–66). Hermsprong finds that English ladies have "too little liberty of mind;" they have "minds imprisoned,—which, instead of ranging the worlds of physics and metaphysics, are confined to the ideas of . . . routs and Ranelaghs. . . . " Fittingly, since Bage takes all his essential arguments in this section from *A Vindication of the Rights of Woman,* Hermsprong refers to Mrs. Wollstonecraft who "in two octavo volumes . . . affirms that the mode of [women's] education turns the energies of their minds on trifles." Mrs. Wollstonecraft "has presumed to say . . . that the homage men pay to youth and beauty is insidious; that women for the sake of this . . . permit themselves . . . to submit to this inferiority of character. . . . " He insists that women should be educated to use their minds as fully as their mental endowments permit, and he would encourage them to attempt any endeavors for which they feel capable. But "the change, if change there can be, must begin with men. Lovers must mix a little more wisdom with their adoration. Parents, in their modes of education, must make less distinction of sex" (vol. II, p. 167 ff.).[11]

These are serious censures of the ways in which society educates women, and quoting Mrs. Wollstonecraft would have emphasized further their radical nature. We have already seen a more detailed exposition of these same arguments in Holcroft's *Anna St. Ives*.[12] Both Holcroft and Bage have an ideal of human beings as they should be, and women in this vision have the same responsibility and right in the furthering of the social order as men. It is as an individual, rather than as a member of a group, that a man or woman assumes personal and social responsibility. Bage draws the same corollary from this premise that Holcroft does: if the responsibility for spreading truth and enlightenment is individual, no authority, not even that of the family, supersedes the individual's duty to govern himself by truth. A person must make his own moral judgments, and duty to a parent does not excuse the grown child from carrying out his own moral imperatives. Frank Henley in *Anna St. Ives* owed no particular allegiance to the dishonest and selfish Abimelech, and in Bage's novel, Caroline Campinet owes no respect to her gross father Lord Grondale.

But Hermsprong has to work hard to make Caroline understand that. She feels that no matter what her father demands, she must obey him. Lord Grondale is a tyrant, and Caroline as child and daughter makes an easy object for his tyranny. Lord Grondale rejects Hermsprong as a suitor for his daughter, and Caroline accepts his decision because such obedience seems to her a duty. If she meets Hermsprong even by accident, Lord Grondale rages; Caroline is treated much like a prisoner, being told with whom she may speak, when she may go out, and even when she must stay in her room. Lord Grondale demands complete power over her, and Caroline, because of her own misunderstanding of what she owes him as a father, allows herself to be tyrannized—almost but not quite to the point of allowing him to choose the ridiculous Sir Philip Chestrum (whose rent-roll is sufficient, Lord Grondale himself remarks, even if his wit isn't) for her husband.[13] We have seen this particular form of intimidation before in *Caleb Williams*, where Tyrrel tortures his ward Emily with the prospect of a forced marriage to an unsuitable mate. Gary Kelly's observation that Bage "treats parental oppression of romantic lovers as a domestic variety of the same tyranny that led to [political persecution]"[14] is accurate, and parental oppression as a form of social tyranny is examined by several of the protest novelists. Their conclusion, whether we think of Godwin, Holcroft, or Bage, is that the guardian role does not bring with it the right to limit another's freedom. The rule of reason should extend to all relationships, including that between parent and child. I have examined the arguments of Holcroft and Godwin; Bage devotes even more of his novel to an analysis of the limits of parental power. Note that this is a different concern from education; here we speak specifically of the limits of power itself.

Caroline's initial assumption is that "he is my father; I say every thing in that. . . . I refer to the duty I owe; a duty which forbids my giving him offence" (vol. II, p. 12). She ignores Miss Fluart's suggestion that such duties imply reciprocity. Miss Fluart insists that Lord Grondale essentially keeps Caroline shut out from larger society—only to have Caroline retort that that too is his right, if he so wishes. Lord Grondale's restrictions extend not only to Caroline's social life but to her family life as well. He has decided to ignore her aunt Garnet and insists that she ignore that worthy woman as well. Here the matter becomes one of morality, for it is clearly Caroline's duty to visit her aunt and it is also a duty to obey her father's commands. In response to Hermsprong's remonstrance on her error, Caroline in some dismay wonders that

> "filial obedience [can] ever be error? . . ."
> "An illegal act you must not do, even by the command of a father; and ought you to do a wrong one?"
> "But surely it may be wrong to do a right thing, when prohibited by a father."
> "What, if that right thing be a duty also, and the prohibition pride, prejudice, or caprice?"
> "And ought a child to erect herself into a judge of her father's motives?" (vol. II, pp. 62–63)

Bage answers yes. The parent's opinions are worth no less, but no more, than any other person's, and each individual must choose for himself his moral path. In this case, it is wrong for Caroline to hurt her aunt by refusing to see her, and it is irrelevant that such a visit would be against the wishes of her father. Caroline finally decides that she will, indeed, meet with Mrs. Garnet.

As Maria Fluart tells Caroline, it is fine to keep the commandment about honoring your father "when it is possible to be performed. Where it is not, children must do as well as they can" (vol. II, p. 112). Bage presents an entirely new perspective for the relationship: to make parent and child equal is, after all, to deny much of a parent's accustomed power. Even further, Bage insists that in those issues preeminently affecting the child (marriage in particular) the parent's say is negligible. Thus to Caroline's complaint that although Hermsprong seeks her affection, "upon no occasion [do] you take the trouble to conceal your contempt of my father" (vol. II, p. 221), his response is that he loves her, not her father. Her father's feelings about Hermsprong, or Hermsprong's about Lord Grondale, are irrelevant. Like Holcroft in *Anna St. Ives*, Bage argues that "father's ought to be known by their cares, their affections" (vol. III, pp. 32–33). They do not have the right to make other people miserable simply because traditionally they have held so much power. Caroline finally brings herself to tell Lord Grondale that she will not accept his choice of Sir Philip Chestrum as her husband: "it is no part of my duty to make myself miserable for life" (vol. III, p. 73). For this rebellion, Lord Grondale threatens to disinherit her and confines her to her room. He tells Miss Fluart, when she protests on her friend's behalf, that this is "prudence," not "cruelty." Miss Fluart, however, finds that such "protection" is really a guise, used by "father, or brother, or guardian, or husband" to "protect [women] from liberty" (vol. III, p. 90). It is unacceptable repression, not made any the more palatable because it has been sanctioned by custom.

Bage, like Holcroft, recognizes the filial tie, but as a tie of respect and help, not of repression. In almost exactly the same words used by Frank to explain why he feels bound to Mr. Trenchard rather than to Abimelech, his natural father, Hermsprong explains that "merely for existence . . . I owe nothing. It is for rendering that existence a blessing, my filial gratitude is due. . . . Suppose me preserved and educated by a stranger, whose compassion would not permit me to perish. Is it to the author of my existence, or of the happiness of that existence, to whom I am in debt?" (vol. III, pp. 173–74). Such statements have radical implications. If authority, even parental authority, is to be accepted only after rational analysis, then any form of authority must justify itself. Power may no longer be based on tradition. The redefinition of parental privilege is another aspect of the attack on corrupt institutions, no matter how sacred.

Caroline is convinced; with the help of her friends, she escapes from the incarceration she has endured at Lord Grondale's hands and joins Hermsprong. Just as reason triumphed in the public sector at Hermsprong's trial, it triumphs here on a personal level. And they all, with the exception of Lord Grondale, live happily ever after. He dies, but not without having first blessed the union of his daughter and Hermsprong. Bage takes a last chapter to tie up all the ends: the good people are happily provided for, and the unpleasant ones, Dr. Blick in particular, are mildly punished. For a book that has made so many basic criticisms of society and its institutions, it is a very happy ending indeed. And like Inchbald's ending, it is a withdrawal from the issues raised.

Bage has exposed a society in which institutional and personal corruption is rampant. Advancement in politics is a matter of rank and money; advancement in the church is a matter of pandering to that rank and money. The rich are for the most part interested only in themselves, but even their selfishness does not keep them happy or healthy. Women are repressed, children helpless. The laws are frequently bent to the will of the rich, and when they are not, justice is often due to a fortunate fall of circumstances, as when Hermsprong intercedes for a man Lord Grondale had tried to have jailed for a trumped-up debt (vol. III, p. 102) or when Hermsprong is fortunate enough to have at his own trial one judge who is a defender of truth. Individual morality and benevolence are set against institutional corruption; Hermsprong, as his banker Mr. Sumelin reports to Miss Fluart, is "engaged in the oddest business . . . [one that] many a gentleman would be ashamed of. . . . It is the condescending to notice poor objects in distress, and taking the trouble to relieve them" (vol. II, p. 153). That is admirable but not tremendously reassuring, for Hermsprong is clearly the exception, and whatever efforts he makes can only haphazardly relieve misery. Thus he helps Mrs. Garnet, or Lord Grondale's other would-be victims, but if Hermsprong himself were not on hand, what recourse might these people find? Like Falkland in the early part of *Caleb Williams*, Hermsprong is available to help, but when he is not available—as when Falkland was away while Tyrrel victimized the Hawkinses—then what? Bage suggests no more reliable social safety net than the goodness of individuals like Hermsprong. In fact, although Bage makes so many basic criticisms of his society, he posits no very definite or detailed reforms. Even education, which is such a central concern in the majority of these novels, receives relatively little attention here: it is true that the savage system of education seems to have much to recommend it over the European, but Bage does not go on to draw any conclusions from that. Certainly he is not suggesting that Europeans give up reading and learn to hunt, so that contrast, too, rests finally as a criticism without a program for reform.

As the century drew to its close, it became harder and harder to posit reforms; too much that had seemed promising had turned out in the end to hold horror rather than hope. Bage at one point talks about the Birmingham riots, "where a quantity of pious makers of buttons, inspired by our holy mother, had pulled down the dissenting meeting houses, together with the dwelling houses of the most distinguished of that . . . sect" (vol. II, p. 34).[15] Dr. Blick in fact preaches a sermon on this very subject, and although he does not "say this was exactly right," he does note that

> "Now, when the atheistical lawgivers of a neighboring country, have laid their sacrilegious hands upon the sacred property of the church; now, when the whole body of dissenters here have dared to imagine the same thing. These people, to manifest their gratitude

for the indulgent, too indulgent toleration shewn them, have been filling the nation with inflammatory complaints against a constitution, the best the world ever saw, or will ever see; against a government, the wisest, mildest, freest from corruption, that the purest page of history has ever yet exhibited." (vol. II, p. 35)

Dr. Blick, in short, is delighted to take the pillaging of that mob as a text not against lawlessness but against the dissenters, the French, and any who would dare to criticize the institutions of society as they stand at that moment. It was indeed, this Birmingham mob's action, such as would make a most enjoyable text for the likes of Dr. Blick, and it would certainly have been a most depressing spectacle for a man like Bage.[16]

The premise of *Hermsprong* is that reason must shape all human relationships and institutions, and Bage defines reason not in terms of complex philosophizing but of common sense. It does not make sense to dine for hours to the point of sickness; it makes sense to eat. It is not reasonable to submit to lifelong misery because one's parent chooses an unfitting mate; one must make a rational choice oneself. But although Bage would like to believe that applying reason to human affairs will improve the state of society, it must have been difficult in the light of recent events to assume that that would happen. Not only must the enlightened man contend with a corrupt government and clergy, but with a people who would turn on those who tried to help them, as Bage suggests they had in the Birmingham riots. Bage makes a number of positive statements in the book—the outcome of Hermsprong's trial, Hermsprong's successful reeducation of Caroline—to balance some of his criticisms, but he provides no system for reform. The corruptions he has detailed throughout the book are not cleaned up because Lord Grondale dies at the end or because on his deathbed he blesses dear Caroline. Bage can only arrive at his happy ending by ignoring the larger issues he has raised. The reader does not even have to resolve the question of whether Caroline should marry beneath her; Hermsprong, as the heir, is of course a most fitting husband. Like Holcroft in *Hugh Trevor* and Inchbald in *Nature and Art,* Bage at the end of *Hermsprong* retreats from his position as critic to leave us with a sunny image, indeed, of man as he is not.

1. Robert Bage, *Hermsprong or, Man As He Is Not,* 3 vols. (London: Minerva Press, 1796), vol. I, pp. 35–38. All further references are to this edition. The 1796 text is available in a 1979 photographic reprint by Garland Press (New York and London) that is identical to the original except for two pages of advertisements for Minerva Press books that appear at the end of volume two in the original and are omitted in the reprint. The 1796 text is also available in a 1982 photographic reprint in Stuart Tave's annotated edition for the Pennsylvania State University Press (University Park and London).

2. Stuart Tave notes that "Cornwall was the most notoriously over-represented county in the unreformed Parliament and its saleable boroughs a center of corruption and of Crown influence." Introd., *Hermsprong, or Man as He Is Not,* by Robert Bage (University Park, Pa.: Pennsylvania State University Press, 1982), p. 3.

3. John Sekora's incisive analysis of the concept of luxury in the eighteenth century is relevant to this passage. Sekora shows that many in England, especially in the early part of the century, were extremely suspicious of consumption as a means to happiness; they saw in the increasing desire for goods a sinister fascination with consumption for its own sake—that is, as luxury. See especially Sekora's second and third chapters in *Luxury: The Concept in Western Thought, Eden to Smollett* (Baltimore: The Johns Hopkins University Press, 1977).

4. The positive view of commerce that I have noted in these novels of the mid and late 1700s is in marked contrast to much of the comment earlier in the century, when commerce and trade were seen as contributors to display and an ever-increasing need for goods. The view that commerce serves largely to contribute to the development of artificial needs is, as I noted, less prominent as the century wears on. Of the novelists of the last half of the century, only Smollett espouses this view of luxury, and one of Sekora's main points about Smollett is that his view of luxury and commerce was already old fashioned in his own time. Thus, when at the very end of the century Bage makes his complaint about the relation between commerce and "the parade of life," he is renewing an argument that had lain dormant for a good many years.

5. For a fuller account of this justice and his trials see G. D. H. Cole and Raymond Postgate, *The British Common People, 1746–1938* (New York: Alfred A. Knopf, 1931), pp. 141–44.

6. Cole and Postgate, pp. 41–42. For discussion of the atmosphere surrounding the outbreak of war with France see also Leonard W. Cowie, *Hanoverian England: 1714–1837* (New York: Humanities Press, 1967), pp. 370 ff.

7. However, this statement must be qualified by noting that by the time Hermsprong is brought to his hearing, which will determine if he goes to

trial, he has established his reputation in the community and thus stands in some measure as Lord Grondale's social equal, while Caleb is Falkland's social inferior.

8. *The English Jacobins: Reformers in Late 18th Century England* (New York: Charles Scribner's Sons, 1968), p. 187. Cone provides a detailed description of the trials as well as an authoritative account of their context within English political and social history.

9. Cole and Postgate, p. 147.

10. Cole and Postgate, pp. 147–48; see also Cone, pp. 218–24.

11. Bage follows quite closely the arguments and emphases of the early part of the *Vindication*. Wollstonecraft's main concern is that the education of women forces them into a subservient and socially harmful role. Until the modes of education are changed, women will not be able to turn their energies to the betterment of themselves, their families, and society but will continue to expend them on the "trifles" that their faulty educations have convinced them are the proper sphere of women's interests. Hermsprong's argument that men's homage to women is destructive also is taken from Wollstonecraft, as is the remark about esteem versus love. See particularly the introduction and the first three chapters of the *Vindication*, most conveniently available in the critical edition edited by Carol Poston (New York: Norton, 1975). It is interesting to note that although Bage alludes to "two octavo volumes," apparently only one volume was published; Wollstonecraft had promised a second volume in her "advertisement," but as Poston tells us, "so far as is known from Wollstonecraft's papers, she never began the other volume."

12. Holcroft and Wollstonecraft both enthusiastically reviewed *Hermsprong;* Godwin on his tour through the midlands in the summer of 1797 went out of his way to make the personal acquaintance of its author. See also Tave, pp. 3–5, and Peter Faulkner, *Robert Bage* (Boston: Twayne Publishers, 1979), p. 31.

13. It had been well over a century since parental choice of a child's mate had been the rule; by the time Bage was writing the decision-making power belonged to those directly involved. Lawrence Stone notes that "between 1660 and 1800 . . . the children [were] normally making their own choices, and the parents [were] left with no more than the right of veto over socially or economically unsuitable candidates." *The Family, Sex and Marriage in England 1500–1800* (New York: Harper and Row, 1977), p. 272.

14. *The English Jacobin Novel: 1780–1805* (Oxford: The Clarendon Press, 1976), p. 46.

15. Bage's long-time friend (and customer for the entire production of his paper mill) William Hutton was one of those who were forced to flee from the mob. Bage wrote to Hutton that "in this country, it is better to be a churchman, with just as much common sense as heaven has been pleased to give on average to Esquimaux, than a dissenter with the understanding of a Priestley or a Locke. I hope Dear Will, experience will teach thee this great truth and convey thee to peace and orthodoxy, pudding and stupidity." Quoted by Faulkner, p. 26.

16. Cole and Postgate suggest that it was "highly amusing to the 'Church and King' party that the defenders of 'the people' should be harassed by the people itself" (p. 138). The incident had started with a hotel dinner celebrating the storming of the Bastille held by the Birmingham "Friends of Freedom." A mob collected that night to burn down dissenting chapels (the church was against the revolution; enemies of the church were presumed to be revolutionaries). The mob then went to Fair Hill and destroyed Priestley's laboratory, wrecking and finally setting his house aflame. The next day the mob went on to destroy the homes of lesser known reformers. The authorities did not interfere; Faulkner (p. 25) suggests that the magistrates probably did not have the means to control the rioters.

CONCLUSION

I have tried in this book to offer a broad range of coverage that is selectively comprehensive. It is the least I could do for a group of novels that expanded the range of the genre itself. Politics, the church, the aristocracy, the family, the educational structure—all became objects for critical inspection.

The eighteenth-century novelists are mainly idealists rather than reformers. None is programmatic; none has a plan for specific reform of this or that, with the possible exception of Godwin. This differentiates them from nineteenth-century reformist writers like Disraeli, Reade, and Kingsley, though not so much, perhaps, from Dickens. The eighteenth-century novelists open up the genre to social protest, and they institutionalize a posture of strident moral outrage that is taken over whole cloth by the Victorians.

But the Victorians' subject is different, and this fact in part explains the difference in practicality of approach, that is, in the specific nature of the reforms called for. The Victorian protests are largely made about economic forces, and their complaints relate to the destruction of individual human beings by the tyranny of barely understood economic movements. I have alluded to the general paucity of revolution in the eighteenth-century novels of protest; it should be noted that the nineteenth-century novels advocate even less the dismantling of faulty social institutions. Hand in hand with expressions of horror at the destruction of industrialization come injunctions to the victims that industry and thrift, and above all religion, are virtues to be cultivated. In the mid-nineteenth century, the fear of violent disturbances was shared by the public and the government to a greater extent, I think, than was true of the fear of political revolution in the 1790s. Thus while the Victorian novelists were protesting against horrendous social conditions, they were not advocating the overthrow of whatever social institutions they saw as responsible: in fact, in the face of "progress," it would have seemed both ungrateful and impossible to try to stop the economic forces about which they wrote. Rather, there were specific, and somewhat remediable, social ills that could be attacked in Charles Kingsley's and Mrs. Gaskell's and Disraeli's novels. Dickens, in the breadth of his censure and the concomitant generality of his injunctions for reform, is closer to his eighteenth-century forbears.

In the eighteenth century the novel had not yet been understood as a vehicle for the real reformist, except perhaps in Godwin's use of it in *Caleb Williams.* The failings of social institutions are seen as a kind of cumulative failing of corrupted individuals, like Justice Thrasher in *Amelia,* who in their turn produce more corruption. The depredations of individuals upon one another produce social evils. Thus to improve society, the heart and mind of the individual must be reformed. Brooke and Day criticize the education of aristocrats rather than the class structure itself. In *Nature and Art* Inchbald reserves her primary anger for William, the powerful and callous man who destroys Hannah by willfully seducing her; only secondarily does she lament the support his individual action takes from the structures of society. Like Godwin and Bage, she sees the need for societal safeguards to protect the individual from abuse, but the abuse itself stems first from distorted relationships among men. Even Holcroft, whose *Hugh Trevor* comes very close to attacking the institutions themselves, stops short and attacks instead individual corrupted members such as the bishop and Lord Idford. Only Godwin carries through the logical premises of his novel to indict directly not only corrupt individuals but the institutions that corrupted them. In *Caleb Williams* the tyranny of society is so oppressive that nothing can save Caleb or Falkland.

The abuse of power is a common theme in the eighteenth-

century novels of protest and so too is the misuse of power—
the first being deliberate, the second in error. Critics have remarked on the depictions of arbitrary power that are so frequent in these novels, but it has not been noted that many of
the novels attribute the misuse of power to misguidance rather
than to malice. Brooke, Day, and Inchbald suggest that aristocrats are badly educated and that an education in benevolence
and usefulness for them would create a better society. Godwin,
in one context, attributes Falkland's character to his education
in an outdated chivalry. Education is seen as a tremendously
powerful force, and although several of these novelists complain that it is misused in many cases, especially with upper class
children, they also suggest that society has an extraordinary
potential for good precisely because of the promise that a socially healthy education holds out. In *Anna St. Ives* Holcroft
insists that it is possible to "contribute to the great, the universal
cause . . . the general perfection of mind." While young
William in *Nature and Art* is the unhappy product of his education, his cousin Henry is the wonderful human being *his* education should make him. Belief in the power of education as a
force for the improvement of society colors the protest, for it
suggests that there is a relatively easy and likely cure for much
of what is wrong. Brooke, Day, Inchbald, Holcroft (in *Anna St.
Ives*), and Bage all imply that any man will choose goodness and
productivity if he is enlightened to those goals, and a society of
such enlightened men will be a juster society. Except for *Caleb
Williams*, the various protests are made within this context. The
prevailing spirit of these novels is that the failings of society,
once they are exposed, will be ameliorated by rational men of
good will.

The attack on arbitrary power is largely fueled by this expec-
tation, for the notion of arbitrariness is antithetical to ra-
tionality. Arbitrary power is attacked in most of the novels I
have studied here, as well as in almost all of Smollett's novels,
Goldsmith's *The Vicar of Wakefield*—Walter Allen finds it a
theme in Richardson. What has not been remarked by critics is
the extent to which the questioning of traditional relationships

of the powerful to the less powerful extends even to the most basic and sanctioned hierarchical relationship, the family. Authority figures in every walk of life are viewed negatively in these novels, and parents often seem just another variety of tyrant. Some novelists, as I have shown, even go so far as to redefine the parent-child relationship: a human being owes his love, honor, and respect not to the biological parent but to the person who guides and educates him—to the nurturer of the mind, not of the body.

This notion of education as the primary function of parenting is central to the latter part of the century. If biological parents cannot educate their children properly, then the children must be taken away and raised by more fit preceptors. Aristocratic parents especially seem to be poor risks; their children are brought up to believe in the same corrupt values that have distorted the moral nature of the parents. But to suggest that it is necessary to remove children from the authority of their parents is to attack the family itself. If a child may be better off under the guidance of someone other than his parents, then he may have the right to question the opinions and decisions of those parents. In the third quarter of the eighteenth century, novelists go so far as to remove children from their parents to the care of more fit guardians; in the 1790s the novelists go even further and question the very basis of the parent-child relationship.

In the earlier books, the basic challenge to the family structure does not come from the child. None of the children in *The Fool of Quality* and *Sandford and Merton* questions authority; as far as the children are concerned, they obey their guardians just as they would their parents. Clarissa in Richardson's novel and Sophia in *Tom Jones* believe in parental authority even while defying it. It is the given premise of the books that is the challenge to the family structure: the child, and society, may be better off if the child is removed from his parents' influence.

Fanny Burney presents the same pattern a few years later in *Evelina*. Evelina is a very well brought-up young lady, but she is raised by the clergyman Mr. Villars, not by her father. Nevertheless, her feelings of love and respect for her father are undiminished—even if she has never met the man and knows only detrimental facts about him. Although Burney recognizes that a natural parent may be unfit to raise his child and that the child and society will both gain if the child is in someone else's care, she also insists on the sanctity of the relationship between the natural parent and his offspring. It is an inconsistent attitude that questions the traditional view of parent-child relationships while at the same time confirming its validity. That questioning becomes much more dominant in the novels of the nineties.

In the 1790s the assumption that parents have unlimited authority over their children merely by virtue of their parenthood is no longer accepted. Parents are to be judged by the same rules as everyone else. A stupid parent should not be respected; a tyrannical parent should not be obeyed. It is each person's duty to become the most productive member of society he can be, and anything that interferes with that goal, a bad or misguided parent included, must be avoided. In these later novels, reason rather than custom is the ideal mover in human affairs, and so in *Anna St. Ives* for example, it is not acceptable to say, as Evelina does, that one must obey a father just because he is a father. One must obey only the dictates of one's reason.

The hero and heroine of *Anna St. Ives* act according to these principles, and they live happily ever after. Not only do they run their own lives by rational design, they also influence others, thus improving society. But as I have shown, neither of them is blessed with regard to parents. As happens quite often in the novels of this period, there is no female parent in sight for either of them. The venal and crafty Abimelech Henley and the silly Baronet St. Ives are clearly, each in his way, models to be avoided. Thus neither Frank nor Anna has a parent who is worthy of respect. The revolutionary aspect of the book is that, this fact being evident, neither Frank nor Anna feels compelled to behave according to his parent's wishes or precepts. Frank and Anna try in all things to act in accord with reason, and when reason contradicts a parent's injunction, it is reason that is obeyed. *Anna St. Ives* is the earliest novel in this study in which the authority figure is directly questioned. In *Anna St. Ives,* the parent has no special authority just because he is a parent; authority is earned in a relationship rather than assumed by hierarchical right. This is the pattern in all four of the novels of the 1790s I examine.

In Robert Bage's *Hermsprong,* Caroline Campinet at first insists that she owes obedience to Lord Grondale just because he is her biological parent. Like Evelina in Burney's novel, Caroline does not consider whether her father's actions are right or wrong; she believes she must honor his commands only because they are his. Hermsprong, the hero of the book, has very different ideas, and by the end of the novel Caroline has been converted—although not without a considerable struggle. Bage insists that human beings must be of use both to themselves and to others. It is as an individual, rather than as a member of a group, that one assumes personal and social responsibility. Bage draws the same corollary from this premise that Holcroft does: if the responsibility for spreading truth and enlightenment is individual, no authority supersedes the individual's duty to govern himself by truth. Duty to a parent does not excuse the grown child from carrying out his moral imperatives. Frank Henley in *Anna St. Ives* owed no particular allegiance to the dishonest and selfish Abimelech, and in Bage's novel Caroline Campinet owes no respect to Lord Grondale.

Godwin, in *Caleb Williams,* postulates the case of the person who is tyrannized by a guardian and who has no friends to help in the escape from tyranny. Falkland is in a sense a father-figure to Caleb. He cares for Caleb until Caleb disobeys, and then Falkland hounds him constantly, punishing yet sustaining him in a bizarre relationship that is powerful enough to reach Caleb no matter how far he runs from his former protector. And when one man is destroyed, the other is as well. The Falkland-Caleb relationship is paralleled and preceded in *Caleb Williams* by the story of another guardian and his dependent, Tyrrel and Emily. Because Emily is under his care, Tyrrel believes that he should have complete control not only over her actions but over her emotions as well, and the law supports him in this view. Godwin finds that the existing legal structure gives so much latitude to the domestic tyrant that he can murder his ward before any restraining hand will be raised against him. For Godwin, domestic tyranny is no different from any of the other tyrannies to which society subjects the helpless. Godwin's is the bleakest of these novels, but his analysis differs from Holcroft's or Bage's in degree, not in kind. As I have noted, Lord Grondale in *Hermsprong* is capable of very serious mischief—left to his care, Caroline's life would be blighted in a marriage to the odious Sir Philip Chestrum.

Other institutions of society come in for equal, if less surprising, criticism. The corruption complained of within the family is seen on the larger scale in the church and in politics. In all of the novels that discuss both, the two are closely linked, as in the "state of the nation" pamphlets of Dean William in Inchbald's *Nature and Art*. William's career, in fact, although it is in the church, closely approximates a politician's. He curries favor with his superiors, he plots his upward moves, and, of course, he evaluates the state of the nation solely in terms of his satisfaction with his professional progress. The needs of those whom he is supposed to serve, the poor and the helpless, do not concern him. William is an example rather than an exception; the bishop whose favor he cultivates and whose place he waits patiently to inherit is no better a churchman. The church is a powerful institution, and men like the dean and the bishop are power brokers. Instead of helping to temper the harshness of society, they contribute to the oppression of the poor. The dean and his family are so much of society that they are even the stuff of the scandal sheets, or that is what Lady Clementina believes.

Holcroft so closely identifies the corruption of church and state in *Hugh Trevor* that at one point, as I noted, Hugh concurrently is writing pamphlets for a corrupt bishop and an equally corrupt politician. Holcroft's parallel figures, Lord Idford and the bishop, like William and his bishop in *Nature and Art*, are guided only by principles of self-aggrandizement. Bage in

Hermsprong also pairs political and religious corruption in Lord Grondale and his toady Dr. Blick. Lord Grondale, like Holcroft's Lord Idford, changes his allegiance each time the opposition party offers him a new inducement. And Dr. Blick is another in the series of clerics who care only to please those in power in order to become richer and more powerful themselves. Bage explicitly contrasts Dr. Blick with Mr. Woodcock, a fine, caring cleric. Mr. Woodcock, like Hermsprong himself, stands as a measure of appropriate behavior.

There is a dual sense in many of the novels that corruption in society is pervasive, but that a grand potential for a clean, rational world also exists. The improvement scheme may be based on Brooke and Day's middle-class merchant morality or on Holcroft's *Political Justice*-like utopia, but the premise is that society can be reformed. The reader is distanced from any shock of dismay by the content of the discussions. Because the assumption is that faults in society are remediable through rational means, exposing those faults brings the reader to a sense not of despair but of hope. Although the mode for playing on the reader's emotions already had been developed, sentiment is only used in these novels at particular moments. Even *The Fool of Quality,* which has often been dismissed as "merely" a sentimental novel, presents almost all of its major demands for reform not to the reader's heart but to his mind. Brooke explains why the producing merchant is more valuable to society than the consuming aristocrat in a reasoned rather than an emotional appeal. Bage, at the end of my time span, shows the reader that Lord Grondale is a ridiculous and potentially dangerous tyrant, and the effect is intellectual amusement rather than emotional distress at the foibles Bage is presenting. It is frightening that Lord Grondale has quite so much power, but the safeguards in the social structure do work—even if their protection is only barely adequate—and Hermsprong's voice of reason is, with no real struggle, totally triumphant. Bage, like most of the other novelists I have discussed, gives us a social world marred by serious flaws but still essentially ordered.

Godwin's *Caleb Williams* presents a different premise, and in its uniqueness is remarkable not only in terms of its place within the eighteenth-century novel but as it prepares us for the nine-teenth century. *Caleb Williams* suggests that the flaw in the social structure is so deep as to be irremediable; for the first time in the protest novel, the flaw is seen as a schism of class.

When the other novelists discuss rank, it is within an egalitarian context. The rich and powerful are not necessarily better than other people; because they have means, they owe it to others to be as socially productive as possible. None of the authors wants to strip the upper classes of either position or power; each requires from them only responsibility. Bage's Lord Grondale is not bad because he is a lord but because he is an overbearing, ignorant tyrant. Hermsprong himself is of equal rank and, as the real owner of Lord Grondale's estate, he possesses much greater wealth. Burney's Lord Orville is a para-gon, and lovely Evelina, fortunately, not only is of equally good character but of appropriately high rank. Holcroft's Frank Henley may be a commoner, but Anna is the daughter of the baronet. Most of these authors are still fascinated by rank even as they talk of equality.

The ideal is the unostentatious, responsible aristocrat: "the father of Lord Bottom, who came in a plain napped coat" in Brooke's novel. Brooke does not claw at the idea of rank—his little hero is, after all, an aristocrat himself—but he does re-define the role of the aristocrat in society. What C. J. Rawson says of Fielding in *Henry Fielding and the Augustan Ideal Under Stress* is true as well for Brooke: the "assumption is that it is more important for the highly-placed to fulfil the ideal respon-sibilities of their rank, than to relinquish their claims to high titles." Both aristocrats and merchants can be fine men, and there need be no conflict between them. There is not even an economic class between them; one of the most affecting stories in *The Fool of Quality* is the tale of Mr. Clement, the gentleman's son who, along with his wife and child, nearly dies of hunger because he has no skill with which to make a living. Holcroft's Hugh Trevor feels inferior to the carpenter Clarke because the simple workman is more fit to make a living than the higher class Hugh.

Holcroft, surely a more radical writer than Brooke, in *Anna*

St. Ives delimits the institution of rank in much the same terms Brooke had used. Social usefulness rather than rank determines the worthiness of a person. Coke Clifton is wrong to consider himself a better person than Frank Henley. But Coke's rank does not itself make him reprehensible nor does it preclude his transformation into a valuable member of society. For Holcroft, rank is an irrelevancy between human beings, a premise that he exemplifies in the courtship between the plebeian Frank and the aristocratic Anna. As Anna insists, "The word gentleman . . . is a word without a meaning. Or, if it have a meaning, that he who is the best man is the most a gentleman." Rank creates artificial distinctions among men, and it must therefore be ignored because it is only a prejudice, and rational men as they join in that "universal benevolence which shall render them all equals" will overcome prejudice and go beyond it. Holcroft, like the other novelists in this study, sees class schisms as irrational rather than irreparable.

In the nineteenth-century novel, the class question becomes a paramount concern; novels like Mrs. Gaskell's *Mary Barton* chronicle the clash of irreconcilable forces, forces so powerful that it seems irrelevant even to attempt to fix blame for the resultant destruction. *Caleb Williams* presents just this viewpoint in the eighteenth century: Godwin seems to show that it is not so much the fact of class as it is the inevitable corruption and inevitable collision between classes in the struggle toward equity that is profoundly destructive—socially, politically, personally. This is a dimension of the protest novel that is without precedent before Godwin but very prominent after him. Falkland's position in society gives him both the power and the motivation to destroy Caleb; Caleb's position prevents him from defending himself. As Caleb finds in his anguished response to the prosecution he has finally won, there is no righting of the wrongs he and Falkland have suffered. His last, revealing lament is "I have no character to vindicate."

"Things" are out of control in *Caleb Williams*. Godwin is the only one of all the novelists I have dealt with in this study who does not force his characters and events into a semblance of order before the final scene. The reader is not distanced from the horror in *Caleb Williams;* there is no scaffolding of the rational by which Caleb and Falkland can be led from their misery, as Coke Clifton in *Anna St. Ives* could be. Falkland is both a good man and an intelligent one—he knows that what he is doing is heinous, and yet he is no more in control of the situation than Caleb. This is a large part of the horror. Such lack of control marks much of Romantic literature, the poetry in particular, and is a primary chord in the Victorian novel. And as in Romantic poetry and the later novel, emotion is close to the surface and is wrenching rather than politely moving. One of the conclusions to which the discussions in this book lead is a new appreciation for Godwin's achievement in *Caleb Williams.* Although it has been recognized as one of the more important of the late eighteenth-century novels, *Caleb Williams* has not, I think, been accorded quite the stature it deserves as a pivotal work. Not only does Godwin delineate what will be perhaps the central question for the social novel of the following fifty years, he also sets the tone of those novels. For finally we must recognize that protest in the novel of the eighteenth century is a quite civilized affair: irony, satire, and a great deal of rationalistic optimism intervene between the reader and the social pain. Only Godwin put the pain first.

INDEX